# Alaska Native Land Claims

by

Robert D. Arnold

with

Janet Archibald
Margie Bauman
Nancy Yaw Davis
Robert A. Frederick
Paul Gaskin
John Havelock
Gary Holthaus
Chris McNeil
Thomas Richards, Jr.
Howard Rock
Rosita Worl

With a Foreword by Emil Notti

the alaska native foundation

*Alaska Native Land Claims* was written and published by
the Alaska Native Foundation under terms of a contract with
the Alaska Unorganized Borough School District.
Funds made available through the Indian Education Act were
provided by that district and the Anchorage School District.
Supplementary funding was provided by the Alaska Native Foundation,
supported in part by the Ford Foundation.

The activity which is the subject of this report was supported in
part by the U. S. Office of Education, Department of Health,
Education, and Welfare. However, the opinions expressed herein do
not necessarily reflect the position, or policy, of the U. S. Office of
Education, and no official endorsement by the U. S. Office of Education
should be inferred.

Preparation and production supervised by Robert D. Arnold
Book designed by Rena Arend and Rick Peck,
Arctic Environmental Information and Data Center, Anchorage
Cover designed by Lydia L. Hays and Clyde Van Cleve
Maps prepared by Mary Aho, Karen Cramer, and Larry Sugak,
Arctic Environmental Information and Data Center, Anchorage
Translation assistance provided by Alaska Native Education
Board, Anchorage, and Alaska Native Language Center,
Fairbanks and Bethel
Typed by Pam Lekanof and Gloria Lorah
Text set by Computor Composition, Anchorage
Titles by the Type Shop, Anchorage
Printed by Graphic Arts Center, Portland, Oregon

# Foreword

Congressional passage of the Alaska Native Claims Settlement Act in late 1971 could, perhaps, be considered an ending of more than a century of endeavor by the Native people of the state to secure to ourselves our lands. But this settlement is more than an ending; it is a beginning and, in Alaska and elsewhere, swells generated by this historic act are washing unexpected shores.

Working together, reasonable men had compromised to arrive at what appeared to be the best possible resolution of the land claims issue. Like any compromise, it made no one entirely happy. It provided that new paths must be trod, sometimes by people who were uncertain as to just where these paths would lead. Today — four years after passage — we see some destinations more clearly.

No Alaskan — Native or non-Native — is unaffected by the settlement. To some it has meant money and title to lands and the growing assurance that comes from waging a successful fight and becoming a little more a master of one's own fate; to others it means they are no longer so free to move across the face of Alaska as millions of acres become private property.

There was economic as well as social impact. Millions of settlement dollars were funneled into the Alaskan economy in the form of both short-term purchases and long-term business enterprises. The land freeze was lifted and the door opened to construction of the Alaska pipeline and resumption of state land selection. Land use planning was mandated and millions of federal acres were set aside to await this planning.

In the villages, where subsistence living had been a way of life for generations, little appeared to be changed, but increasing concern was being voiced that this way of living would soon be irretrievably lost. In larger communities, there was much talk of corporations and stockholders, boards of directors and annual meetings. Speculators waited in the wings to acquire settlement dollars and lands. Most were quietly put aside.

But it was not in Alaska alone that the impact of the settlement was felt. The Native people of Canada were stirring. They watched with interest what was happening across the border and began to organize and to voice their own claims to the lands they had used since earliest days.

Across half an ocean, the people who had settled the Hawaiian Islands and greeted the European when he came late to their shores, began to call for their own settlement.

Both these causes have the expressed support of Alaska's Native people. Just what settlement either of these groups is likely to win is unclear at this time, but the winds of change are blowing.

Whatever the future holds, assuredly there will be change, brought about by passage of the Alaska Native Land Claims Act.

Emil Notti, President
Alaska Native Foundation

November, 1975
Anchorage, Alaska

# Preface

As its title implies, this book is broader than the topic of the Alaska Native land claims settlement itself. The 1971 act, however, is the event around which the book is organized. Achievement of the settlement act shaped the historical sketches which make up the first half of the book; the act's provisions — as implemented in 1975 — defined the topics for the second half.

In this book the subject of our focus is Alaska Natives and their destinies. As a result, our narratives are unlike those of writers who have the destinies of European colonists, frontiersmen, or goldrushers as their subjects. Their accounts and ours are both true, we trust, but not to the exclusion of the other.

The writing of this book has been a collaborative effort by Alaskans, both Native and non-Native. Some inspired its preparation, some helped write it, others reviewed it, and yet others gave it trial use in their classrooms.

Preparation of *Alaska Native Land Claims* was encouraged by the Statewide Parents' Indian Education Committee of the Alaska Unorganized Borough School District. We commend that committee, the District's Director of Indian Education Act Programs, Nettie Peratrovich, and its Director of Community Advocacy, Laura Bernhard, for their encouragement and support of the project.

We express our appreciation to members of the Textbook Review Committee appointed by the District. Its members — Harry Carter, Ralph Eluska, Oscar Kawagley, Jim LaBelle, Frank Smith, and Philip Smith — gave generously of their time in reading and commenting upon the chapters. We also thank those teachers and students in Anchorage, Kenai, Kivalina, and Nulato who gave us the benefit of their criticism, and presidents and staffs of regional corporations who provided information to us.

Chapters of the book are based upon articles especially commissioned for this purpose. The writers of these articles were Janet Archibald, Margie Bauman, Nancy Yaw Davis, Robert A. Frederick, Paul Gaskin, John Havelock, Gary Holthaus, Chris McNeil, Thomas Richards, Jr., Howard Rock, and Rosita Worl. The information, intelligence, and perspectives which they brought to the task contributed importantly to the strengths of the narratives.

As editor and project director, I am especially grateful to Lydia Hays, who wrote the teacher's manual and student's workbook to accompany this book. Her review of the narratives contributed immeasurably to whatever clarity the text has achieved and her examination of the galleys has certainly reduced the incidence of errors.

Finally, I thank the Alaska Native Foundation, and its president, Emil Notti, and the Ford Foundation, and its president, McGeorge Bundy, for making this book possible. Although funding for its preparation came principally from the Indian Education Act, supplementary funds provided by these two foundations helped assure that no sacrifice was required in the quality and format of the book itself.

Robert D. Arnold

November, 1975
Anchorage, Alaska

# Table of Contents

# Figures

x

# Maps

# UNIT ONE

National Park Service (Robert Belous)

# EARLIEST TIMES

*"All this region has neither past nor present, and it may confidently be said of the future, that it is far and impenetrable."*

*Russian government memorandum, 1867*

The story of Alaska Native land claims begins in the distant past with migrations of people from Asia into what was an uninhabited land. Use and occupation of the land by these migrants and their descendants preceded the arrival of others by more than 11,000 years.

But discovery of Alaska by a Russian expedition in 1741 was to lead — beginning in 1766 — to claims of ownership by Russia. Then, after a century of exploitation but limited settlement, Russia was to sell what it called its possessions in America to the United States.

# Alaska's First Settlers                              Chapter 1

It is not known for certain when man first entered the western hemisphere from Asia. Scientists are in general agreement, however, that his earliest route was through Alaska when America and Asia were joined by land. Based on this conclusion, and evidences of ancient occupation, it is generally believed that the first migrations took place 25,000 to 40,000 years ago.

What is today known as the Bering Sea was — for thousands of years at a time — a tundra plain. Today's St. Lawrence, Nunivak, Diomede, and Pribilof Islands are the tops of mountains of that plain. The name given to the plain when migrants crossed it is the Bering Land Bridge.

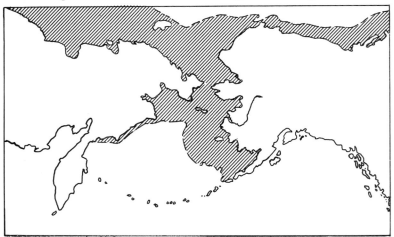

MAP 1 BERING LAND BRIDGE

The Land Bridge existed during periods in which the earth's climate cooled. Because much of its water was locked up on land as ice, the sea level fell by more than 300 feet. One such period began more than 40,000 years ago and lasted for perhaps 15,000 years. After several thousand years the Land Bridge was formed again, then flooded again, and it has been a sea for at least 10,000 years.

Although much of the continent was covered by glaciers, there was an ice-free corridor across Alaska and through Canada. Many of the earliest migrants from Asia apparently continued southward along this corridor. Over thousands of years, their descendants developed physical and cultural differences as they spread across the continents of North and South America. These migrants — these first Americans — were the ancestors of the peoples who would become known to the world later as American Indians.

But not all of these early peoples turned southward. At Old Crow Flats in the Yukon Territory, just to the east of the Alaska boundary in an area never glaciated, there is evidence that man was present between 25,000 and 30,000 years ago or more.

The migrants who travelled eastward across the Land Bridge and settled in Alaska over several thousands of years — the first Alaskans — were the ancestors of today's Eskimos, Indians, and Aleuts.

Evidence of human occupation of Alaska is not as ancient as elsewhere on the American continent. In the southwestern parts of the United States scrapers and other crude tools have been uncovered that are estimated to date back 35,000 years. In Alaska the oldest evidence dates to about 11,000 years ago.

**Antiquity of settlement**

More than 2,700 archaeological sites have been identified in Alaska. The age of most of them has not been determined and may not ever be because of the costs of such field work and analysis.

**Extent of early settlement**

Portrayal of a few of the ancient sites suggests the wide distribution of some of Alaska's first settlers.

National Park Service, U. S. Department of the Interior (Keith Trexler)

*House pits at Cape Krusenstern*

National Park Service, U. S. Department of the Interior (Pete Sanchez)

Onion Portage. Located on a bend of the Kobuk River, 125 miles east of Kotzebue, is a site occupied successively by different peoples over the last 10,000 years. This site, named for its abundance of wild onions, is Onion Portage. Located on the forest-tundra boundary with an abundance of fish and caribou, this site was an attractive and desirable home for man over a very long period of time. It was still being used in the 1970's as a hunting camp. The early investigations at this site were carried out by J. Louis Giddings of Brown University.

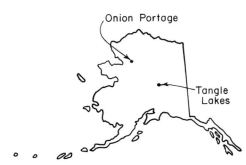

Tangle Lakes. Some of the oldest sites in Alaska are in the interior. One cluster, located 130 miles southeast of Fairbanks, has been designated the Tangle Lakes Archaeological District. More than 150 sites dating back perhaps 10,500 years, have been located in this district. Field work at the sites, largely carried out by Frederick Hadleigh-West of Alaska Methodist University, has resulted in the recovery of artifacts resembling those of Central Siberia.

Doug Reger

Doug Reger

Anangula Island. The oldest Aleut village site yet discovered is on Anangula Island, an island a mile and half long in Nikolski Bay off Umnak Island. Based on scientific analysis, the site is estimated to be about 9,000 years old. More than 30,000 stone scrapers and other tools have been recovered. In August, 1974, a team of Soviet and American archaeologists announced that several kinds of tool blades unearthed on Anangula matched other blades previously discovered in Siberia. The head of the U. S. group, archaeologist, W. S. Laughlin of the University of Connecticut declared, "This is the first direct link we've had that Aleuts came to (Alaska) . . . via the Bering Land Bridge . . ."

Ground Hog Bay. Only a few prehistoric sites have been located in Southeastern Alaska where towering rain forests and heavy undergrowth obscure most of the places where early man probably lived. One of these sites is at Ground Hog Bay on Icy Strait opposite Hoonah. Excavations made at locations back from the shore by Robert E. Ackerman of Washington State University have revealed occupation at several different periods. Cores and chopping tools dating back 9,000 years have been found here. The site is the oldest so far discovered in southeastern Alaska.

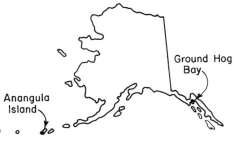

Washington State University (Robert E. Ackerman)

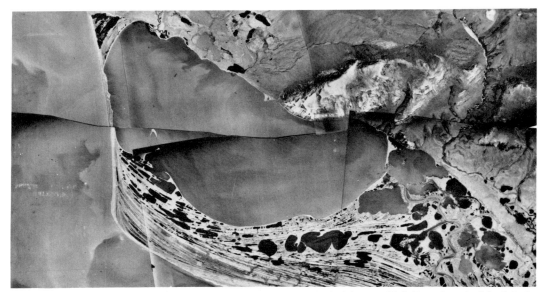

Geological Survey, U. S. Department of the Interior

Cape Krusenstern

Healy Lake

Cape Krusenstern. At Cape Krusenstern, 35 miles northwest of Kotzebue, are 114 beach ridges formed over thousands of years as the shoreline changed. Groups of ridges reveal different periods of settlement: the latest sites are near the current beach; the oldest sites — 5,000 years old — are further back. Beyond the lagoon are sites that are much older. Investigations of J. Louis Giddings produced evidence that the ridges showed a succession of all the major prehistoric cultures of the Arctic.

Healy Lake. Another site in interior Alaska is Healy Lake, about 115 miles southeast of Fairbanks. Artifacts recovered from the top two inches at the site are about 1,200 years old; a piece of bone from the lower levels dates to the ancient past — about 11,000 years ago. Most of the work at Healy Lake was carried out by John P. Cook of the University of Alaska.

Doug Reger

**Kukulik Mound.** Kukulik Mound, near Savoonga on St. Lawrence Island, is a prehistoric site which was occupied from about 2,000 years ago until about 100 years ago, when the people died of disease. The huge mound (800 feet long and 140 feet wide) was first investigated by Otto William Geist of the University of Alaska. Elaborately carved artifacts recovered from the site included those of the Old Bering Sea Culture (1,500 to 2,000 years ago) and the later Punuk culture (900 years ago or more).

**Birnirk.** Another relatively recent site is Birnirk, near Barrow, which represents a culture which began to develop about 1,500 years ago. Excavations carried out in the 1950's by James A. Ford produced thousands of artifacts, including hunting and fishing gear, utensils, musical instruments, and remains of kayaks and sleds. The dwellings were situated below the ground, were rectangular, and had sod roofs.

7

The world first learned of the existence of northwestern America as the result of the voyage of Vitus Bering in 1741. Over the next 50 years its coastline was more fully defined, and names were applied by explorers and navigators to its harbors, bays, and other features. Much of the interior was to remain unknown to the world for another hundred years.

Geographic features of the land were already known and named, of course, by people who would in time become known as Alaska's Eskimos, Indians, and Aleuts. It was — and had been for thousands of years — their homeland.

But the world's knowledge of these Americans — as they were appropriately called by their first foreign visitors — was but slowly acquired. Their existence and their lifeways became known to the world only through the eyes of foreign voyagers, fur trappers, miners, missionaries, and others. It is necessary to draw upon their observations gathered over a century and a half, together with later research, to portray the people of Alaska before the arrival of the first Russians in the mid-1700's.

Alaska State Museum, Juneau (Lutke's Voyages)

*Aleut hunters in kayaks, 1820's*

Alaska was then the home (according to James Mooney) of an estimated 74,000 Eskimos, Indians, and Aleuts. They belonged to one or another of several dozen linguistic and cultural groups. Each group lived in identifiable geographic regions. To varying degrees, the groups' territories were recognized and respected by others. To the extent they could support life, the accessible lands and waters were used and occupied by these native inhabitants.

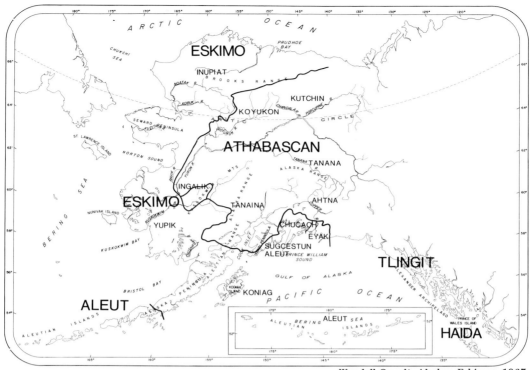

Wendell Oswalt, Alaskan Eskimos, 1967

MAP 2 GENERALIZED GEOGRAPHIC DISTRIBUTION OF ESKIMOS, INDIANS AND ALEUTS IN ALASKA

**Aleuts**

Most Aleuts lived in coastal villages on islands named after them stretching 1,000 miles across the North Pacific. Some few lived at the lower end of the Alaska Peninsula.

The population of about 15,000 Aleuts lived in numerous small villages, most of which were located on the Bering Sea side of the islands. One island, Umnak, once had 16 villages. A typical village was made up of six or seven houses; each household consisted of 20 to 30 people who were related to one another. Their houses were half underground and covered with a warm dome of sod.

Every village with its cluster of houses had its own sea hunting areas, which had to be respected by other villages. Use of these areas without permission meant war.

Adult men hunted seals, sea lions, and whales in the open sea from kayaks, perhaps the most seaworthy of watercraft. Roots, berries, birds, and eggs were available on the land. The food resources of the Aleuts were so abundant that anyone who could walk, young or old, could survive by gathering food from the beaches and the reefs.

The material culture of the Aleuts included 30 kinds of different harpoon heads and a great variety of nets and darts. Rainproof clothes made of sea mammal gut and wooden hats (often highly decorated) were useful in this rainy and foggy territory. Baskets of finely woven grasses were used for many purposes.

Dentalium and amber were so highly prized for ornamental purposes the Aleuts used them in trade. Their trade took them great distances — and there was always risk, for they might run into enemies on the way.

The Aleuts also had considerable knowledge of the human body. They had surgeons who could perform operations, and they skillfully embalmed the dead before respectfully burying them in caves.

Sarychev's Voyages

*Man and woman of Unalaska, 1780's*

Aleuts spoke three distinct dialects which were remotely related to the Eskimo language. Aleuts and Eskimos may have spoken the same language a few thousand years earlier but isolation from one another led to differences in languages and cultures over time.

According to anthropologist J. Ellis Ransom, the Aleut word "Alaxaxaq" is the origin of the word "Alaska." Its meaning was the mainland — "the object toward which the action of the sea is directed."

**Koniags and others**

The people of Kodiak Island, the southern Kenai Peninsula, and the Prince William Sound area were similar to Aleuts in their general lifeways and in their reliance upon sea mammals. These people — the Koniag, the Sugcestun, and the Chugach — were to consider themselves in the 20th century as Aleuts. In language and physical type they showed a clear relationship to Eskimos.

*Russian portraits of Koniag man and woman, 1780's*

By far the largest of these groups was the Koniag. According to anthropologist Wendell Oswalt, most of the 6,500 Koniag people lived on Kodiak Island, but some lived opposite the island on the Alaska Peninsula. Their population density may have been the greatest of any group in Alaska. Both the Chugach of Prince William Sound and the Sugcestun Aleuts on the Kenai Peninsula appear to have been far fewer in number.

**Tlingits and Haidas**

Two major groups of Indians lived along the Gulf of Alaska, on the islands of the Alexander Archipelago, and on the mainland bordering Canada. Most of this territory — from Controller Bay southward — was the home of the Tlingits. Haidas lived principally on Prince of Wales Island (and on Canada's Queen Charlotte Island to the south).

Tlingits and Haidas spoke different languages and each culture had unique features, but there were many similarities. The economy of both was based primarily on the harvesting of fish. At least a dozen species of saltwater fish were caught, including salmon, halibut, cod, and candle fish. Shellfish and sea mammals were also harvested. Unlike Aleuts, they did not pursue the whale. Many species of land plants were named and utilized. No famines are known to have existed in this richly endowed, wooded, warm and rainy area.

Because of the abundant resources available, large villages were possible. An estimated 10,000 Tlingits lived in 14 major territories. Winter villages sometimes included as many as 700 persons.

Because their area was so rich in resources which could readily be obtained, a surplus could be acquired. This allowed time for extensive art work, large competitive potlatches, and long trading expeditions.

Their material culture included much wood working, large houses, fish traps, and wrap-around clothing. Their art style included the display of both sides of an animal figure on a flat surface. The head and face of the animal were often emphasized in size.

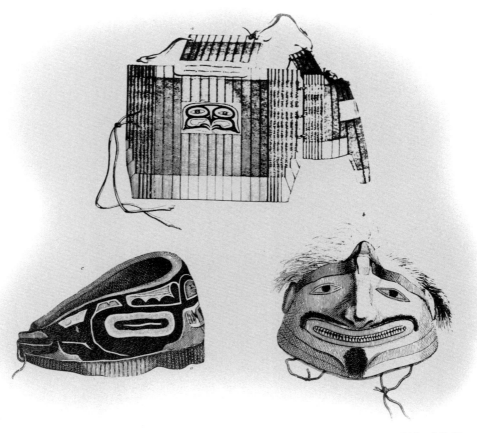

*Tlingit armor and masks, 1805*

Lisianski's Voyages

Trading occurred up and down the coast as far south as California and through passes into the interior of Alaska and Canada. Some of the goods obtained on these expeditions and much of the stored surplus food were given away at potlatches — competitive festive occasions given for many purposes such as honoring the dead, establishing prestige and reputation, changing a name, absolving an insult, avoiding open conflict, or completing a house.

Both groups of Indians had many subdivisions. Within Tlingit villages there were clans and these were further subdivided. Generally speaking, clans owned names, songs, crests, berry patches, clam beaches, fishing areas, and trade routes. Violation of these rights could and did lead to warfare.

The vast interior of Alaska in the 18th century was the home of several thousand Athabascans. They lived along the rivers, generally in or near wooded areas, but their territories included a variety of landscape and terrain. Only three were located near and along the coast.

Among the major groups of Athabascans were the Kutchin, Tanana, Koyukon, Ingalik, Ahtna, and Tanaina. The Kutchin lived in the northeastern interior along the Yukon, Chandalar, and Porcupine rivers and their tributaries. To their south lived the Tanana, principally along the river of the same name. To the west lived the Koyukon, along the Yukon and Koyukuk rivers, and the Ingalik, in a small area along the Yukon and Anvik rivers. The Ahtna lived along the Copper River, including at its mouth. The Tanaina lived in the area surrounding Cook Inlet north of Kachemak Bay.

*Copper River Athabascans at Taral, 1885*

Allen's Explorations

One very small group of Athabascan-related peoples lived on the coast between the territory of the Chugach and the Tlingit. These were the Eyak. Their culture was a blend of Chugach and interior Athabascan.

Each of these groups was made up of people who spoke one or another of several Athabascan languages and who occupied a common territory. The groups were not organized as tribes.

For most Athabascans the village was the basic social unit. This was often only a winter village. In the summer, bands of people who were related to one another would separate to move to fishing camps. Depending upon the game resources available, they might also separate into smaller groups for hunting.

*Athabascans hunting moose, Yukon River, 1867*

All Athabascans hunted, fished, and gathered, but there was variety among the groups depending upon their locations. The Ingalik, for instance, relied heavily for subsistence upon the seasonal run of salmon in their rivers; hunting moose and small game animals was supplementary. The Kutchin, on the other hand, depended principally upon moose, caribou, bear, goats, and sheep; fishing, for them, was supplementary. The Tanaina, the only Athabascans along the coast, were hunters of the beluga whale and seal, as well as land animals. They were also fishermen.

To the extent that Athabascans depended upon large land animals, they faced an uncertainty of subsistence. There were periods of serious shortage of food and even famine. Generally speaking, the food resources of the interior were far less abundant than along the coastal areas.

Athabascans had many kinds of tools for river fishing — nets, traps, lures, and hooks. They had a variety of techniques for obtaining game animals including construction of snares and pits.

Some fishing sites and hunting areas were owned by individuals, but sometimes they were owned by the band. For example, among the Kutchin, hunting territories and fishing sites were common property of the bands, but caribou fences were individually owned. Boundaries between groups were understood and protected.

Western and northern Alaska was the home of most Eskimos. Lands they inhabited stretched from the Bristol Bay region around the coast and across northern Canada. In addition, as noted earlier, there were the Koniag, Sugcestun, and Chugach along the northern Gulf of Alaska.

Most of the estimated 40,000 Eskimos spoke one of two languages — Inupiat or Yupik (or a dialect of Yupik). The linguistic boundary was in the Norton Sound area. Inupiat speakers lived to the north; Yupik speakers lived to the south.

Alaska State Museum, Juneau (Beechey's Voyages)

*Eskimos of the Cape Thompson area, 1826*

Permanent winter villages were the pattern among both northern and southern Eskimos. The larger villages were generally in the north, and of these, the largest was Wales with 500 persons.

Although the village was the basic unit of organization, villagers identified themselves with other villagers as part of a larger group. According to Oswalt, there were 21 groups (including those of the Gulf of Alaska) each of which occupied a recognized area, and each of which had a sense of shared identity.

Describing northwest Alaska, anthropologist Dorothy Jean Ray wrote:

> The Eskimos were extremely conscious of their tribal affiliations, extent of their territory, and relations with foreign groups. Inhabitants of the smaller villages felt a strong tie with members of the larger capital. Wherever they went they identified themselves as belonging to the specific larger group and were acutely aware of their crossing over into other tribal territory.

There was much similarity in the material culture of Eskimos, insofar as they depended upon the same resources — the use of kayaks, harpoons, and spears by seal hunters, for example. But because there was much variety in resources available, there was also much diversity.

Eskimos engaged extensively in trade, especially the Inupiat speakers from the coast, who traded with those who lived inland. Coastal Eskimos exchanged seal oil, walrus and seal skins, ivory, and other products for caribou and wolverine skins. Coastal Eskimos also traded with the Chukchi of Siberia. There was some trade between northern Eskimos and Athabascans but it was very limited, partly because of hostility that existed between them. Less extensive trading took place among Yupik Eskimos, but there was some; seal oil from the coast was an important commodity to inland Eskimos. There was also some trade between Yupik Eskimos and neighboring Athabascan groups.

**Northern Eskimos**

Northern Eskimos lived on the Seward Peninsula and on the lands bordering the Chukchi Sea and the Arctic Ocean. If they were not on the coast, they typically lived along rivers, including the Kobuk, Noatak, and Kuzitrin rivers. Only one group — the Nunamiut — lived almost entirely inland.

The Inupiat Eskimos living along the northern coasts were hunters of the enormous bowhead whale, walrus and seal. They supplemented their sea-based activities by hunting on land, fishing in inland waters, and gathering plants and berries.

Alaska State Museum, Juneau (Kotzebue's Voyages)

*Kotzebue Sound Eskimos, 1820's*

Along the rivers flowing into the area of Kotzebue Sound, Eskimos relied less on sea mammals and more upon land animals and river fishing. At the northwestern tip of the Seward Peninsula lived Eskimos who — like those of the northern coast — were principally whalers. Others on the Seward Peninsula depended largely upon caribou, as did the people of the upper Noatak and Kobuk rivers, and of the Brooks Range.

Most southern Eskimos lived along the Bering Sea coast from Norton Sound to the Bristol Bay region and along the rivers flowing into the Bering Sea. These Yupik-speaking people were primarily hunters of the bearded seal along the southwestern coast, and salmon fishermen along the Yukon, Kuskokwim, Nushagak, and other rivers. Over a wide area they were also hunters of caribou and small game animals.

The other speakers of a Yupik dialect were on St. Lawrence Island, where they pursued the great whale and walrus; on Nunivak Island where they were seal and beluga whale hunters and fishermen; and in the earlier-noted Gulf of Alaska areas, where they were sea mammal hunters.

Whymper's Travels

*Eskimo from the Unalakleet area, 1867*

Alaska was a populated country thousands of years before Russians were to claim it on the basis of Bering's voyage. The native inhabitants extensively used and occupied the land. The intensity of use of any specific area depended upon the availability of resources. Though boundaries were not constant or precisely fixed, recognizable boundaries did exist among groups of Eskimos, Indians, and Aleuts.

"I was a boy of nine or ten years," the old man of Kodiak Island recalled, "when the first Russian ship with two masts appeared . . ." The man, Arsenti Aminak, was looking back many years on the arrival of the first Russians in 1762. In his recollection (reported by historian Hubert H. Bancroft), Aminak said, "his people had traded with Tanainas and others, but "ships and white men we did not know at all." He said most of his people were afraid upon sighting the ship, but,

> Among our people there was a brave warrior named Ishinik, who was so bold he feared nothing in the world; he undertook to visit the ship and came back with presents in his hand, a red shirt, an Aleut hood, and some glass beads. He said there was nothing to fear, 'they only wish to buy our sea-otter skins and to give us glass beads and other riches for them.'

Alaska State Museum, Juneau (Cook's Voyages)

*A sea otter*

A council of the old and wise urged caution in dealing with the strangers, but the islanders were "dazzled by the sight of such quantities of goods." Once trading began, Aminak related, the Russians set upon the islanders, killing 30 of them and taking their sea-otter skins.

The attack upon Kodiak Islanders was a continuation of what had begun with the arrival of Russian fur hunters in the Aleutian Islands about 20 years earlier. The Aleuts had suffered terrible cruelties and mass killing at the hands of the Russian hunters. Because the Aleuts were skilled hunters of the highly valued sea otter, the Russians wanted their services. When they resisted becoming slaves, the Russians killed them in order that those remaining could be forced to submit.

As the sea otter and other fur bearers became more scarce the Russians moved further eastward along the Gulf of Alaska. Before 1800 their vessels had traveled into Cook Inlet, Prince William Sound, Yakutat Bay, and Sitka Sound. Like the Aleuts and Koniags, the Tanainas and Chugach had only spears and bows and arrows, which were not very effective against the firearms of the Russians. Tlingits, who were of fierce reputation, had traded with other foreigners for guns and were a continuing menace to the Russians even into the 1850's.

During these years of eastward expansion a few trading companies took the place of the independent fur hunters.

## SHELIKHOV'S CONCLUSION

On one of his voyages to Alaska waters, trader Gregory Shelikhov successfully traded strands of blue glass beads at a number of coastal villages for a large quantity of beaver and otter furs. He also buried at each location small copper plates inscribed "Land of the Russian Crown." A later report from the Russian Ministry of Marine told of Shelikhov's reaction to the 1788 voyage:

"On examining the stock of furs obtained by way of exchange, Shelikhov found that its value amounted to half a million of rubles, and was astonished not so much at the great benefit obtained, as at the subjection to the Russian Crown of so many tribes, by such easy and simple means. On sound reflection he understood that all that occurred so by God's will, deigning to favor the elevation of Russia to glory, because everywhere Russia's name has been pronounced, there the populations with eager readiness obeyed and recognized subjection."

Source: Memorandum from the Russian Ministry of Marine, quoted in *Alaska Boundary Tribunal.*

Then, in 1799 one firm — the Russian-American Company — was granted a royal charter giving it exclusive hunting and trading privileges in what was becoming known as Russian-America. It was owned by fur-trading companies, merchants, and by Russia's royal family. It was both a commercial enterprise and an arm of the Russian government. Subject to the provisions of its charter, the company was the administrator of colonial affairs in the North Pacific.

Alaska State Museum, Juneau (Lisianski's Voyages)
*Russian-American Company headquarters at Kodiak, 1805*

**Russian settlement**

Colonization of Russian-America by Russians was very limited. During the years 1799-1867, the number of Russians averaged 550 persons. There were never more than 823 Russians in the colony. Apart from Kodiak and Sitka, permanent settlements were very small, often including as few as a dozen Russians. Most locations were simply trading posts, often manned by one or two Russians.

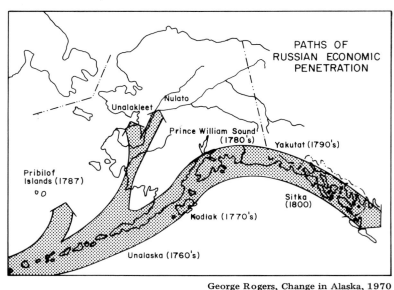

George Rogers, Change in Alaska, 1970

MAP 3  PATHS OF RUSSIAN ECONOMIC PENETRATION

## ALEUTS COMPLAIN TO
## THE CZAR, 1799

"The Russians are coming to America and to our Fox Islands and Andreanof Island to hunt sea and land animals." We receive them in friendly fashion, but they act like barbarians with us. They seize our wives and children as hostages, they send us early in the spring, against our will, five hundred versts [about 330 miles] away to hunt otters, and they keep us there until fall, and at home they leave the lame, the sick, the blind, and these, too, they force to process fish for the Company and to do other Company work without receiving any pay ... The remaining women are sent out on Company labor and are beaten to death. They are removed by force to desert islands, and the children are taken away from those who walk with crutches, and there is no one to feed them."

Source: *The Russian-American Company*, S.B. Okun, Harvard University Press, Cambridge, 1951.

Until about 1819, Russian settlement and activity was largely confined to the Aleutians, the Pribilofs, Kodiak Island, and to scattered coastal locations on the mainland. With the continuing decline in the numbers of sea-mammals, Russians began moving into the western mainland — along the Nushagak, Kuskokwim, and Yukon rivers. They established trading posts as far north as Unalakleet and Nulato.

**Status of Natives**

By the 1820's, the cruelty and mass killing of natives in Alaska was ending. The long-time chief manager of the company, Alexander Baranov, had been replaced by an officer of the Russian navy. Hostile encounters between Russians and natives continued to take place, however, at scattered locations.

The Russian government classified natives for purposes of their law as "dependent," "not wholly dependent," and "independent." As the labels imply, it was primarily the "dependent" natives who were subject to Russian laws and requirements.

The "dependent" or "settled" groups were the Aleuts, Koniags, Chugach people, and perhaps a few Tanainas. Considered Russian subjects, these people were required to supply half of their male population between the ages of 18 to 50 as hunters for the Russians. These men held such compulsory employment for three years. During this period, the company supplied all equipment and clothing and paid a

*View of Russian Settlement at Sitka, 1820's*

small salary. Although they could hold private property, they could not sell furs to any other buyer than the Company.

The other two classes of natives were generally beyond control of the Russian authorities. Some of them, like the Tlingits, were in continuing contact with the Russians, but were considered independent. Others who were classed as independent were Athabascans and Eskimos with whom the Russians had no contact. Some southwestern Eskimos (classed as not wholly dependent) simply engaged in trade with the Russians.

The children of Russian and native parents were not considered to be natives, but were classified as a separate class they called "creoles." They had no compulsory service or other obligations to the Company unless they had been educated at Company expense.

**Land use**

Since the Russians were engaged in fur gathering, not agriculture, and they were few in number, taking land was not necessary. While the Company's Charter (1821) did not provide for deeds or titles to land, it appeared to respect the natives' right to land used:

> The Company shall be obligated to leave at the disposal of [the dependent tribes] as much land as is necessary for all their needs, at the places where they are settled or will be settled . . .

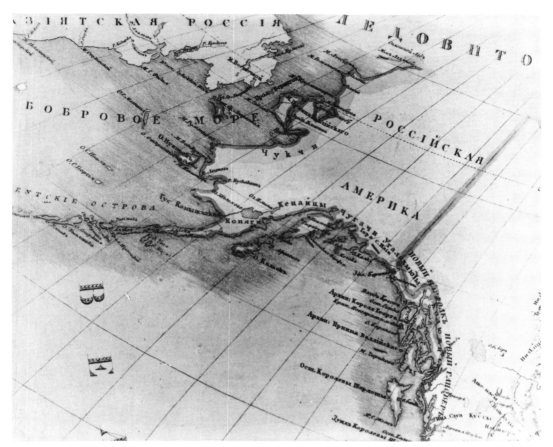

MAP 4 RUSSIAN AMERICA, 1827

Although the lives of thousands of natives were affected by the Russians, their lands were not taken. This was made clear in a memorandum prepared by the Russian government shortly after its sale of Alaska. The memorandum, written by Kostlivtzov, summarized the situation area by area:

> Northern islands: '... neither the imperial government nor the Company ever had any influence upon the mode of division of lands between said Natives, who to the present time, use such lands in perfect freedom, without any foreign interference or restrictions.'

> Aleutians: '... The division of lands between the Aleutian settlements was established at a time anterior to the Russian occupation and continues to be inviolably preserved ...'

> Other regions: '... no attempts were ever made and no necessity ever occurred to introduce a system of land ownership.'

*Michaelovski (Fort St. Michael's), 1867*

---

**"PERMITTED"? "ENTITLED"?**

"The natives not employed by the Company are permitted to enjoy fishing along the shores where they live . . . in order to procure food for themselves and their families . . . They are entitled also to catch the sea animals and wild beasts on these islands and places where they are living . . ."

Source: Sec. 56 of the second charter of the Russian-American Company (1821).

---

**Purchase by the United States**

By the 1860's Russia had good reason to consider selling Russian-America. Russia's recent war with the British in Crimea had drained the government's treasury. Its experiences in the war suggested that the government would be powerless to defend its possession against other nations. There was increased American and British trading along the coasts. Furthermore, the Russian-American Company was no longer financially profitable.

Once launched, negotiations with the United States were quickly concluded. The Treaty of Cession was signed on March 30, 1867. Russian-America was formally transferred to

*Fort Yukon, a Hudson's Bay Company post within the boundaries of Russian-America, 1867*

the United States on October 18 of the same year with the lowering of the Russian flag at Sitka and the raising of the American flag. "Thus, without further ceremony," wrote historian Bancroft, "this vast area of land, belonging by right to neither, was transferred from one European race to the offshoot of another."

Negotiations were conducted with such speed that the treaty itself was hastily drawn. It failed to define clearly the status of natives, their rights, or matters of land ownership. Only one paragraph (part of Article III) was devoted to the inhabitants of Russian-America:

**Treaty of Cession**

> The inhabitants of the ceded territory, according to their choice, reserving their natural allegiance, may return to Russia within three years; but if they should prefer to remain in the ceded territory, they with the exception of uncivilized native tribes, shall be admitted to the enjoyment of all rights, advantages and immunities of citizens of the United States, and shall be maintained and protected in the free enjoyment of their liberty, property and religion. The uncivilized tribes will be subject to such laws and regulations as the United States may, from time to time, adopt in regard to aboriginal tribes in that country.

*Stockade separates Tlingit and Russian settlements at Sitka, 1860's*

It was clear that Russians were free to return to Russia or to remain within the United States. Further, if they chose to remain, they were to be accorded the full rights of citizenship. But what about natives?

Almost 30 years later a court held that creoles and "dependent" tribes — being Russian subjects — should have been entitled to citizenship under the treaty. Nonetheless, from the time of the transfer, the United States apparently viewed all natives as uncivilized and therefore falling under the final sentence:

> The uncivilized tribes will be subject to such
> laws and regulations as the United States may,
> from time to time, adopt in regard to aborigi-
> nal tribes in that country.

Natives, then, would be subject to policies adopted for "aboriginal tribes" by the United States. Their futures would be linked to those of the American Indians. Given that fact, it is necessary to turn aside from Alaska to look at the situation of American Indians in the years surrounding 1867 and the policies that had been pursued to that time.

# UNIT TWO

The Indians, Time-Life Books (L. A. Huffmann)

# AMERICAN INDIANS AND THEIR LANDS

*"On the whole, the people of the United States have not paid an exorbitant price for the ground upon which to build a nation. Trinkets and trickery in the first instance, followed by some bluster, a little fighting, and a little money, and we have a very fair patch of earth, with a good title, in which there is plenty of equity, humanity, sacred rights, and star-spangled banner. What we did not steal ourselves we bought from those who did, and bought it cheap."*

*—H. H. Bancroft,* History of the Pacific States of North America, *Vol. XXVIII, Alaska, A. L. Bancroft and Company, San Francisco, 1886*

By 1867, the American nation stretched from the Atlantic Ocean to the Pacific. For more than a quarter of a century, miners, cattlemen and other settlers had poured into the west. Through war, treaty, and purchase, all of the land area that was to become the 48 United States had been acquired from other nations.

The recently ended Civil War had caused widespread destruction of property and a staggering loss of life. Now the whole southern region was being rebuilt; several million former slaves, now free, were facing uncertain futures; prosperity stimulated by the war was continuing in the north; and a railroad was being constructed in the west to aid the transportation of settlers and goods.

Throughout this period of upheaval and reconsolidation, settlers were moving ever westward. Their arrival in the great plains and upper midwest was creating new conflicts with American Indians, but most Indians had been subdued. What they and their ancestors considered theirs was now largely lost to the American government or its farming, mining, and cattle-raising citizens.

Three centuries earlier virtually all of the land had belonged to several hundred tribes and bands of American Indians numbering about a million people. The United States, a nation founded upon principles of equality of men and respect for property, had largely dispossessed them of their land by the end of the 1800's. Some understanding of how this came to be may be gained from the sketches which follow.

# The Dispossessed                                   Chapter 4

In the same year that Congress ratified the Treaty of Cession, which would make "uncivilized tribes" subject to laws adopted for American Indians, one of its committees described the conditions of such Indians. As reported by historian S. Lyman Tyler, the committee concluded that:

> First. The Indians everywhere, with the exception of the tribes within the Indian Territory, are rapidly decreasing in numbers from various causes: By disease; by intemperance, by wars among themselves and with the whites; by the steady and resistless emigration of white men in the territories of the west, which, confining the Indians to still narrower limits, destroys that game which, in their normal state, constitutes their principal means of subsistence.

# SELECTED DATES
## 1789-1887

1789     Under the new Constitution, the Congress is given the specific authority "to regulate commerce with foreign nations, and among the several States, and with the Indian tribes"; the Congress continues the use of the Secretary of War to manage Indian affairs.

1819     A fund is created by the Congress for the "civilization of the Indians."

1830     The Indian Removal Act is passed by the Congress.

1831     Landmark decision is handed down by the Supreme Court in *Cherokee Nation* vs. *Georgia.*

1832-1842     Federal government removes portions of "Five Civilized Tribes" from southeastern states to Indian Territory.

1849     By Congressional action the Bureau of Indian Affairs is transferred from the War Department to the new Department of the Interior.

1850's     With the opening of Indian Territory west of the Mississippi to settlement it becomes government policy to set aside reservations for Indian tribes.

1869     The completion of the transcontinental railroad and the beginning of the end of the buffalo herds bring great change in the lives of the Plains Indians.

1870-1876     Following federal Indian policy the remaining tribes are placed on reservations, with the help of the military when necessary. Rations of food and clothing are made available in lieu of the privilege of hunting in "customary places."

1871     The negotiation of treaties between the United States and Indian tribes is ended by Congressional action.

1887     The General Allotment Act (Dawes Act) makes the allotment of land to individual Indians and the breaking up of tribal landholdings the official policy of the United States.

Source: Excerpted from S. Lyman Tyler, *A History of Indian Policy*, U. S. Government Printing Office, Washington, D. C., 1974.

Second. The committee are of opinion that in a large majority of cases Indian wars are to be traced to the aggressions of lawless white men, always to be found upon the frontier, or boundary line between savage and civilized life. Such is the statement of the most experienced officers of the army, and of all of those who have been long conversant with Indian affairs.

Third. Another potent cause of their decay is to be found in the loss of their hunting grounds, and in the destruction of that game upon which the Indian subsists . . .

"Confining the Indians to still narrower limits" had been the practice of the national government since the earliest days. During the years from 1830 to 1890, the practice developed into formal policy as Indians were forced to cede part of their lands to the government in exchange for modest annual payments. That part of their land which they did not give up was reserved for their exclusive use and occupancy. It was, in other words, a reservation. Although the reservation was for Indians, they did not own it. They could not sell or otherwise dispose of it. It was held in "trust" by the government and any action relating to it was subject to government control.

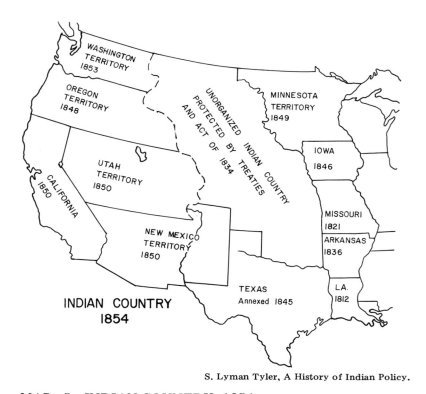

S. Lyman Tyler, A History of Indian Policy.

MAP 5 INDIAN COUNTRY, 1854

Indians resisted reservations fiercely and with good reason. At a large conference called by the government in October, 1867, to arrange for the settlement of western Indians upon reservations, a chief of the Comanches, Ten Bears, explained:

> . . . there are things which you have said to me which I do not like. They were not sweet like sugar, but bitter like gourds. You said you wanted to put us on a reservation, to build us houses and to make us medicine lodges [schools and churches]. I do not want them.

Smithsonian Institution (Alexander Gardner, 1872)

*Ten Bears, Comanche.*

> I was born upon the prairie, where the wind blew free, and there was nothing to break the light of the sun. I was born where there were no enclosures, and where everything drew a free breath. I want to die there, and not within walls . . .
>
> When I was at Washington, the great father told me that all the Comanche land was ours, and that no one should hinder us in living

upon it. So why do you ask us to leave the rivers, and the sun, and the wind, and live in houses? Do not ask us to give up the buffalo for the sheep.

Earlier the same year, a chief of the Kiowas, Satanta, had told military representatives of the government:

I have heard that you intend to settle us on a reservation near the mountains. I don't want to settle. I love to roam over the prairies. There I feel free and happier, but when we settle down we grow pale and die.

But protests were unavailing against the superior force of the government. Both Kiowas and Comanches were among the many tribes settled on reservations.

**Conditions of life**    By the late 1890's, the Indian population of the United States had been reduced to 350,000; two-thirds of them were living in tragic circumstances on reservations. There had been little choice for them. They either had to move from their ancestral home to desolate reservations or be killed by the U. S. Army. For those who were accustomed to roaming

Museum of the American Indian, Heye Foundation

*Two ration tickets for Sioux Indians.*

across the great sweep of the western prairie such reservations were like prisons. For others who were from eastern agricultural communities, such reservations were alien lands to try to farm.

Administration of reservations was assigned to Indian agents, virtually all of whom were white representatives of the federal government. Their powers, backed up by force when it appeared necessary, were far-reaching. They were, in effect, lawgivers as well as law-enforcers. And many of them were corrupt.

Subsistence resources upon which the plains tribes depended for food and clothing had been destroyed by the growing numbers of immigrants moving across Indian land. When the buffalo, an especially important game animal, was hunted almost to extinction by white settlers, Indians had to rely upon the U. S. government for essentials such as food and shelter. Even though provisions were promised in treaties or provided for in law, they often were not received because corrupt Indian agents had sold them or otherwise arranged for their disposal.

As a result Indians were starving and dying from disease, but could not do much about it. To remain on the reservation meant hunger, but if Indians left the reservation to go hunting, they were declared "hostile" by the agents, and military forces would track them down and bring them back. If they resisted they were killed. If they tried to organize to improve their conditions, their agents had the power to prevent such organization.

Since Indians were not citizens, they could not vote, and thereby help influence the policies of government. Except as conscience or public outrage stirred senators and congressmen, conditions among Indians were unimportant to them. More important were those who wanted Indian lands and protection from Indians — white settlers and miners who had the power the ballot box brings; and railroads, which had the power great wealth brings.

Once Indians were firmly settled on reservations there was a renewed effort at "civilizing" them — making them like white men. Such an effort, called assimilation, required destruction of Indian cultures and social systems. This program was carried out by several agencies including the Army, the Office of Indian Affairs schools, and by various church denominations which were paid by the federal government to provide services to reservation Indians. Since churches were involved in this assimilation process, they sought to replace Indian belief systems with those of their denominations.

**Assimilation efforts**

Although religious groups did successfully convert many Indians to their views, a chief of the Crows, Plenty-Coups, looked upon their efforts with contempt:

> Their wise ones said we might have their
> religion, but when we tried to understand it

*Plenty Coups, Crow.*

we found that there were too many kinds of religion among white men for us to understand, and that scarcely any two white men agreed which was the right one to learn. This bothered us a good deal until we saw that the white man did not take his religion any more seriously than he did his laws, and that he kept both of them just behind him, like helpers, to use when they might do him good in his dealings with strangers.

These were not our ways. We kept the laws we made and lived our religion.

Just as governmental policy dictated changing Indians in fundamental ways, it also demanded superficial changes like requiring wooden dwellings to be constructed and white men's clothing to be worn. Historian Clark Wissler observed that the Indian Affairs Department thought the most important requirement was that Indian men give up their braids

Smithsonian Institution (William Smyth, 1827)

*San Carlos Mission, California.*

and cut their hair short. Explaining the apparent reasoning of the Department, Wissler explained:

> [Cutting his hair] would humble the Indian and give him pain, for he took pride in his hair; and to the white man long hair was the symbol of Indian ways, so he wanted to blot out the symbol and then believe he had civilized the Indian.

Museum of the American Indian, Heye Foundation

*Group of Apache, Carlisle Indian School, Pennsylvania.*

*Piles of buffalo hides intended for market.*

Tribes such as the Sioux, Northern Cheyenne, Nez Perce and others which resisted the reservation system, the reduction of their lands, or the arrival of white settlers, engaged in countless battles with soldiers in the last third of the 19th century. But their victories — such as that of Crazy Horse and the Sioux over General George A. Custer in 1876 — were only temporary gains. In time, the great warriors were also pursued, killed, or imprisoned.

**Consequences of settlement**

In 1881 the extent to which once-Indian lands now belonged to whites was described by a U. S. Senator from Oregon. In a speech to the Senate (quoted by Tyler), he also pointed out what he saw as the consequences:

> Our villages now dot their prairies; our cities are built upon their plains; our miners climb their mountains and seek the recesses of their gulches; our telegraphs and railroads and post offices penetrate their country in every direction; their prairies are plowed and their wildernesses opened up. The Indians cannot fish or hunt. They must either change their mode of life or they must die.

# Three Centuries Earlier                    Chapter 5

The western hemisphere had been inhabited for tens of thousands of years before Columbus sighted the islands he mistakenly thought were the Indies. Within two decades the lands would be renamed the Americas, but the name Columbus gave the original inhabitants — the people of the Indies — persisted.

At the time of the European discovery of the Americas, there were about one million Indians in the area that was to become the 48 United States. They lived throughout the land

Library of Congress

*Iroquois warrior, 1787.*

in more than six hundred diverse societies, and they used and occupied the land in varying ways. They were the sole owners of the land.

What white colonists saw when they arrived in America were patterns of living very different from their own. There was no single "Indian" culture, but one took shape in the minds of colonists: Indians were noble savages; they did not work, but instead, led simple and natural lives; they roamed the forests like wild animals, had no homes, no government, and no law. Such conceptions — though false — helped colonists justify to themselves the taking of Indian land.

**Government and law**

Like other human societies, Indians were organized into political systems designed to resolve conflicts.

Conflict came about, for instance, by a shortage of something — food, land, weapons, or prestige. Leaders and political systems emerged to help resolve such issues. In addition to establishing means of dividing valuable resources, they provided for resolution of other conflicts, control of anti-social forces, and regulation of trade and commerce.

Indian rules of conduct had the force of law, and dealt not only with criminal matters like theft or violence, but with other issues such as trade among tribes. Because these laws were not in writing, Indian societies were seen as lawless by Europeans whose laws were written.

**Social organization**

North American Indian societies were organized as bands, tribes, and chiefdoms. Bands, the smallest of the three, consisted typically of an extended family which used and occupied a limited area of woodland and streams. Tribes, the most common form of governmental organization, were larger than bands, but were usually made up of less than three thousand people. They controlled land areas ranging from 500 square miles to 20,000 square miles. Tribes generally were able to obtain resources such as food, tools, and weapons beyond their immediate needs, but the size of tribes was also limited by their need for resources such as grass for horses. In both bands and tribes, each family generally had to obtain its own food, make its own clothing, and in other ways, meet its own needs.

*Division of labor among Florida Indians, 1564.*

*John White's view of Indians fishing.*

In chiefdoms, which were larger than tribes, there was some division of labor among members. Some men might engage in hunting or warring, for instance, on behalf of all of the members of the groups, not just their families. Women frequently were given the role of gardeners or food gatherers for the entire group.

In addition to the three basic forms of Indian governmental organization, there were ethnic and diplomatic confederacies. Usually, such confederacies would be made up of tribes of the same language stock and ancestry which joined together for common defense, trade, or hunting. Tribes which had no relation to one another also combined in a confederacy from time to time for similar reasons. These confederacies were formed only for specific purposes or occasions, such as war. Each tribe still maintained its ability to rule itself without interference from the confederacy. Members of a confederacy rarely fought against one another.

Such confederacies were formed before the coming of Europeans. They were first established by tribes to resolve conflicts among themselves. Points at issue were often negotiated and resolved through the skill of a confederacy's leaders. At other times, a confederacy warred upon other Indian groups to resolve conflicts. It was only later in time that they were utilized for defense against the white intruders.

There were many kinds of Indian leaders — war chiefs, religious leaders, and those who determined when to move or where to hunt, for example. Europeans typically viewed war leaders as leaders over all aspects of Indian society, and this was an error.

**Land ownership and use**

Indians of North America had clear conceptions of land ownership, for land was a primary value in their societies. Being of value, it was frequently an object of dispute and cause of conflict between Indian groups. Although there was much variation in specific rules relating to ownership among the many groups, some few generalizations are possible.

Smithsonian Scientific Series, Inc.

*Granary of Florida Indians, 1564.*

One important aspect of band or tribal ownership was that it was generally exclusive ownership. The land was not available to other groups for hunting, for settlement, or for other purposes. Land belonging to bands or tribes usually had clearly identified boundaries which were known to all parties in the area. These boundaries were often so specific that they were used to describe the lands ceded by Indians to the U. S. government. Trespassing on another tribe's property was a serious matter and was done at risk of war.

Smithsonian Scientific Series, Inc.

*Fortified Indian town in Florida, 1564.*

Another important aspect of Indian ownership was that most land was not individually owned. Cultivated tracts or fishing sites held by families, for instance, were only scattered parcels in the large areas controlled by bands or tribes. Use of these large areas was communal; in that sense, the ownership was shared by all members of the group.

Varying with their locations, Indians were hunters, fishermen, or trappers. All were gatherers of whatever food grew naturally in their territories. Many Indian groups engaged in agriculture — sowing and harvesting corn, beans, cotton, and other plants. According to the noted authority on American Indians, John Collier, "These societies existed in perfect ecological balance with the forest, the desert, the waters and the animal life."

Whatever the ownership or use pattern which particular tribes developed, Collier pointed out that, "At the time of white arrival there was no square mile unoccupied or unused."

It is this fact of occupation and use by organized Indian groups which is the foundation of "aboriginal" or Indian title: the lands which later became the United States were owned by tribes or bands of Indians who had exclusive use and ownership which they could transfer to others. In brief, they exercised the powers of land owners just as did Europeans who held deeds, patents, and titles to land.

But Indians did not have the pieces of paper which proved their ownership; they had no deeds or titles. In the eyes of English settlers accustomed to paper transactions, Indians did not own the land. Their use of land was acknowledged, however, and lands ceded to colonists were almost invariably purchased from the tribes who used them.

**Indian title**

41

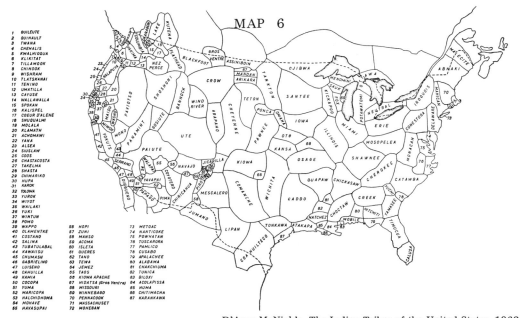

MAP 6

| | | | | | |
|---|---|---|---|---|---|
| 1 | QUILEUTE | | | | |
| 2 | QUINAULT | | | | |
| 3 | TWANA | | | | |
| 4 | CHEHALIS | | | | |
| 5 | KWALHIOQUA | | | | |
| 6 | KLIKITAT | | | | |
| 7 | TILLAMOOK | | | | |
| 8 | CHINOOK | | | | |
| 9 | WISHRAM | | | | |
| 10 | TLATSKANAI | | | | |
| 11 | TENINO | | | | |
| 12 | UMATILLA | | | | |
| 13 | CAYUSE | | | | |
| 14 | WALLAWALLA | | | | |
| 15 | SPOKAN | | | | |
| 16 | KALISPEL | | | | |
| 17 | COEUR D'ALENE | | | | |
| 18 | SNUQUALMI | | | | |
| 19 | MOLALA | | | | |
| 20 | KLAMATH | | | | |
| 21 | ACHOMAWI | | | | |
| 22 | YANA | | | | |
| 23 | ALSEA | | | | |
| 24 | SIUSLAW | | | | |
| 25 | COOS | | | | |
| 26 | CHASTACOSTA | | | | |
| 27 | TAKELMA | | | | |
| 28 | SHASTA | | | | |
| 29 | CHIMARIKO | | | | |
| 30 | HUPA | | | | |
| 31 | KAROK | | | | |
| 32 | TOLOWA | | | | |
| 33 | YUROK | | | | |
| 34 | WIYOT | | | | |
| 35 | WAILAKI | | | | |
| 36 | YUKI | | | | |
| 37 | WINTUN | | | | |
| 38 | POMO | | | | |
| 39 | WAPPO | 56 | HOPI | 73 | METOAC |
| 40 | OLAMENTKE | 57 | ZUNI | 74 | NANTICOKE |
| 41 | COSTANO | 58 | MANSO | 75 | POWHATAN |
| 42 | SALINA | 59 | ACOMA | 76 | TUSCARORA |
| 43 | TUBATULABAL | 60 | ISLETA | 77 | PAMLICO |
| 44 | KAWAIISU | 61 | QUERES | 78 | CUSABO |
| 45 | CHUMASH | 62 | TANO | 79 | APALACHEE |
| 46 | GABRIELINO | 63 | TEWA | 80 | ALABAMA |
| 47 | LUISENO | 64 | JEMEZ | 81 | CHAKCHIUMA |
| 48 | CAHUILLA | 65 | TAOS | 82 | TUNICA |
| 49 | KAMIA | 66 | KIOWA APACHE | 83 | BILOXI |
| 50 | COCOPA | 67 | HIDATSA (Gros Ventre) | 84 | ACOLAPISSA |
| 51 | YUMA | 68 | MISSOURI | 85 | HUMA |
| 52 | MARICOPA | 69 | WINNEBAGO | 86 | CHITIMACHA |
| 53 | HALCHIDHOMA | 70 | PENNACOOK | 87 | KARANKAWA |
| 54 | MOHAVE | 71 | MASSACHUSET | | |
| 55 | HAVASUPAI | 72 | MOHEGAN | | |

D'Arcy McNickle, The Indian Tribes of the United States, 1962.

## LOCATION OF INDIAN TRIBES AT THE TIME OF EUROPEAN ARRIVAL

The concept of aboriginal or Indian title was developed to distinguish between the land title of the English legal system and land ownership among American Indians. Indian title is founded on use and occupancy since ancient times; that is, "from time immemorial," a recurring phrase in Indian treaties.

Rare Book Division, New York Public Library

*Swedish settlers and Delaware Indians, late 1600's.*

When Indian groups ceded land to the government, Indian title to it was said to be extinguished. Ownership was transferred to the government. It became part of the public domain — land available for sale or other disposition under laws adopted by the Congress.

# Chapter 6                                    European Attitudes

The total accumulation of governmental actions affecting Indians to the end of the 1800's came to be known as "Indian policy." Its roots were deep in European traditions and in European settlers' perceptions of American Indians. Neither European tradition nor the Indians' heritage had produced attitudes which would enable their cultures to live

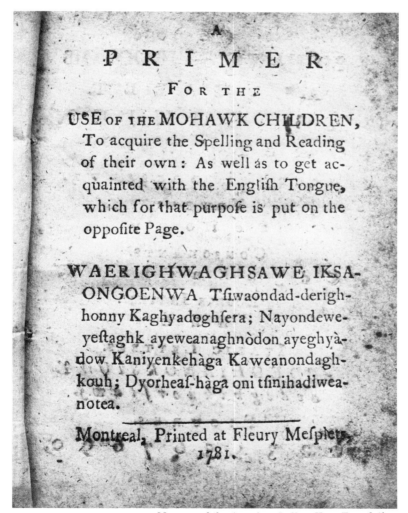

Museum of the American Indian, Heye Foundation

*Title page of Mohawk primer, 1781.*

together in easy harmony. As historians Harold E. Fey and D'Arcy McNickle pointed out, "When Europeans and Indians met for the first time . . . neither side was prepared for the event."

Attitudes of European settlers had been molded by centuries of experiences which had produced not only a different material culture from that of Indians, but different expectations as well. Those experiences, "prepared one for victory, the other for vanquishment," noted Fey and McNickle. Europeans had a conviction that their customs and institutions were superior; they also had an unquestioning faith in their destiny. Their material culture, which included guns, helped convince them they were superior and that their faith was well placed. The fact that they had a writing system, which Indians did not have, likewise made them believe themselves to be of an advanced civilization.

**A key difference**

There was another critical difference in attitude which was never resolved during early Indian-settler contacts, and which was a source of ill will, misunderstanding, and war, from the earliest days to the end of the 1800's. That

*Silver peace medal presented to Indians.*

*Baptism of Delawares and Mohicans by Moravians, 1758.*

difference was in the attitude toward land. As Fey and McNickle explained:

> To the European, land was merchantable. Law and usage had developed a complicated system of privileges and obligations, all deriving from the notion of a transferable fee title in land. Land that was not encompassed within some form of recorded title was outside of law itself . . . When these Europeans found that Indians had no proceedings for recording title, indeed had no titles, they readily assumed that there was no ownership. They were beasts that ranged the land rather than occupied it.

As a result of basic differences between themselves and Indians, European settlers felt free to take land because they would put it to "higher use" than "illiterate savages." They believed the advance of civilization should not be slowed by savage Indians who stood in its path. Among the several options available, then, an important policy became to "civilize" the Indians.

Differences in material culture, conceptions of land ownership, patterns of life, and the lack of written languages, all indicated to Europeans that Indians were not civilized. They were, in their eyes, still in a state of savagery which

**The idea of savagery**

45

Europeans had outgrown centuries earlier. This view was given additional weight by some Puritan clergymen who declared that savages were children of the devil, and therefore it was fit to acquire their lands and wipe them out.

In a study of race prejudice in the western hemisphere, Lewis Hanke cited the religious attitude of some colonists which permitted them to take Indian land. The views of one New England assembly are expressed with simplicity in the resolutions it adopted in the 1640's:

1.  The earth is the Lord's and the fullness thereof. Voted.

2.  The Lord may give the earth or any part of it to his chosen people. Voted.

3.  We are his chosen people. Voted.

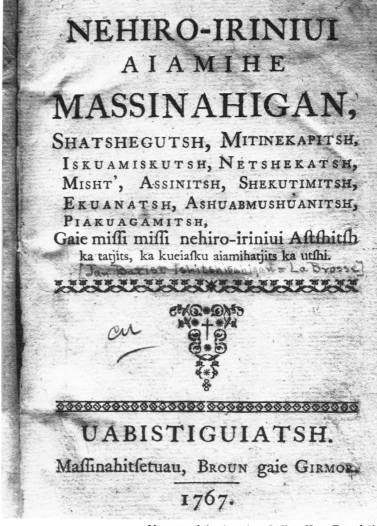

Museum of the American Indian, Heye Foundation

*Title page from prayer book.*

In an analysis of the role of beliefs in shaping Indian policy, Roy Harvey Pearce wrote:

> The New England Puritan of the 1630's knew, in the very intensity of his Puritanism, that he too must be a civilizer and Christianizer, and thus a savior of the Indians, and that God would show him the truest way with the savage. He knew that Pilgrim experience with the Indians, some ten years before, had been fortunate: God had sent a "wonderful plague" among the savages to destroy them and to leave most of their lands free for civilized occupation.

The perception of Indians as representatives of a lower, less civilized estate allowed European settlers to take Indian lands and feel morally right in doing so. An expression of this view, quoted also by Pearce, is found in a 1634 letter from John Winthrop: "The natives are neare all dead of the small Poxe, so as the Lord hathe cleared our title to what we possess."

That this view persisted even three centuries later is clear in the remarks of General Francis C. Walker, quoted by historian Jack Forbes. Walker, a Commissioner of Indian Affairs, said:

> There is no question of national dignity, be it remembered, involved in the treatment of savages by civilized powers. With wild men, as with wild beasts, the question of whether in a given situation one shall fight, coax, or run, is a question merely of what is easiest and safest . . . The Indians should be made as comfortable on and as uncomfortable off, their reservations (as possible) . . .

For Indians the outcome of such perceptions, together with the settlers' desire for land, was the loss of Indian territory and the destruction of much of their culture.

# Chapter 7                                                    Treaties

Origin of Treaties

When America first became an independent nation, it was not a strong world power. Its government was fearful of external threats to the young country's existence. As early American leaders saw it, such threats included the Indian tribes. Although the settlers believed themselves more civilized than Indians, they were fearful of the danger Indians posed to their fragile society. Because of the Indians' governmental organizations and their ability to make war, the American government recognized them from the beginning as independent nations and sought agreements with them for mutual benefit. These agreements — treaties — carried the force of law and were expected to be binding upon all participants.

**Treaty provisions**

Treaties between Indian tribes and the U. S. government usually included several provisions: the parties agreed that hostilities between them would cease; the Indian tribe would forever give or cede certain of its lands to the U. S. government; and the Indian tribe in return would be guaranteed the right to keep a specified amount of land forever. Some treaties also guaranteed perpetual payments to the Indian tribe in compensation for ceded land; other treaties promised food, supplies, and training for Indians.

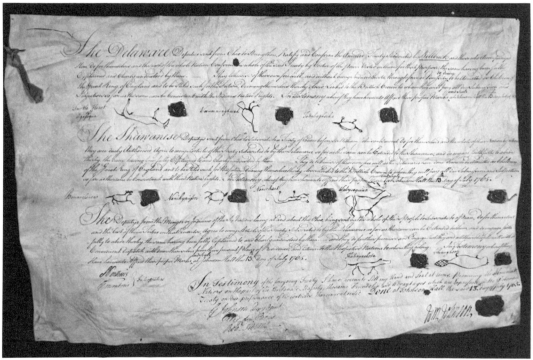

Museum of the American Indian, Heye Foundation

*Treaty with Delaware, Shawnee, and Mingo nations, 1765.*

**Breakdown of Treaties**

The practice of treaty-making was often marred by unfair dealing. The government frequently threatened Indian tribes if they were reluctant and forced them to sign treaties. Unless the tribe signed a treaty, the government would take the land anyway, and then the Indians wouldn't receive any compensation. Another problem was that the government frequently signed treaties with Indians who lacked tribal authority to make such agreements on behalf of their people.

Neither the Indian tribes nor the U. S. government found the treaty system satisfactory. Treaty provisions imposed upon the tribes were often harshly restrictive or unreasonable. Still the government was uneasy that raids might take place. Both sides often felt that the other had violated the intent of the treaties.

An example of the problem of the treaty system from the Indian standpoint was in the government's ability to declare a treaty null and void if any single member of the tribe broke any one of the treaty provisions. A common provision was that Indians were not to leave the reservation without permission from the government. When hunting was the purpose, permission was often denied for fear weapons of the hunt would be used for war. But Indians starving on the reservation had little choice but to leave to get food. Such a hunting expedition, even by one man, would risk ending the treaty which entitled their tribe to provisions from the government.

Museum of the American Indian, Heye Foundation

*Treaty transferring land, 1683.*

In still other instances, Congress made new laws which eliminated the Indian treaty or special provisions of it. Often such action was taken without informing the tribes of the changes. At other times the government ignored solemn promises made to Indians.

**The end of treaty-making**

The widespread dissatisfaction with treaties finally became the focus of debate in Congress. In 1869 during a discussion of appropriations to pay for land purchased by treaty, the failure of the government to live up to its promises was sharply criticized. As reported by McNickle, one Congressman said:

> When we were weak and the Indians were strong, we were glad to make treaties with them and live up to those treaties. Now we have grown powerful and they have grown weak, and it does not become this nation to turn around and trample the rights of the weak.

Smithsonian Institution (Alexander Gardner)
*Cheyenne and Arapahoe Indians meeting with General Sherman and Indian Commissioners, 1868, Fort Laramie, Wyoming.*

Others argued against the appropriation, one saying that the Indians, "never owned a foot of land. They were roving savages." Another insisted that "every dollar appropriated for Indians tends to prevent the Indians from becoming civilized."

A fundamental problem for the United States in maintaining treaties or agreements was the subject of a U. S. Senator's remarks during the 1869 debate. He suggested that it arose from "the misfortune of the Indian." As reported by McNickle, he said:

> Their misfortune is not that they are a dwindling race, not that they are a weak race. Their misfortune is that they hold great bodies of rich lands, which have aroused the . . . [greed] . . . of powerful corporations and powerful individuals.

The United States continued to make treaties with Indians until 1871, when the U. S. Congress decided Indian tribes would no longer be considered sovereign nations. Agreements between the government and Indian tribes were made, however, until a number of years later when the entire system was abandoned.

*Oto delegation in Washington, D. C., 1881.*

# Chapter 8            Congressional Action

Throughout the period of treaty-making, as well as subsequent to it, Congress enacted legislation affecting Indians. Two acts of significance for Indian lands adopted by Congress in the 19th century were the Indian Removal Act and the General Allotment Act. One of these — providing for the removal of Indians from eastern states — began before the extensive development of the reservation system. The other — providing for individual ownership of land by Indians — came later. Like the reservation system, both policies led to the loss of additional Indian lands.

Indian removal

Up to the 1820's treaties generally included land cessions which allowed Indians to retain some of their homeland. But with the policy known as Indian removal, Indians had to give up even those tracts in exchange for other lands.

Of the dozens of tribes and thousands of Indians affected by the removal policy, perhaps none was more tragic than the case of the Cherokees in Georgia. Following their defeat in 1814, the Cherokees began adopting white ways. By 1830 the tribe had created local governments, churches, writing systems, newspapers, and school systems. They owned livestock in large numbers and were relatively prosperous. They had established a well-ordered society that had won respect

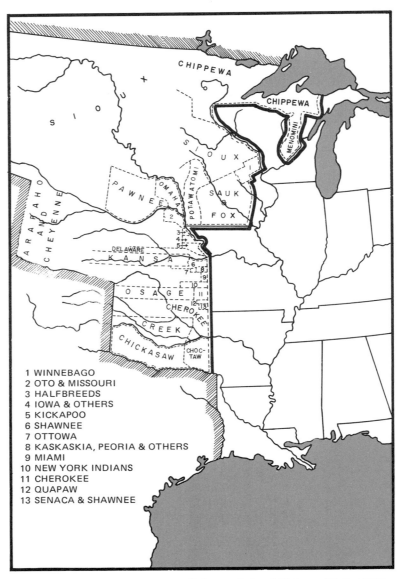

1 WINNEBAGO
2 OTO & MISSOURI
3 HALFBREEDS
4 IOWA & OTHERS
5 KICKAPOO
6 SHAWNEE
7 OTTOWA
8 KASKASKIA, PEORIA & OTHERS
9 MIAMI
10 NEW YORK INDIANS
11 CHEROKEE
12 QUAPAW
13 SENACA & SHAWNEE

S. Lyman Tyler, A History of Indian Policy

MAP 7  LOCATION OF TRIBES AS A RESULT OF INDIAN REMOVAL, 1841

*John Ross, Cherokee, 1858.*

from whites in the longer-settled areas of the country. As Marquis James, a biographer of President Andrew Jackson, pointed out, "They gave their neighbors no trouble."

Unfortunately their neighbors in Georgia did not share that respect. Instead, according to James, they were "alarmed at the success of the Indians' cultural experiments," and "saw the red man on the road to permanent possession of their soil." Respect gave way to jealousy and fear. The policy-makers of Georgia became determined to move the Indians to some other land.

The Indians were given no choice. The Cherokees had to leave their homeland and move west of the Mississippi. This area had been so defined as Indian country (in the Indian Trade and Intercourse Act of 1834) to prevent white settlement and regulate traders and others.

Forced to walk most of the way in the dead of winter, thousands of Indians died from starvation and exposure on the journey. One military officer reported that the men were manacled and forced to march double file. It was "very slow moving them in irons, chained together," he wrote.

The Chickasaws, Choctaws and Creeks were removed from Alabama and Mississippi and the Seminoles were taken from Florida. Nearly three hundred Seminoles drowned in a forced crossing of the Mississippi River on the way to their final destination in Arkansas and Oklahoma. Though their new lands were strange to them, their right to keep them forever was guaranteed by treaties. Later, these and other "removal Indians" were to lose most of their lands in the west through governmental action.

The period after passage of the Indian Removal Act was one of consolidation. There were several removals and they took time. While the U. S. government continued treaty making for another 40 years, acquiring more and more Indian lands, white settlers continued to move westward. When the California gold rush began in 1849, settlers began moving into Indian country from both directions — from California eastward and from the Atlantic Coast westward. During this time Indian tribes were forced to live upon smaller and smaller tracts of land reserved for their use, and the U. S. government increased control over many areas of Indian life. In such circumstances, the government believed it would at least be able to civilize Indians by replacing aboriginal culture with white men's ways and Christianity.

*Flag-raising at Rosebud Reservation for Brule Sioux, South Dakota.*

**General Allotment Act**

By the late 1870's the government realized that the expectation of "civilizing" Indians on reservations was not being met. They decided to try a new approach, for they came to believe reservations — with their shared use of tribally held lands — were hindering them in their efforts. It was believed that giving every Indian a tract of land for his individual ownership would allow him to experience the pride of possession felt by white settlers, and hasten the process of civilization.

In 1887, this belief became the basis of a new law enacted by Congress. Senator Henry Dawes from Massachusetts was the primary force in passage of the General Allotment Act of 1887, so it is also referred to as the Dawes Act. Like many others, Senator Dawes believed that private property was the Indians' door to white civilization. This act divided reservations into 80- and 160-acre tracts which were to be owned by individual Indians. After each eligible tribal

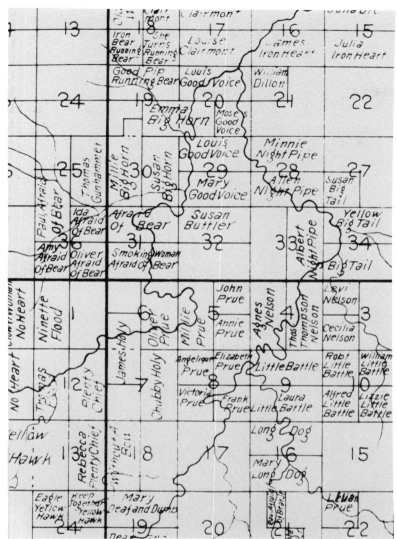

The Sioux of the Rosebud from the Bureau of Indian Affairs

*Indian allotments on the Rosebud Reservation, 1903.*

member was allocated his tract, the remaining tribal lands were declared surplus and put up for sale by the government. By this means, Indian landholdings were reduced, according to historian Tyler, from about 156 million acres to about 78 million acres by 1900.

The General Allotment Act was also aimed at breaking down Indian culture. Indians themselves were aware of this danger and had protested passage of the act. Nineteen tribes sent their representatives to an "International Council of Indian Territory." Among other things, they unanimously opposed allotments. As quoted by Fey and McNickle, they explained why:

> Like other people the Indian needs at least a
> germ of political identity, some governmental
> organization of his own, however crude, to

which his pride in manhood may cling and claim allegiance, in order to make true progress in the affairs of life. This peculiarity in the Indian character is elsewhere called 'patriotism,' the wise and patient fashioning and guidance of which alone will successfully solve the question of civilization. Exclude him from this and he has little to live for. The law to which objection is urged does this by enabling any member of a tribe to become a member of some other body politic by electing and taking to himself the quantity of land which at the present time is the common property of all.

With the allotment of land the ancient Indian system of common ownership of land was destroyed; the Indian identified less with his tribe; and the importance of tribal government declined. The sense of community and the combined power of people had been the tribes' best hope for political influence, and now it was lost. This was nearly as stunning a blow as the loss of land.

*Oglala Sioux delegation to Washington, D. C. (before 1876).*

By the end of the 19th century, education and health services were being provided on a modest scale to Indians by the federal government. Because such services were looked upon by some citizens as charity, it is important to review why they were begun and then continued.

The source of federal authority regarding Indians is in the United States Constitution. Article I, Section 8(c) sets out:

> The Congress shall have power . . . To regulate commerce with foreign nations, and among the several states, and with the Indian tribes.

**Source of federal authority**

As Supreme Court Justice John Marshall described the Constitution's effect on Indian/government relations, both Congress and the executive branch had certain obligations. Congress, Marshall ruled, had the power to make war, authority to confirm treaties, and to regulate commerce with Indian tribes. The executive branch was responsible for negotiating treaties and administering them.

The relationship of Indians to the federal government was spelled out in treaties, laws, and court decisions. A definition of the relationship that was to influence Indian policy for the next century and beyond was also given by Chief Justice Marshall. In *Cherokee Nation v. Georgia* (1831), Marshall wrote that the tribes could not truly be called "foreign nations," but, in his opinion:

**The federal "guardian"**

> They may, more correctly, perhaps be denominated domestic dependent nations . . . They are in a state of pupilage; their relation to the United States resembles that of a ward to his guardian. They look to our government for protection; they rely upon its kindness and its power; appeal to it for relief of their wants; and address the President as their Great Father.

Though it was not John Marshall's intent, the descriptions of Indians as "wards" lingered for many years. As Fey and McNickle explained, "The initial intent was not to subject Indian people to the proliferating controls which ultimately consumed them . . . He [Marshall] did not mean that the Indians had turned over their persons and their estates for management, as if they were legal wards in fact." Yet the idea caught hold and developed force comparable to law.

Federal services for Indians often had their beginnings in treaty commitments made by the United States. For

**Origins of services**

*Sauk, Fox, and Kansa delegations with U.S. Commissioner of Indian Affairs, 1867.*

instance, when the Sauk and Fox tribes ceded land in 1804 to the government, the treaty provided as follows:

> In consideration of the cession and relinquishment of land made in the preceding article, the United States will deliver to the said tribes at the town of St. Louis or some other place on the Mississippi yearly and every year goods suited to the circumstances of the Indians of the value of one thousand dollars . . .

*Blacksmithing class, Forest Grove School, Oregon.*

58

In 1824, upon a further cession of land by the tribes, the United States further promised (1) "to provide and support a Blacksmith, as long as the President of the United States may think proper," (2) to furnish them farming utensils and cattle, and (3) "to employ such persons to aid them in their agriculture, as the President may deem expedient."

Services not required by treaty commitments were often begun to protect white settlers, Indian agents, or soldiers. As summarized by Felix Cohen, in his *Handbook of Federal Indian Law:*

> The erroneous notion is widely prevalent that in their relationship with the federal government the Indians have been the regular recipients of unearned bounties. In reality, federal services were, in earlier years, largely a matter of self-protection for the white man or partial compensation to the Indians for land cessions or other benefits received by the United States.

Education was originally seen as the instrument by which Indians might be "civilized," and thus prevent the destructive raiding and death entailed by war. And education was less costly than war. Reporting that it was estimated to cost one million dollars for each Indian killed, Cohen observed that education offered "a practical alternative to a policy of warfare." Federal appropriations for Indian education were first made by the Congress in 1802. Teachers and schools were also often provided for in treaties.

Museum of the American Indian, Heye Foundation

*Pupils and teachers at day school, Pueblo Isleta, New Mexico, 1904.*

Health services were initiated, in part, to protect whites by "providing a service" to Indians. Cohen described the development as follows:

> Reservations were located in the vicinity of army posts. In the panic of an epidemic of smallpox, as a matter of protection to prevent the spread of the disease through the entire population, a statute was enacted which provided for vaccination of Indians by army surgeons.

Provision of health services also developed because of the relationship between health and education. When the government undertook to educate Indians, some responsibility for the health of students was also assumed. In fact, the first expenditures for health services were taken from the money appropriated for "education and civilization."

Services for Indians having these origins were continued, in part, because of the failure of state governments to provide them. Their treaties had been negotiated with the federal government, not with states. Most Indians were on reservations which were administered by the federal government or on lands belonging to the federal government. They were on lands which were not taxed by the states. As a result of the unique relationship of Indians to the federal government, 19th century state governments did not see the health, education, or welfare of Indians as their responsibility.

Museum of tne American Indian, Heye Foundation

*Ration day, Crow Reservation, Montana.*

# UNIT THREE

# ALASKA NATIVES AND THEIR LANDS

*"I am glad that I lived to see the Americans in the country. The Aleuts are better off now than they were under the Russians. The first Russians who came here killed our men and took away our women and all our possessions; and afterward, when the Russian American Company came, they made all the Aleuts like slaves, and sent them to hunt far away, where many were drowned and many killed by savage Natives, and others stopped in strange places and never came back. The old company gave us fish for nothing, but we could have got plenty of it for ourselves if we had been allowed to stay at home and provide for our families. Often they would not sell us flour or tea, even if we had skins to pay for it. Now we must pay for everything, but we can buy what we like. God will not give me many days to live, but I am satisfied."*

—Peter Kostromitin, Makushin
1878

(Quoted in Bancroft, History of the Pacific States of North America.)

Replacement of Russian colonial administrators by Americans meant little to most Eskimos, Indians, and Aleuts of the former Russian-America, now called Alaska. About 20,000 Eskimos and Indians lived in the interior and along the western and northern coasts where Russian traders had rarely traveled. Most of the Eskimos and Indians had been ignorant of Russia's claims of ownership, and for a number of years were to be unaware of the sale of the vast territory to the United States.

Many of the remaining 10,000 Eskimos, Indians, and Aleuts were also largely unaffected by the change. They lived in the southern coastal regions where their contacts with Russians went back 50 years or more. During the early years under the American flag, however, most of them would not even see any representatives of the United States.

Taken together, these 30,000 people were considered to be the "uncivilized native tribes" referred to in the Treaty of Cession. As noted earlier, the treaty had provided that "uncivilized native tribes" would be excluded from citizenship and they would be "subject to such laws and regulations as the United States may from time to time adopt in regards to aboriginal tribes of that country."

# New Migrants                                      Chapter 10

Upon the 1867 transfer to the United States, Alaska became a military district, governed by the War Department. Its commanding officer, Brevet Major General Jeff C. Davis, who later was to win distinction as an Indian fighter in California, was charged with providing protection to American citizens, Russian subjects, and the aboriginal tribes. His orders said he would act as the general superintendent of the tribes, "protecting them from abuse and regulating their trade and intercourse with our own people."

Because the principal posts established were in the southeastern part of the territory, it was the Tlingits who were most affected by the Army, then later by the Navy, during Alaska's first 17 years as an American colony.

**Tlingit reaction to sale**

When Tlingit chiefs first learned that Alaska had been sold to the United States, they objected and advised the U. S. officials that the Russians had lived in their country only with their permission. Although they had not previously united politically, they organized to discuss their objections to the sale. An agent of the U. S. Treasury Department reported in 1869 that:

> The dissatisfaction among the tribes on account of the sale of the territory did not arise from any special feeling of hostility, but from the fact that it was sold without their consent, they arguing that their fathers originally

owned all the country, but allowed the Russians to occupy it for their mutual benefit, in that articles desired by them could be obtained from the Russians in exchange for furs; but the right of the Russians to sell the territory, except with the intention of giving them the proceeds, is denied.

Some of the chiefs were in favor of waging war and driving out the "Boston men,"their name for the Americans. However the chief of the Chilkats warned that the locations of the coastal villages made them easy targets for possible bombardment from U. S. war vessels. He persuaded the other chiefs to wait and see what the Boston men would do.

U. S. Army

*Brevet Major General Jeff C. Davis, commanding officer of the Military District of Alaska, 1867-1870.*

**Military occupation**

Their wait was not long. In 1869, when two Tlingits were killed by a soldier, Tlingit leaders demanded a settlement from the Army in keeping with their system of law. When the Army failed to pay for the loss of life with blankets or other articles of value, Kake Tlingits retaliated by killing two prospectors. The Army then bombarded three Kake villages, destroying homes, winter food supplies, and canoes. A special agent of the U. S. later reported that the punishment of Kake was for acts that had been provoked by the Army itself.

# SELECTED DATES
## 1867-1959

1867        Alaska is purchased from Russia by the United States. Treaty of Cession provides that " 'uncivilized Native tribes' to be subject to such laws and regulations as the United States may from time to time adopt in regards to aboriginal tribes of that country."

1867-1884    Governance of Alaska by the Army, then by the Collector of Customs, then by the Navy.

1878        Beginning of salmon industry; first canneries established.

1880        First important gold discovery in Alaska (Juneau).

1884        The Organic Act makes Alaska a District with appointed governor and other officers; protection for lands used and occupied by Natives promised.

1906        Native Allotment Act provides first opportunity for Natives to obtain land under restricted title.

1912        Alaska becomes a territory with a two-house legislature; capital at Juneau.

1912        Alaska Native Brotherhood is founded in Sitka.

1924        Citizenship Act extends citizenship to all Alaska Natives who had not become citizens earlier.

1924        First Alaska Native — William L. Paul — elected to territorial legislature.

1926        Native Townsite Act provides opportunity for Natives to obtain restricted deeds to village lots.

1934        Provisions of Indian Reorganization Act extended to Alaska permitting establishment of reservations for Native groups.

1958        Congress approves the Statehood Act; right to Native lands is disclaimed; State to choose 103 million acres.

1959        Court of Claims rules that Indian title of Tlingits and Haidas was not extinguished and that they were entitled to compensation for lands taken from them by the United States.

Historians from H. H. Bancroft to Ernest Gruening agree that the Army's influence over the decade of its rule was not only demoralizing for the Tlingits, but that the Army was largely responsible for the incidents of violence which occurred.

Many of the problems of these years were caused by liquor. Although there was traffic in alcohol before the transfer, historian C. L. Andrews reports that it was an ex-soldier who taught Indians how to make "hootch," a liquor made from molasses. In 1877, when the Army was withdrawn to battle Nez Perce Indians in Idaho, a missionary observed that, "sending of soldiers to this country was the greatest piece of folly of which a government could be guilty."

That soldiers were not necessary to protect whites was shown during a two-year period between the time the Army left and the Navy arrived. Sitka Tlingits did destroy the Army stockade, however, and they occupied the abandoned buildings. Departure of the Army also led to a declaration by Chief Annahootz about retaking their country. As reported by historian Ted Hinckley, Annahootz said:

> The Russians have stolen this country from us
> and after they have gotten most of the furs
> out of the country, they have sold it to the
> Bosten Men for a big sum of money, and now
> the Americans are mad because they have
> found that the Russians have deceived them,
> and have abandoned the country, and we are
> glad to say that after so many years hard fight
> we get our country back again.

The absence of soldiers also contributed to the fears of the white population. The customs agent at Sitka was alarmed that the Tlingits would attack the white citizens, since, as he said, "many of these Indians have wrongs to redress and injuries to be made good, inflicted upon them while the country was in the hands of the military." The Sitka agent added:

> . . . as the Indians are roaming at their leisure
> and pleasure all over the place night and day,
> the probabilities of some murderous out-
> break, ending in a general massacre, are
> exceedingly great.

On the other hand, the customs agent at Wrangell, where there was a gathering of white miners, expressed fears for the safety of the native population.

With 1,500 Indians in the vicinity of Sitka and only 20 American citizens and Russians, the sense of threat may have been real. But no "massacre" occurred. The period during which the American government was represented only by a customs office was generally free of violence.

*Tlingit Chief Annahootz.*

**No extinguishment
of title**

During Alaska's first decade as an American colony there was but little interference with traditional uses of the lands and waters, even among the Tlingits and Haidas. And there was no extinguishment of aboriginal or Indian Title.

No laws had been adopted by Congress to allow persons to obtain title or other rights to land, and partly for this reason, there was very little movement of white settlers into Alaska. Since there was not the same urgency to extinguish Indian title as existed in the American West, there was no need to make treaties with native tribes. The designation of "Indian Country" was formally applied to Alaska in 1873 to prohibit the sale of liquor, but the designation did not extinguish Indian Title.

*Tlingits of Killisnoo arrive at Sitka for potlatch, 1904.*

## "... INHABITED BY, BUT NOT BELONGING TO THEM ..."

An archbishop and members of his party journeying to the Yukon Territory in 1886 were stopped by a chief of the Chilkat Tlingits and told to pay a fee for passing through their area. When the archbishop protested, the chief reportedly assaulted him. Upon hearing of the complaint, Governor A. P. Swineford (along with 12 men) traveled to Chilkoot village and arrested the chief, who "boldly asserted the right to exact payment for the privilege of passing through the country he claimed as belonging to him and his people." Swineford then talked with the Chilkats, warning them that they "must abandon their pretentions of right to collect toll from white men passing through the country inhabited by but not belonging to them in a political sense ..."

Source: Letter from Governor A. P. Swineford to the President, October 1, 1886.

There were, however, intrusions into aboriginal lands. One such instance was the recording of squatters' and miners' claims by the U. S. Customs office even though such claims could not lawfully be made. Further, the claimants were not removed from their claims, despite the military's authority and obligation to do so.

**Intrusions**

67

Intrusion into Native lands was made possible in 1880 during the Navy's rule. Chilkat Tlingits had steadfastly refused to allow the movement of whites through their territory into Canada and the Navy's commander saw this as a deterrent to the development of Alaska. He sent a warship carrying a Gatling gun to escort five sailboats of armed prospectors to the Chilkat country. The ship's officer explained to the Chilkat chiefs how the gun worked and read a letter to them assuring them that the prospectors would not interfere with their fur trade. The Chilkat chiefs then agreed to open Dyea Pass into Canada to gold hunters.

Later during the period of Navy rule, its commanding officer disrupted traditional patterns of land and water use by encouraging a treaty of peace between the Stikine (Wrangell area) and Hutsnuwu (Angoon) Tlingits. In the treaty they agreed that members of each tribe "shall be free to travel, hunt, or fish in the territories of either." Such a provision effectively weakened tribal laws governing land and water ownership.

Another kind of intrusion, which also took place during the Navy's period of rule, involved the removal of Aukwan Tlingits from the mining settlement called Rockwell (now Juneau). Despite the Navy's obligation to expel the miners — owing to the absence of any land laws — it did not. The officer in charge reported, in explaining the Navy's action, that the Tlingits had been paid for the land. Such transfers of land rights were not legal, for there were no land laws.

**The Organic Act (1884)**

The first land law for Alaska provided specific protection to claims of miners and lands used by missionaries, but gave only promise of continued use and occupancy of lands to holders of aboriginal rights. The law was the Organic Act,

*Potlatch dancers at Sitka, 1904.*

adopted by Congress in 1884 to provide the first civil government for the territory.

While mining interests stimulated passage of the Organic Act, the rights of Natives* affected its provisions. The stated intention of the committee sponsoring the measure was "to save from all possible invasion the rights of Indian residents of Alaska" until such time as "the Secretary could ascertain what their claims were." During debate on the measure, Senator Plumb of Kansas had said:

> I do not want to impose a government on several thousand Indians, for the purpose of assuming to consult the convenience of about four hundred white people, which shall do the Indians more hurt than it will do the white people good. Pending an investigation of this question I propose that the Indian shall at least have as many rights after the passage of this bill as he had before.

While the provision of the act regarding Native lands did not permit them to acquire title, it was a provision of much future importance:

> Indians or other persons in said district shall not be disturbed in the possession of any lands actually in their use or occupation or now claimed by them but the terms under which such persons may acquire title to such lands is reserved for future legislation by Congress.

*the word "Native" is capitalized to make clear that the reference is to persons of Eskimo, Indian, or Aleut birth, not to all persons born in Alaska.

University of Alaska Archives (Frederick Hadleigh-West Collection)

*Klinkwan, Prince of Wales Island, 1899.*

## KOBUK RIVER PEOPLE, 1884

"The fact that these interior tribes are better morally than their brethren of the coast is so apparent that even the dullest observer must see the difference between the two, and wonder how it happens that these natives who have been brought into contact with our boasted civilization are more objectionable in their manners and less trustworthy than those who have not enjoyed these advantages. A few words will suffice to show the moral character of these gentle hyperboreans. They are honest in their dealings with strangers and amongst themselves, as we had ample means of finding out. They are simple and credulous, and easily deceived, showing that they are not liable to deceive others. They are hospitable, and although intensely curious, are not prying or intrusive. In their domestic relations they are kind and devoted to each other, and the universal consideration paid by all to the very old and feeble is one of the touching and admirable traits of their character. The extraordinarily kind and indulgent treatment of their children is a trait which is common to all these northern tribes."

Source: J. C. Cantwell in *Cruise of the Revenue Steamer Corwin in the Arctic Ocean in the year, 1884,* by M. A. Healy, Government Printing Office, Washington, 1889.

The U. S. policy of "civilizing" American tribes was also reflected in the act. Grants of up to 640 acres could be made to missionary stations to allow continuation of their activities.

At the time of passage, greater importance lay in the act's extension of mining laws to Alaska. Those with mining claims could obtain title to their claims unless such claims were located on a site physically occupied or improved by members of Native groups. The land office established by the act quickly made legal the mining claims recorded illegally over the preceding 17 years. Among other events, the earlier dispossession of the Aukwan Tlingits was made legal.

However important the Organic Act was to become in the future in its recognition of aboriginal use and occupancy, it effectively denied Natives at the time the opportunity to obtain title to their lands under the white man's system of title recognition. It provided the legal means for miners to deprive Natives of their land and resources. Although title to land apart from mining claims could not be acquired, other lands were staked, posted, and recorded.

Passage of the Organic Act launched a period of growth in the white population of the territory and the development of business and commercial enterprises. In 1880 there had been 430 whites; by 1890 there were about 6,700 non-Natives in Alaska. With this growth was to come new intrusions on lands used, occupied, or claimed by Natives.

| | Figure 1 | | |
| | POPULATION OF ALASKA | | |
| | 1880-1970 | | |
| Year of Census | Eskimos, Indians, and Aleuts | Non-Natives | Total |
| --- | --- | --- | --- |
| 1880 | 32,996 | 430 | 33,426 |
| 1890 | 25,354 | 6,698 | 32,052 |
| 1900 | 29,536 | 34,056 | 63,592 |
| 1909 | 25,331 | 39,025 | 64,356 |
| 1920 | 26,558 | 28,478 | 55,036 |
| 1929 | 29,983 | 29,295 | 59,278 |
| 1939 | 32,458 | 40,066 | 72,524 |
| 1950 | 33,863 | 94,780 | 128,643 |
| 1960 | 43,081 | 183,086 | 226,167 |
| 1970 | 51,712 | 250,461 | 302,173 |

Source: Rogers, George W., "Alaska Native Population Trends and Vital Statistics, 1950-1985," Institute of Social, Economic, and Government Research, University of Alaska, Fairbanks, Alaska, November 1971.

University of Alaska Archives (Charles Bunnell Collection)

*Home of Chief Ko-Teth Sha-Doc, Ketchikan, 1905.*

Encroachments upon the lives and lands of Eskimos, Indians, and Aleuts multiplied with the passage of time. Aboriginal land rights were ignored by American citizens and others as they sought profits from the natural resources of Alaska. By 1900 these new migrants numbered about 34,000 persons, making Natives for the first time a minority in their own land.

**The gold rush**

It was the discovery of gold in Alaska and the neighboring Yukon Territory of Canada which led to the first great migration of whites to Alaska. The small number of miners who sought gold at Juneau in the 1800's became a swarm with discoveries in the Klondike district of the Yukon, and later in interior and western Alaska.

As noted in the last chapter, the first to be affected had been the Aukwan Tlingits who gave way to prospectors at the site of what was to become the city of Juneau; and as early as 1880, Chilkat Tlingits had been forced by threat to allow prospectors passage through their country. Following the discoveries in the Klondike district in 1896, thousands of prospectors made their way across the mountain passes.

Alaska State Museum, Juneau

*Klondikers climbing Chilkoot Pass.*

## A REQUEST FOR A
## "RIGHT TO HOLD A CLAIM," 1902

Karta Bay, Alaska, July 17, 1902.

Dear Sir: I am a native born of Fort Wrangell and would like to know if there is any chance of getting papers for holding mineral lands in Alaska. I was educated in the East, in Philadelphia, and at Carlisle Indian School. I was almost brought up as a white person, and I have lived up to it ever since I left school.

If you want to find out about my reputation you can find it out from my brother-in-law, John Kelly, who has lived in Killisnoo and Sitka for a good many years. Also, you can inquire of any merchant in Wrangell.

I like to prospect, but as a native have no right to hold a claim, and I never know what to do with the prospects that I have found, and there are only a few white men that can be trusted, to my knowledge, in a case of this kind.

I am 26 years of age, and I think I could do well if I could succeed in getting my citizen papers or rights for holding mineral lands in Alaska. I want you to advise me what to do to get it, or if you can do anything for me let me know it soon and oblige.

My address will be Loring, Alaska.

Yours, very truly,

Thomas Jackson.

Governor Brady, Sitka, Alaska.

Source: "Report of the Governor of Alaska" in *Annual Reports of the Department of Interior*, Government Printing Office, Washington, D. C., 1902.

Eskimos of western Alaska and Athabascans of the interior were next to experience the flood of gold seekers. By 1900 the beaches of Nome had drawn nearly 20,000 people from elsewhere in the world. Thousands of others were scattered along western and northern rivers and creeks in search of gold. With the strikes in 1902 in the vicinity of what was to become the city of Fairbanks, disappointed stampeders poured into interior Alaska from the Seward Peninsula, the Klondike, and from the United States. They also went to Cook Inlet, the Copper River area, and elsewhere.

*The gold rush settlement of Nome, 1903.*

By 1908, over $140 million in gold was taken from Alaska. Some had certainly struck it rich, but Natives were not among those who did. Although Kowee, an Aukwan Tlingit had led Joe Juneau to gold, he did not share in the wealth. Nor did Tom Guarrick, the Eskimo who had located one of the first gold deposits on the Seward Peninsula. Mining claims could lawfully be staked only by citizens. Since Natives were considered to be members of "uncivilized tribes," they were not accorded citizenship by the Treaty of Cession.

For Natives, the gold stampede meant a drastic reduction in moose, caribou, and small game as prospectors hunted these animals for their food supply. In many areas, gold mining resulted in siltation of salmon streams, destroying them. But contact with the white men had even graver consequences. In the words of William H. Dall, a scientist associated with Alaska for over 40 years, "civilization and the greed of gold [had brought] drink, disease, and death."

*Successful gold miners.*

*Barge of salmon at Egegik.*

University of Alaska Archives (C. H. Whetherbee Collection)

**The salmon industry**

Even before the first gold strikes, the salmon — the most important single food resource of Natives — was being harvested and marketed by others. Tlingits of southeastern were the first to be affected as canneries were established in 1878 at Klawock and Old Sitka. Eskimos and Aleuts were next as the number of canneries grew and spread to Prince William Sound, Cook Inlet, Kodiak Island, the Alaska Peninsula, and Bristol Bay.

Native catches of salmon had been based upon their need for immediate use and for drying or smoking for the winter months. Some additional quantities were taken to be used in trace. Each year thousands of fish were taken. The interest of the commercial salmon packers, however, was to catch as many as could be processed and sold. Using a variety of methods — seines, nets, and traps as appropriate — the packers and their fishermen took millions of fish from the creeks and streams.

In 1895, a special agent of the U. S. Treasury Department visited the salmon canneries of Alaska and prepared a comprehensive report. He warned of the destruction of the salmon streams and described the complaints of Natives. At Karluk, located on "the finest salmon stream in Alaska," he wrote:

> we met a committee of native men who, through an interpreter, told us of how they were denied the right to fish for themselves, and refused employment by the canners as well. It seems that owing to the fact that seines were stretched across the mouth of the river the salmon could not ascend the stream

75

*Salmon cannery on Karluk River, Kodiak Island, 1897.*

and consequently there were no fish for the natives to get whenever they did attempt to get any; and being refused employment as regular hands along with the foreigners, they could not make a living.

The effect of the salmon industry upon Natives was also the subject of complaint in southeastern Alaska. In 1897 the commander of the *Albatross*, a government fisheries survey vessel, told of visits to his ship by Tlingit and Haida chiefs. He reported:

They are essentially fish-eating Indians, depending upon the streams of the country for a large amount of food supply. These streams, under their own administration, for centuries have belonged to certain families or clans settled in the vicinity, and their rights in these streams have never been infringed upon until the advent of the whites. No Indians would fish in a stream not their own except by invitation, and they cannot understand how those of a higher civilization should be — as they regard it — less honorable than their own savage kind. They claim the white man is crowding them from their homes, robbing them of their ancestral rights, taking away their fish by shiploads; that their streams must soon become exhausted; that the Indian will have no supply to maintain himself and family; and that starvation must follow.

The commander, Jefferson Moser, said his sympathies were with the Indians and that he would "gladly recommend, if the way were clear, the establishment of ownership in streams." But, he said, "it is impracticable, and I only ask for him a consideration of his claim, and whatever law is framed, that a liberal balance be thrown in his favor."

---

## AN APPEAL FOR HELP, 1889

Afognak, Alaska, June 22, 1899.

Sir: We, the natives and all the Russian population of Afognak, appeal to your excellency to help us to retain possession of the fish streams where we are dependent upon getting our winter's supply of food for ourselves and families. We can not get any chance of fishing in the streams, as the cannery fishermen of all the companies operating here have taken possession of the mouths of the rivers. They stretch a rope across the water, and as the rope vibrates from the force of the current, they frighten the fish. In the meantime they seine fish directly at the mouth of the stream.

We tried to remonstrate with them and they threatened to smash our skulls. We lay these facts before your excellency so that you may give us some assistance. We can not allow our families to starve, and if the canneries are allowed to carry away all our fish—the main food—we will be obliged to starve.

Hoping you will look kindly upon our petition,

We are, very respectfully, your obedient servants,

Vasili Alexandroff,
Radion Shangen,
Radion X. Malutin,
Chiefs for the Afognak Population.

His excellency Hon. John G. Brady,
Governor of Alaska.

Source: "Report of the Governor of Alaska" in *Annual Reports of the Department of the Interior*, Government Printing Office, Washington, D. C., 1899.

---

**Sea mammals**

Northern and western Eskimos and Aleuts who depended upon sea mammals were not spared as white men sought the resources of Alaska's waters.

American whalers were active in the Arctic long before the transfer of Alaska to the United States. As early as 1846 several hundred ships pursued the whale for its oil and baleen. In 1852 the value of the catch was set at $14 million.

*Four whaling vessels and the U. S. Revenue Cutter Bear.*

By the time of the transfer, the number of whales was so reduced that only a few dozen ships were off Alaska's coast. If they failed to obtain the number of whales they wanted, they killed walrus for oil and ivory tusks. Historian C. L. Andrews says that 100,000 walrus were taken between 1870 and 1880. The result, he reports:

> . . . was almost to exterminate the animals in the Pacific, causing suffering and death among the Eskimos because of the taking of their food supplies in whale and walrus, thus throwing them onto the caribou and seal, which were insufficient. The caribou were nearly exterminated, and the natives perished from famine and consequent pestilence.

In these same years, the numbers of fur seals and sea otters were sharply reduced by hunters employed by American companies. A California corporation had been granted a

*Seal harvest, Pribilof Islands, 1897.*

lease to harvest the fur seals of the Pribilof Islands on a regulated basis, but the slaughter of the seals at sea by others was rapidly depleting the herd. Aleuts employed by the corporation at St. Paul and St. George harvested 140,000 seals the year after the purchase. Twenty-five years later, the total number of seals taken on the islands was 7,390. The taking of the even more valuable sea otter of the Aleutians was not regulated after the departure of the Russians. In the 1880's almost 5,000 pelts were taken annually by American companies but, as Andrews reports, in 1910 only 29 pelts were taken. The sea otter had been virtually exterminated.

In 1909, a former senior Army officer in Alaska, Major **Effects** General A. W. Greely, wrote a *Handbook of Alaska.* Drawing upon his nine years in the territory and the works of others, he portrayed the grandeur of its scenery and the wealth of its natural resources. His enthusiasm for what the "great and prosperous country" had become was only diminished when he wrote of the situation of Alaska Natives. He said that the conditions of Natives caused by the advance of whites in the territory "can only be viewed as disgraceful to a nation claiming to be civilized, humanitarian, or Christian." After reviewing the history of several decades, he asked:

> What, if anything does the General Government owe the natives of Alaska, and in what form shall the payment be made? It is a problem great in its moral as well as in its practical aspects. Having largely destroyed their food supplies, altered their environment, and changed their standards and methods of life, what does a nation that has drawn products valued at $300,000,000 owe to the natives of Alaska? Will this nation pay its debt on this account?

# Chapter 12                                   Unacknowledged Title

Aboriginal title had not been extinguished by the Treaty **Land transfers:** of Cession and it appeared to be accepted by the Organic **others** Act. But just as the act did not prevent the taking of the resources of the land by others, it did not prevent the taking of the land itself. Until Natives became citizens and until they could organize for their cause there was little they could do about it.

With the cession of Alaska to the United States all of its lands and waters had become public domain — land held and controlled by the federal government. Transfers to private ownership or designation for specific uses required Congressional action.

*Rev. Duncan's Town Hall, Metlakatla, 1895.*

Apart from land rights granted through mining claims, the first land rights transferred by Congress went to a group of Tsimshians who had migrated to Alaska from Canada in 1887. Under the leadership of William Duncan, a white lay missionary, they had established a community called New Metlakatla on Annette Island. Although the island was in the territory of the Cape Fox Tlingits, Congress established in 1891 an 86,000-acre reservation for the Metlakatlans "and such other Alaskan natives as may join them."

The same 1891 act of Congress opened land for townsites and trade and manufacturing sites, and authorized the President to set aside timbered areas as public reserves. There was no provision for Natives of Alaska to acquire legal title to land.

Under the 1891 law and subsequent acts of Congress, millions of acres were withdrawn from the public domain to establish Tongass and Chugach National Forests, Mt. McKinley National Park, and to serve a variety of other public purposes.

**Land grants:**
**Natives**

The first of two Congressional acts that allowed Alaska Natives to obtain title to land was adopted in 1906. The second was adopted in 1926. Neither was based upon aboriginal title, nor did they recognize it. Neither was appropriate to Native uses of the lands and waters.

The Native Allotment Act of 1906 provided for conveyance of 160 acres of public domain to adult Natives. Any single tract could be selected as long as the ground did not include mineral deposits. A few allotments were issued in southeastern Alaska, but most Natives did not even know that such allotments could be obtained.

Under the second act, the Native Townsite Act of 1926, villages were to be surveyed into lots, blocks, and streets, and individual lots conveyed to Native adults.

Both of these acts provided only for the conveyance of "restricted" title. The Native to whom it was issued could not sell or lease the lot or allotment without the approval of the Secretary of the Interior. The land was, in other words, held "in trust" by the Secretary, who was a guardian of the Native as he was of the American Indian. Such restricted title meant also that the land would not be taxed.

Neither the Allotment Act nor the Townsite Act were effective in protecting lands used and occupied by Natives. Allotments were fine for farmers, but not for hunters and fishermen. And what protection for a large food-gathering territory was to be afforded by a small lot in the village?

The continuing movement of whites into interior Alaska, brought about planning for a railroad (which would bring even more settlers). According to Stanton Patty, writing in the *Alaska Journal*, this led to what may have been the first conference devoted to Native land rights. It was held in July, 1915 at the Thomas Memorial Library in Fairbanks.

**Land rights conference**

The conference had been called by former Judge James Wickersham, Alaska's delegate to Congress. Wickersham brought the group together because area Athabascans had asked him how they could preserve their lands against settlement by others. It was attended by 14 persons, including six Tanana chiefs. What the chiefs wanted, in the words of Chief Alexander of Tolovana was that the government "not let the white people come near us. Let us live our own lives in the customs we know."

Through an interpreter, Wickersham explained that the government couldn't stop the white people, but that Indians could protect their land (1) by obtaining 160-acre allotments for their homes, or (2) by asking for establishment of a reservation.

After some deliberation, the Athabascan chiefs reported that the two choices offered were not acceptable. The allotments would separate members of the community, they explained; and besides, their people lived at many locations throughout the year, not just at one. And, as for a reservation, Chief Ivan of Coskaket (also called Crossjacket) spoke for all:

> We don't want to go on a reservation, but
> wish to stay perfectly free just as we are now,
> and go about just the same as now.

Wickersham argued that the reservation would not be a prison, but the chiefs were not persuaded. "I tell you that we are people on the go," said Chief Alexander of Tolovana,

*Tanana chiefs, 1915, (left to right), Alexander of Tolovana, William of Tanana, Thomas of Nenana, interpreter Paul Williams, Ivan of Coskaket, Charlie of Minto, and Alexander William of Tanana.*

"and I believe if we were put in one place, we would just die off like rabbits."

Perhaps Chief Joe of Salchaket best expressed the request of the Tanana Chiefs when he asked, "We are suggesting to you just one thing, that we want to be left alone. As the whole continent was made for you, God made Alaska for the Indian people, and all we hope is to be able to live here all the time."

The chiefs expressed the hope that Wickersham could accomplish their request before he sought re-election as delegate. In reply, Wickersham said he was pleased at their interest in who would be delegate to Congress. He asked the interpreter to tell the chiefs that "as soon as they have established homes and live like white men, and assume the habits of civilization, they can have a vote."

**Alaska Native Brotherhood**

Winning citizenship was a primary goal of the first Native organization to be formed on more than a local basis. This new organization was the Alaska Native Brotherhood (ANB).

The ANB was founded by a Tsimshian and nine Tlingits from Sitka, Angoon, Juneau, and Klawock at a meeting in

*Founders of the Alaska Native Brotherhood (left to right), Paul Liberty, James Watson, Ralph Young, Eli Katinook, Peter Simpson, Frank Mercer, James C. Johnson, Chester Worthington, George Field, William Hobson, and Frank Price.*

Sitka in 1912. Within three years, a women's organization, the Alaska Native Sisterhood, was established. Within a decade, chapters (called camps) were established in most towns and villages of southeastern Alaska.

Along with the goal of winning citizenship the ANB had two related concerns: education for themselves and abandonment of aboriginal customs which were seen by whites as "uncivilized." The Dawes Act, it will be recalled, provided that citizenship could be obtained by Indians who "severed tribal relationship and adopted the habits of civilization."

Although the Dawes Act permitted Natives to become citizens, many whites in Alaska resisted the idea of Natives having citizenship rights. In part because of ANB efforts, the territorial legislature adopted in 1915 a similar act for the specific purposes of allowing Natives to become citizens. A few additional Natives became citizens under the 1915 act, but most Natives did not become citizens until adoption by the U. S. Congress of the Citizenship Act of 1924.

**Citizenship**

One right of citizenship — the right to vote — was exercised by some southeastern Indians two years before the national legislation was enacted. This came about as the result of efforts by William L. Paul, a Tlingit, attorney, and active member of the ANB. Charlie Jones, also known as Chief Shakes, had been denied the right to vote by Wrangell election officials. Paul defended Jones, pointing out that he had voted before and that he was a responsible member of the community. Jones was found not guilty. While the case "did not really affect the legal status of Natives," according to anthropologist Philip Drucker, "it was accepted as doing so in the popular mind, both white and Indian." As a result, there was increasing acceptance that the Indians had the right to vote.

## LEGAL STATUS
## OF ALASKA NATIVES, 1932

"In the beginning, and for a long time after the cession of this Territory Congress took no particular notice of these natives; has never undertaken to hamper their individual movements; confine them to a locality or reservation, or to place them under the immediate control of its officers, as has been the case with the American Indians; and no special provision was made for their support and education until comparatively recently . . .

"Later, however, Congress began to directly recognize these natives as being, to a very considerable extent at least, under our Government's guardianship and enacted laws which protected them in the possession of the lands they occupied; made provision for the allotment of lands to them in severalty, similar to those made to the American Indians; gave them special hunting, fishing and other particular privileges to enable them to support themselves, and supplied them with reindeer and instructions as to their propagation. Congress has also supplied funds to give these natives medical and hospital treatment and finally made and is still making extensive appropriations to defray the expenses of both their education and their support.

"Not only has Congress in this manner treated these natives as being wards of the Government but they have been repeatedly so recognized by the courts . . .

"From this it will be seen that these natives are now unquestionably considered and treated as being under the guardianship and protection of the Federal Government, at least to such an extent as to bring them within the spirit, if not within the exact letter, of the laws relative to American Indians . . ."

—from Office of the Solicitor,
U. S. Department of Interior,
February 24, 1932

Source: Anderson, H. D. and Eells, W. C., *Alaska Natives*, Stanford University Press, Stanford, California, 1935.

From its beginning, the ANB had addressed politics and political issues. Until Natives secured the right to vote, however, their effectiveness was very limited.

In 1924, the man who had won a reputation as a champion of Native rights, William L. Paul, won election to the Territorial House of Representatives. He was the first Native to win a legislative seat.

Even though one legislative seat had been won, it represented very little political power in a 40-person legislature. And even though the right to vote was secured, Natives living in remote settlements away from southeastern Alaska were not generally aware of it. Their children were enrolled in schools as they were established, but most adult villagers had but little formal education. By and large they were not concerned about elections and the operation of territorial government. Their concern was, instead, to continue to live on the land as they had for generations.

**Political action**

Alaska State Museum, Juneau

*William L. Paul, third from left, the first Native elected to the Territorial legislature, 1925.*

Even with citizenship it would be more than a generation before Natives acquired enough political importance to significantly affect the legislative process. In the meantime — in the 1930's, 1940's, and 1950's — there was renewed promise that Native rights to land would be protected or, if not, that these rights would be purchased. This promise was suggested in three ways — the Indian Reorganization Act, the Alaska Statehood Act, and the Tlingit-Haida court decision.

**Reservations**

Preserving large areas for the use and occupancy of Alaska Natives became a possibility in 1936. This came about by Congressional action extending the Indian Reorganization Act to Alaska.

The Indian Reorganization Act (also called the Wheeler-Howard Act) was enacted in 1934 to curb the loss of Indian lands and to restore lands already lost under the Dawes Act of 1887. Under its provisions, the U. S. Department of the Interior could establish reservations for Eskimos and Indians in Alaska. Such reservations, it will be recalled, would not mean title for the people living on them. Title would be held in "trust" for them by the Department.

The act became the focus of wide controversy. Both Natives and whites raised objections to it. Non-Natives were fearful that land would be locked up — preventing the development of resources and the growth of the territory's economy. Natives — especially those who were familiar with reservations elsewhere in America — feared that they might be confined to small areas with limited resources.

*View of Sitka Indian Village, 1938.*      U. S. Department of the Interior

*Fish drying racks and food storage cache, Unalakleet, 1939.*

Despite the controversy, seven reservations were established between 1941 and 1946. The largest, which included the villages of Venetie, Arctic Village, Kachik, and Christian Village was 1,408,000 acres; the smallest — Unalakleet — was 870 acres. The others were established at Akutan, Diomede, Hydaburg, Karluk, and Wales.

A court held later that the Hydaburg reservation had not been legally established. Three other villages where reservations were proposed voted them down.

*Two youths in kayak on the Kuskokwim River, 1939.*

One reason for the creation of reservations was the continuing increase in the non-Native population of the territory. Their numbers reached about 40,000 in 1939 and, with the building of the defense systems for World War II, had mushroomed by the mid-1940's. In requesting the reservations, the Secretary of the Interior explained the threat:

> The large influx of population into Alaska as a result of war activities, and the growing encroachment of the whites upon the land and resources of the Indians and Eskimos have served to emphasize the most serious problem confronting the Natives — the protection of their ancestral hunting, trapping, and fishing bases.

By 1950, 80 additional villages had submitted petitions to the Secretary requesting reservations of 100 million acres. What happened in response to their petitions? Writing much later, in *Alaska Natives and the Land*, Esther Wunnicke reported succinctly: "No action was taken." The likely reason for inaction was that public opinion of the 1950's seemed opposed to reservations and what they represented: racial segregation and discrimination.

Under the Indian Reorganization Act only a few villages had obtained protection against encroachments by others.

**Political gains**    Following William Paul's example of 1924, other Natives filed for legislative seats and some won. In 1944, Frank Peratrovich of Klawock and Andrew Hope of Sitka were

Alaska State Museum, Juneau

*Members of the Territorial House of Representatives when it convened in January, 1951 included (second row) James K. Wells of Noorvik, Frank G. Johnson of Kake, Andrew Hope of Sitka, and Frank Degnan of Unalakleet.*

*Territorial Senate President Frank Peratrovich of Klawock (presiding over 1949 session).*

elected to the Territorial House of Representatives; in 1946 Frank G. Johnson of Kake was elected to the House and Peratrovich to the Senate. In 1948, Peratrovich became Senate president. In the same year, the first Eskimos were elected to the Territorial legislature; they were Percy Ipalook of Wales and William E. Beltz of Nome. Then in 1950, Frank Degnan of Unalakleet and James K. Wells of Noorvik won House seats.

*Members of the Territorial Senate when it convened in 1951 included William Beltz of Nome (at left) and Percy Ipalook of Wales.*

# THE CONSTITUTIONAL CONVENTION
## AND NATIVE LAND RIGHTS

Rights of Natives to land were the subject of an extended debate at the 1955 Alaska Constitutional Convention in Fairbanks.

The debate was triggered by a proposal made by Col. M. R. "Muktuk" Marston of Anchorage, who during World War II had organized the Eskimo Scouts of the Alaska Territorial Guard. Marston's proposal was that Eskimos, Indians, and Aleuts be granted title to land parcels of 160 acres they were using and occupying. It also included a provision that would leave open the larger issue of Native claims.

Marston told the Convention that the Native Allotment Act was of no help to most Natives. He explained that he had tried for three years to help George Lockwood of Unalakleet protect his land, but that he had failed. Pointing to a map, he said:

> He lives right there on a little piece of ground and he wants a title to it. He has a fishing camp up here. He would like to have title to that five acres. There is where the military is now occupying camp for three years, and pushed him aside. The cats have destroyed his blueberries, the beach where his kiddies played — they can't play there anymore, and for three years he has been dispossessed of that position by the military who are building a radar station up here. If he had title to that ground, as you and I would have, he would have no complaints, so in the name of decency and honor and common ordinary right, I ask this Convention to adopt this amendment and let George have his ground saved for him and a little camp site where he makes his living by fishing and hunting.

Although a disclaimer regarding Native lands was adopted, Marston's proposal was rejected. Summarizing the five-hour debate in his book, *Alaska's Constitutional Convention*, Victor Fischer wrote:

> Marston had firm supporters who agreed that the convention must do justice to the Alaska Natives. Others, however, expressed concern about interfering with the federal responsibility for safeguarding and compensating aboriginal rights and raised doubts about the state's ability to implement the intent of the Marston amendment. Various delegates also objected to language, to the amount of land involved, and to the special treatment proposed for one class of Alaskans. It was also noted that since 1906, Alaska Natives had by federal statute been entitled to 160-acre allotments, and that their occupancy rights could be taken care of under existing law.

Fischer explained that many revisions were made — including "Alaskans" in place of "Eskimos, Indians, and Aleuts" — that led to confusion about the issues. "Thus," he wrote, "the proposal for granting land rights to Alaska Natives went down to defeat without ever coming to a direct vote on the basic issues involved."

*At Gambell, 1948. Lester Nopawhotak.*

In the legislative session which began in 1952 Natives held seven seats. Although this was a substantial gain from the time Paul was the only Native legislator, it was still but a small minority of the total membership.

When the Organic Act of 1884 had been enacted it appeared to promise protection for lands used and occupied by Natives. It had failed in that promise.

**Statehood**

With the Statehood Act of 1958, the promise was renewed. In the act, the new State and its people disclaimed all right or title to lands "the right or title to which may be held by Eskimos, Indians, or Aleuts" or held in trust for them.

The act, however, did not define the "right or title" which Natives might have. This was left to future action by the Congress or the courts.

Alaska was admitted as a state on January 3, 1959. By 1961, the promise of the disclaimer was to be overshadowed by another provision of the act. This provision — in part the subject of the next chapter — was the grant of about 103 million acres of land to the new state.

While the promise of protection for land rights was again to be unfulfilled, 1959 brought promise of another kind: payment to Natives for lands which were theirs, but taken by others. This was the decision of the Court of Claims in the Tlingit-Haida case.

**Tlingit-Haida decision**

The court action had its beginnings in 1929 at an Alaska Native Brotherhood meeting in Haines. Out of discussions begun there, the Congress passed a law in 1935 allowing Tlingits and Haidas to sue the United States for the loss of their land to others. By this time, nearly all of southeastern Alaska was the Tongass National Forest, Glacier Bay National Monument, or set aside as a reservation for Tsimshian Indians from Canada.

*Diomede Island*

In their suit, long delayed by attorney problems and by the possibility of obtaining reservations, Tlingits and Haidas had asserted that the United States had taken land which was theirs by Indian title. After reviewing the evidence and the arguments of opposing attorneys, the court issued its findings of fact (96 pages) and its decision (26 pages). In conclusion — in the words of the court — the Tlingits and Haidas have established their use and occupancy, i.e., Indian title, to the lands and waters of virtually all of southeastern Alaska. Furthermore, the court concluded:

- that they were using and occupying that land according to their Native manner of use and occupancy in 1867 when the United States acquired Alaska from Russia . . .

- that such use and occupancy was not interferred with by the United States or its citizens until 1884;

- that beginning in 1884 and continuing thereafter, these Indians lost most of their land . . . through the Government's failure to protect the rights of such Indians in such lands and waters through the administration of its laws and the provisions of the laws themselves; and,

- that a large area . . . [was] taken without compensation and without the consent of the Indians . . .

In deciding in favor of Tlingits and Haidas the Court said they were entitled to compensation for "all usable and accessible land which they used and occupied." It was to be another nine years before the Court placed a value upon the 16 million acres taken by the government.

# UNIT FOUR

# THE LAND CLAIMS STRUGGLE

*"A controversy of immense proportions is rapidly coming to a head in Alaska. It is a situation which has lain dormant (except for sporadic outbursts) since Alaska was purchased from Russia in 1867. This problem has been skirted by Congress, alternately grappled with by the Department of the Interior then dropped to allow the furor to settle, kept Alaskan political leaders frustrated, and the courts have ruled time and again — but never with finality nor clarity. The problem is simply this: What are the rights of the Alaskan Natives to the property and resources upon which they have lived since time immemorial?"*

—William L. Hensley (Igagruk)
"What Rights to Land Have
the Alaska Natives?" (1966)

In 1960 Alaska Natives made up about one-fifth of the state's population. Although they were a minority of the total, most Natives lived where they were a majority — in perhaps 200 villages and settlements widely scattered across rural Alaska. Most of the white population lived in a half-dozen cities, principally in Anchorage, Fairbanks, Juneau, and Ketchikan.

Living away from these urban centers, most Natives could use the land as they and their ancestors had for thousands of years. Continued use seemed a certainty.

But the decade of the 1960's was to be marked by the emergence of new threats to Native land rights. In response, Natives formed local and regional organizations to preserve their rights and their lands. Communication among widely separated villagers was improved as a Native newspaper was founded and as government programs began to bring Natives together in planning for the programs affecting their lives. After several unsuccessful attempts, Natives organized in the second half of the decade into a statewide organization.

By this time, claims of Natives to lands traditionally used were being officially recorded. Protests against the transfer of land ownership to others were mounting. There came to be a growing recognition among political leaders in the state and the nation's capital that solving the problem of Native claims was required, partly because the claims were just, and partly because the future of the state itself was tied to finding a solution to the claims.

What began in 1961 as an effort by Natives to preserve their land rights against others was to be concluded with a settlement of Native land claims in 1971 by the Congress.

# New Threats to Land Rights                       Chapter 14

Project Chariot

The first organized efforts of the 1960's to preserve ancient land rights had their beginnings in the proposed use of atomic-age technology. These efforts began in northern Alaska.

When Inupiat Eskimo artist Howard Rock traveled from Seattle to visit his birthplace at the village of Point Hope in 1961, he learned that the U. S. Atomic Energy Commission was planning to set off a nuclear device at nearby Cape Thompson. The experiment, which was called Project Chariot, had brought scientists and engineers into the region to plan for the use of the atomic explosive to create a harbor where none had existed before. The facility was expected to be used eventually for shipment of minerals and other resources from the northwest coast.

Residents of Point Hope, Kivalina, and Noatak worried about the potential danger of radioactive contamination to

*Cape Thompson.*

themselves and to the animals which they hunted for their livelihood. Rock, who soon found himself the spokesman for Point Hope, expressed concern over the failure of the commission to think of the safety and welfare of the people of the Cape Thompson area. "They did not even make a tiny effort," he said, "to consult the Natives who lived close by and who have always used Cape Thompson as a hunting and egging area."

Despite assurances from the federal agency that Project Chariot would be beneficial to the Eskimos of the region and to all of mankind, northwest villagers remained strongly opposed to it.

The strong feeling against Project Chariot in the northwest was matched in Barrow in the outrage felt by other Inupiat Eskimos over limitations being imposed upon their age-old practice of hunting ducks for subsistence at any time of the year. **Hunting rights**

The hunting rights issue had its beginnings in 1960 when State Representative John Nusungingya was arrested for shooting ducks outside of a hunting season established by an international migratory birds treaty. Two days after he was arrested, 138 other men shot ducks and presented themselves to federal game wardens for arrest. By 1961, the charges against all of them had been dropped, but all Natives were warned that future violations would result in arrest and prosecution.

Tundra Times

*First president of Inupiat Paitot, Guy Okakok of Barrow.*

**Inupiat Paitot**

To resolve these issues, northern Eskimos enlisted the support of the Association on American Indian Affairs, a private, charitable organization based in New York City, and held a conference in Barrow in November of 1961. Neither issue was immediately settled, but the conference did win the attention of high officials of the U. S. Department of the Interior. And it led to the development of the first regional Native organization to be established since the founding of the Alaska Native Brotherhood nearly a half century earlier. The new organization, Inupiat Paitot (the People's Heritage), chose Guy Okakok of Barrow as president.

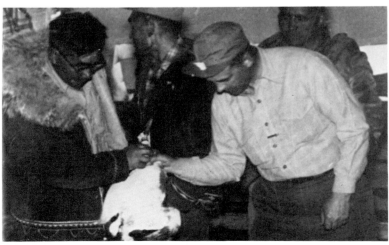

Tundra Times

*An eider duck taken out of season, Barrow, 1960.*

# SELECTED DATES
## 1961-1971

1961      State land selections threaten continued use of lands in Minto area.

1961      Inupiat Paitot meets to discuss protection of aboriginal rights.

1962      *"Tundra Times"* is established.

1963      Proposed Rampart Dam protested by Stevens Village and other Yukon River villages.

         Alaska Task Force calls upon Congress to define Native land rights.

1966      Statewide conference leads to organization of Alaska Federation of Natives (AFN).

         Interior Secretary Stewart Udall imposes a "land freeze" to protect Native use and occupancy.

1967      First bills introduced in Congress to settle Native land claims.

         Native protests and claims to land reach 380 million acres.

1968      Alaska Land Claims Task Force, established by Governor Hickel, recommends 40 million-acre land settlement.

         Governmental study effort *(Alaska Natives and The Land)* asserts Native land claims to be valid.

1969      North Slope oil lease auction produces $900 million for the State of Alaska.

1970      A land claims bill is passed by the Senate, but Natives are disappointed in its land provisions.

1971      Bills pass both houses of Congress, but differences in them require conference committee; its compromise version passes both houses.

         Following acceptance by the AFN convention, President Nixon signs the Alaska Native Claims Settlement Act (P.L. 92-203) on December 18.

A second meeting of Inupiat Paitot, also assisted by the Association, was held in late 1962 in Kotzebue. Twenty-eight delegates from villages as widely separated as Kaktovik on Barter Island and Stebbins on Norton Sound attended. They discussed their need for more schools, employment opportunities, and adequate housing, but they gave their major attention to the problem of growing threats to the continuation of their food-gathering way of life.

Delegates learned at the conference that there was little promise in the one way open to them to obtain legal ownership of land. Although the Native Allotment Act allowed a person to obtain title to 160 acres of land if he could demonstrate use and occupancy over a five-year period, there was a barrier to doing so. The Bureau of Land Management, the federal agency having custody of the public domain, had rejected hunting and fishing activities as proof of use and occupancy under the act. Partly for this reason, only 101 allotments had been made in Alaska in the 56 years since the act had been adopted by Congress.

A guest of honor at this meeting was Alfred Ketzler, an Athabascan Indian from Nenana. Ketzler was chairman of Dena Nena Henash (Our Land Speaks), an association which had been organized earlier in 1962 to deal with land rights and other problems. One of the results of its meetings, he explained, was that "our people learned that almost every village faces the same problems: mainly land and hunting rights; jobs and village economy."

*Howard Rock, Al Ketzler, and Al Widmark, 1964.*

Ketzler was among the first to propose Congressional action to preserve land rights, instead of court action. He said:

> Your grandfathers and mine, left this land to us in the only kind of deed they knew . . . by word of mouth and our continued possession. Among our people this deed was honored just as much as if it was written and signed by the President of the United States. Until recent years, a man's honor was the only deed necessary. Now, things have changed. We need a legal title to our land if we are to hold it. Our right to inherit land from our fathers cannot be settled in court. It is specifically stated in early laws that Congress is to do this by defining the way which we can acquire title. We must ask Congress to do this.

By the time the second Inupiat Paitot meeting was held, at least one recommendation of the first — "that a bulletin or newsletter be published and circulated" — had been fully realized. The first issue of the *Tundra Times* was published on October 1, 1962.

**Tundra Times**

Tundra Times

*Dr. Henry S. Forbes, benefactor of the Tundra Times.*

The editor of the paper was Howard Rock, who had helped organize Inupiat Paitot and who had been urged by villagers to begin the newsletter. His assistant was a Fairbanks reporter who had covered the Barrow meeting, Tom Snapp. Financial support had been provided by Dr. Henry Forbes, a

Massachusetts physician who was chairman of the Alaska Committee for the Association on American Indian Affairs.

In its first issue, the editor told of two purposes. It would be a means of reporting the policies and goals of the Native organizations, and it would become a source of information on Native issues. The first *Tundra Times* editorial announced:

> Natives of Alaska, the *Tundra Times* is your paper. It is here to express your ideas, your thoughts and opinions on issues that vitally affect you . . . With this humble beginning we hope, not for any distinction, but to serve with dedication the truthful presentation of Native problems, issues and interests.

The *Tundra Times* did not have to look very hard to find issues. Many problems, largely ignored by other newspapers, existed in the Native communities — inadequate educational programs, poor health care, substandard housing conditions, incidents of discrimination, and the lack of employment opportunities for Natives.

The appearance of the *Tundra Times* gave Alaska Natives a common voice for the first time. It was to explore a variety of issues, but its impact was to be most far-reaching in the attention it gave to land rights of Eskimos, Indians, and Aleuts.

**State land selections**

The greatest threat to their land rights during the early 1960's came about because of the Alaska Statehood Act. While the act recognized the right of Natives to lands which they used and occupied, it did not provide any means of assuring such use and occupancy. And by authorizing the new State government to select and obtain title to 103 million acres of land from the public domain, the continued use of lands by Natives was endangered.

One of the areas where state land selections first conflicted with Native hunting, fishing, and trapping activities was in the Minto Lakes region of Interior Alaska. The State wanted to establish a recreation area in 1961 near the Athabascan village of Minto and to construct a road so that the region would be more easily accessible to Fairbanks residents and visiting sportsmen. In addition, State officials believed that the area held potential for future development of oil and other resources. Learning of these plans of the State, the village of Minto had filed a protest with the U. S. Interior Department. They asked the federal agency to protect their rights to the region by turning down the State's application for the land.

In response to the protest, a meeting of sportsmen, biologists, conservationists, and State officials was held in 1963 to discuss the proposed road and recreation area. The chief of Minto, Richard Frank, told the group why they had filed a protest:

*Richard Frank of Minto.*

Now I don't want to sound like I really hate you people, no. If we were convinced that everyone would benefit, that the people of Minto would benefit, we might go along. The attitude down there is that you people were going to put a road into Minto Lakes without even consulting the people who live there, who hunt and fish there, who use the area for a livelihood! If you people could live off Minto Flats for one year or even a quarter of a year, you would understand my point.

Frank argued that State development in the region would ruin the subsistence way of life of the Natives and urged that the recreation area be established elsewhere, where new hunting pressure would not threaten the traditional economy. He said, "A village is at stake. Ask yourself this question, is a recreation area worth the future of a village?"

Many others from villages throughout Alaska began to ask similar questions about the danger which State selections presented to their land rights. Leaders such as Ketzler and Rock, accompanied by representatives from the Association on American Indian Affairs, traveled to villages urging them to act to protect their lands from encroachment. They warned them that, unless they filed their claims and protests with the Interior Department, lands they considered theirs would soon end up as the property of the State or others.

In early 1963, about one thousand Natives from 24 villages sent a petition to Interior Secretary Stewart Udall requesting that he impose a "land freeze" to stop all transfers of land ownership for the areas surrounding these villages until Native land rights could be confirmed. The petitioners came from the Yukon River delta, the Bristol Bay area, the Aleutian Islands, and the Alaska Peninsula. No action was taken by the Interior Department in response to the petition.

**Rampart Dam**

Another kind of threat to lands used by Natives during this period was federal withdrawal of lands from the public domain, especially withdrawals like one for the proposed Rampart Dam. The federal project, planned to produce electric power and to create a recreation area, would have flooded numerous villages and vast land areas traditionally used by Athabascan groups.

When Allen John, a resident of Stevens Village, was informed of the proposal, he had this reaction: "We are concerned about the Rampart Dam at which the white man are gonna put in down below us. The project will ruin our hunting, trapping and fishing on which we have lived for so many years . . . What are we supposed to do, drown or something?"

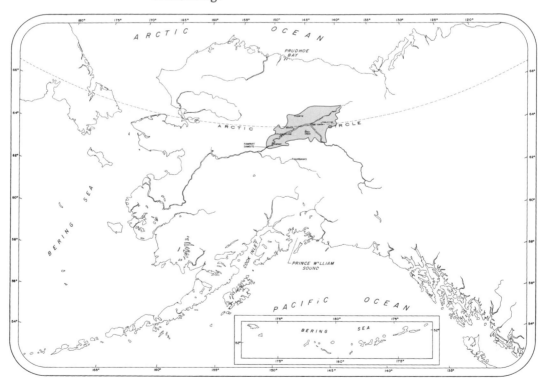

MAP 8 PROPOSED RAMPART RESERVOIR

A combination of the threat of impending State land selections and the proposed dam prompted Stevens Village to file a protest during June of 1963. In a letter accompanying

*The hunter.*

the claim, the Stevens Village Council explained why they wanted to obtain title to an area of more than a million acres. The Council wrote, "We use an area of 1,648 square miles for hunting, fishing, and for running our traplines. This is the way in which our fathers and forefathers made their living, and we of this generation follow the same plan."

Three months later the villages of Beaver, Birch Creek, and Canyon Village also filed claims to land. But there was to be no resolution to their claims, or the claims of other villages, for eight more years.

# Chapter 15            Alternative Solutions

Natives had won recognition from the Interior Department by 1963 that resolution of the issue of Native land rights was long overdue. This was shown in the report of the Alaska Task Force on Native Affairs, a three-man group appointed by Interior Secretary Stewart Udall. The report cited the failure in the Organic Act to provide a means by which Natives might obtain title. It noted that, in the ensuing 78 years, Congress had "largely sidestepped the issue of aboriginal claims," and if Congress was ever to define Native entitlement, it should do so promptly.

Recognition of Native land rights was also demonstrated in the increasing attention given the subject by Alaska's congressmen, by State officials, and by persons or groups outside of the state. These spokesmen offered a variety of solutions to the land claims issue.

Differing approaches were offered by members of Alaska's delegation in Washington, D. C. Senator Ernest Gruening suggested that the claims of Native groups should be settled in the U. S. Court of Claims. But that approach was seen by Representative Ralph Rivers as one that would take too long.

**Land rights recognized**

Rivers said he believed Congress should extinguish Native land rights and award cash compensation. He opposed grants of land to Native claimants. "What would they do with it?" he asked. "They wouldn't use it. It would just lie there."

Senator E. L. "Bob" Bartlett urged that State land selections be allowed to proceed before a land settlement was reached. He said he thought that villages would not require more than one million acres in land and suggested that cash payment could be made for other lands to which Natives claimed ownership.

Joyce Hooley

*Moose and beaver country near Napaimute.*

State officials also urged that the Natives allow the State to proceed with its selections and then enter into cooperative planning with the State for use of the lands. The director of the Alaska Division of Lands told Minto claimants, for example, that federal action might not be helpful to either the State or the Natives. He said:

> My own personal observation is that it is difficult to get anything done through the federal government. The State is more flexible to right wrongs . . . I don't think you people want a reservation. That way it would be under BIA [Bureau of Indian Affairs] contro. wouldn't it? You wouldn't be able to decide anything.

Opinions on how the Native land settlement should be approached also came from sources which were prominent in the field of national Indian affairs. William Brandon, author and historian, wrote President John F. Kennedy in 1962 requesting that he propose legislation for a claims settlement and that he halt land transfers in Alaska until the claims were settled. Early in 1963, the National Council on Indian Affairs, comprised of 16 member organizations such as the American Civil Liberties Union, Association on American Indian Affairs, and national religious groups made similar recommendations.

The report of the Alaska Task Force included specific recommendations for solution. In addition to urging Congressional action, the Task Force called for: 1) the prompt grant of up to 160 acres to individuals for their homes, fish camps, and hunting sites; 2) withdrawal of "small acreages" for village growth; and 3) designation of areas for Native use — but not ownership — in traditional food-gathering activities.

Aided by the Association on American Indian Affairs and its executive director, William Byler, Natives were successful in their efforts to prevent the Alaska Task Force recommendations from being carried out. They opposed them, in part, because there was no provision for cash payment for lands they would lose, and because no mineral rights were guaranteed for the lands on which they would have received title. They opposed the recommendations, too, because the land proposed for Native ownership included only small tracts. As the *Tundra Times* editorialized, "Natives have steadfastly maintained that they need large areas for hunting, fishing, and trapping now and for development of resources later as their economy changes ... Small areas will not be sufficient."

C. D. Evans

*Timber industry, lower Kenai Peninsula.*

**Four alternatives**

To this point, unacceptable solutions were better defined than those that would be acceptable. Alaska Natives were uncertain what course of action might lead to a just solution.

Four basic courses of action appeared to Natives to be open to them. They might seek: 1) to establish reserves under existing law; 2) to resolve their claims in the federal Court of Claims; 3) to obtain legislation at the State level to protect their land rights; or 4) to win a Congressional settlement.

**Reserves**

One possible course — establishment of reserves — was given but little consideration as a means of preserving land for their use. While this would result in designation of exclusive use areas for Natives, these areas would be held in trust by the federal government. Natives would be unable to lease, develop, or sell such land without government permission.

Twenty-three Native reserves had been established in Alaska by 1943. None was established after that time. They ranged in size from about 17 acres (for Chilkat Fisheries) to 1,408,000 acres (for Venetie and Arctic Village).

Joyce Hooley

*Salmon fishing on Iliamna Lake near Kokhanok.*

**Court action**

The experience of the Tlingit and Haida Indians with the courts made Native leaders reluctant to look to judicial settlement of land rights questions. In 1935, The Congress had enacted legislation which permitted the two southeastern groups to sue the federal government in the Court of Claims for land taken by the United States, most of it for the Tongass National Forest, which they historically used and occupied. In 1959, the Court of Claims had supported the claim and decreed that the Tlingits and Haidas were entitled to compensation. The compensation was later set at $7.5 million on the basis of the estimated worth of the land at the time the National Forest was established in 1907.

The Tlingit-Haida settlement took far too long to achieve, and the cash compensation seemed very small, but court action was seen as unsatisfactory for another reason: the Court of Claims had not ever been free to grant legal title to land; its only authority had been to award money for lands lost.

Seeking action by the State government to protect land rights was also only briefly considered by Natives. One proposal introduced into the legislature would have created Native reservations of 20 square miles each surrounding the villages. Natives did not push for its passage because the land area that would be preserved for their use was too small and they were not enthusiastic about reservations. The major reason that the proposal was not adopted was that most state legislators agreed that the Native land rights issue could only be resolved by the Congress.

These legislators were right in pointing out that Congress had reserved to itself in the Organic Act the right to define the terms under which Natives might obtain title. It could be argued in reply, however, that the Congress had done so by providing for reserves, allotments, and homesites.

**State legislation**

Tundra Times

*In search.*

But Native groups knew these acts of Congress were clearly inadequate to the protection of their land rights. New action by the Congress was needed to provide a settlement of aboriginal claims to land.

The problem, however, of seeking congressional settlement of land claims was the enormous uncertainty of what the results might be. The Congress might grant Natives title to only a small part of their land and some cash compensation for lands given up. Or it might award only compensation. Congressional settlement could be the most rewarding or the most damaging of the four alternatives. Even though court action would take time, the legal case based upon use and occupancy might result in a fairer settlement than that which the political process would produce in the Congress.

While these alternatives were being explored in discussions among Native leaders, none was being actively pursued. A decision to do so would have to await the confederation of small, relatively weak Native associations into an organization which would have the power and resources to see it through.

# Organization                                    Chapter 16

The number of regional Native organizations had grown to four with the founding of the Association of Village Council Presidents in southwest Alaska in 1962. In addition, one urban organization which had been established in 1960 — the Fairbanks Native Association — was holding regular meetings and addressing issues of concern to Natives. But each of the organizations was separated by great distances from the others, the cost of communication was high, and there was little contact among the groups.

Tundra Times

*William L. Paul, Sr., Alaska Native Brotherhood, and Al Ketzler, Tanana Chiefs Conference, 1963.*

The first steps toward the development of a statewide organization were taken early in 1963, when leaders of several associations discussed the possibility of its formation. The proposal to unite the associations was made at a meeting of the Tanana Chiefs Conference by Steven V. Hotch, an officer of the Alaska Native Brotherhood. When Hotch called for an affiliation of the Dena Nena Henash and Inupiat Paitot with his organization, the idea was supported by his President Emeritus, William L. Paul, Sr., and by spokesmen for the other two groups. It appeared that the affiliation would be accomplished.

However, some leaders, such as State Senator Eben Hopson, of Barrow, feared there might be an imbalance of regional representation on whatever governing body was set up. Hopson was also concerned that the organization from southeastern Alaska would become the dominant force, overshadowing the other regions. In a letter to *Tundra Times* editor Howard Rock, he warned, "I can just picture you and a handful of other Eskimos sitting at a conference table with a full battery of the members of the Alaska Native Brotherhood, and being voted down on every proposal you might have."

Those who supported the idea of one statewide organization tried to persuade others, but they were unable to overcome a deeply rooted mistrust which many Natives had of people outside of their own geographic regions.

The task of overcoming mistrust became easier as Natives began to realize, in part through the *Tundra Times*, that they were facing a common threat of land loss. There was also increasing communication among Natives from different regions as they gathered together in government-sponsored advisory committees dealing with housing, health, or education programs.

Tundra Times

*Board of Directors, Cook Inlet Native Association. Standing: Emil Notti, John Evans, Lloyd Ahvakana, Al Yakasoff, Flore Lekanof, Shirley Tucker, Carol Bahr, Dorothy Watson, Jim Claymore. Seated: Mike Alex, Laura Bergt, Fred Notti, and Don Watson.*

**New organizations**

In 1964 two new organizations of Natives were established: Gwitchya Gwitchin Ginkhye (Yukon Flats People Speak) made up of Yukon Flats villages, and the Cook Inlet Native Association, founded by residents of the state's largest city, Anchorage. In the same year, another attempt was made to unify the efforts of Native organizations.

This conference of Native organizations was planned by Rock, Al Ketzler, Ralph Perdue, the president of the Fairbanks Native Association, and Mardow Solomon, the president of the newly founded Gwitchya Gwitchin Ginkhye. The

Tundra Times

*Charles Edwardsen, Jr. of Barrow, Jacob Stalker of Kotzebue, Axel Johnson of Emmonak, and Frank See of Hoonah at meeting of Alaska Native Housing Committee, 1966.*

themes of the conference were the need for increased political activity among Natives and the need for cooperative action to achieve common goals. The grand president of the Alaska Native Brotherhood, John Hope of Sitka, chaired the two-day event. Although Roy Peratrovich of Juneau and others stressed the need to hold the conference annually, no further meeting of the group was to take place.

Two more years would pass before a statewide organization would be formed. And for most of that time, little new organization, even on a regional basis, would take place. The establishment of the Tlingit-Haida Central Council, headed by Andrew Hope of Sitka, was an exception. Unlike the other groups being formed in these years, it was not established to protect land rights threatened. Its purpose, instead, was to plan for the distribution of funds expected as a result of the 1959 court determination that southeastern Indians were owed compensation for lands taken.

Apart from a protest by the village of Tanacross against the sale of ancestral lands at George Lake, a protest which stopped the sale, claims to land created little public notice in 1965. There was, however, a growing awareness among villagers of threats to their land and steps they needed to take to protect their rights to it.

Broadening the land rights movement across the state was, in large measure, the achievement of "Operation Grassroots." This community organization effort, headed by Charles Edwardsen, Jr., of Barrow, was an arm of the Alaska State Community Action Program (ASCAP). This state-operated agency was a part of President Lyndon Johnson's antipoverty program funded by the U. S. Office of Economic Opportunity (OEO).

Over the next few years, funding from OEO through ASCAP, and its successor, RurAL CAP, was to be a key factor in claims settlement work of regional Native organizations. Although the antipoverty funds were not targeted to the support of land claims, they were intended to support community and regional organizations, and planning toward the solution of shared problems. Many members of the antipoverty boards and their staffs were, therefore, actively involved in the claims struggle.

During 1965 national focus on problems of village housing, education, and poverty resulted in some overshadowing of Native claims. The subject of Native land rights, however, returned to public attention in early 1966 with the announcement by a new organization in Barrow, the Arctic Slope Native Association, that it was making claim to virtually all of the land north of the Brooks Range. A spokesman said the group was seeking full title to 58 million acres on the basis of aboriginal use and occupancy.

The new organization was established at a meeting called by Charles Edwardsen, Jr. to discuss land rights of Eskimos. It chose Sam Taalak of Barrow as its president.

**Community organization**

**Arctic Slope claim**

Tundra Times

*(Left to right) James Nageak, Abel Akpik, Samuel Simmonds, Walton Ahmaogak, Sam Taalak, Otthneil Oomituk and Herman Rexford. (The man behind Ahmaogak and the woman at right are not identified.)*

In April of 1966, Senator Ernest Gruening pointed out that, because of Native protests against State selection, only three million acres of land had been transferred to the State. He complained that the Bureau of Indian Affairs had encouraged the filing of such protests, and that the Interior Department, of which it was a part, was apparently making "every acre of Alaska subject to questionable claims of rights by Native protests." If there were valid rights, he argued, the Interior Department should propose legislation to allow cash compensation to be paid.

A 24-year-old Eskimo graduate student at the University of Alaska, Willie Hensley, was quick in his reply to the Senator. Hensley criticized Gruening for his failure to consult with Natives before "creating a prejudiced attitude toward them by his statements" and further, for ruling out any land as part of a settlement. He said, in part,

> Compensation in cash would certainly be a simple and quick solution for Congress to buy off Native claims, but it seems we should be given an opportunity to voice our opinions on the matter . . .

The hopes of Native leaders for a unified organization persisted. What was perhaps the most eloquent plea was made by Nick Gray, a founder of the Native organizations in Fairbanks and Anchorage, and more recently, a founder of a Bethel area group, the Kuskokwim Valley Native Association. From his hospital bed, where he lay gravely ill, he wrote:

> It is gratifying to observe the awakening of our people to the necessity of cooperative effort by forming associations, brotherhoods, . . . to protect our heritage . . .

> Our hereditary claims can hardly be denied, since they extend far into the dim pages of history, for outdating the beginnings of most currently established nations. . . . The next logical step for these separate and far-flung groups is affiliation and then eventual amalgamation into a harmonious whole department dedicated to achieve the most good for all.

What Gray envisioned — a statewide organization — was to be achieved shortly before he died.

**Statewide organization**

The meeting which resulted in the establishment of what was to become today's Alaska Federation of Natives was called by the president of the Cook Inlet Native Association, Emil Notti, a 34-year-old Athabascan from Ruby.

In organizing the meeting, Notti had the assistance of Chief Albert Kaloa, Jr. of Tyonek village, Stanley J. McCutcheon, an attorney who had helped Tyonek win

*At left, Nick Gray, founder of Native associations in Fairbanks, Anchorage, and Bethel. At right, Emil Notti, first president of the Alaska Federation of Natives.*

almost $13 million from oil leases on its reserve, and Thomas Pilifant, an area superintendent for the Bureau of Indian Affairs. Tyonek village provided most of the financing of the convention.

The historic meeting began on October 18, 1966 — on the ninety-ninth anniversary of the transfer of Alaska from

*Delegates to the first statewide Native conference. Dan Lisburne of Point Hope, Frank Degnan of Unalakleet, and Billy Beans of St. Mary's.*

113

*At left, Tyonek's attorney Stan McCutcheon of Anchorage, who helped organize the first statewide conference of Natives. At right, Willie Hensley of Kotzebue, Land Committee chairman and later a State Representative.*

Russia. Seventeen Native organizations were represented. The total attendance was estimated at 250 persons.

Notti presided over the three-day conference as it chose a board of directors, named committees, and began flexing its strength politically.

**Land recommendations**

Recommendations of the land claims committee, chaired by Willie Hensley, were unanimously approved by the conference. The three fundamental recommendations were that:

1) a "land freeze" be imposed on all federal lands until Native claims were resolved;

2) Congress enact legislation to enable settlement of the claims; and

3) there be substantial consultation with Natives, including Congressional hearings in Alaska, before any action would be taken on claims settlement legislation.

The conference also adopted specific recommendations for legislation. The proposed bill, the conference said, should authorize court action to settle claims for Native lands taken, and award compensation at current market value. Further, it should award title to other lands which were validly claims.

**Political importance**

In addition to achieving a united stand regarding land claims, the meeting was important in identifying Natives as a significant political force. Delegates were astonished at the attention which they received from well-known political figures in the state. One Native leader in attendance at the convention observed that, if any delegate was seen paying for his own meal, it was probably because he chose to dine alone!

Tundra Times

*John Sackett, Huslia, member of the Alaska House of Representatives, with Tim Wallis, Fairbanks, president of DNH Development Corporation, a contracting firm founded in 1969 by the Tanana Chiefs.*

Tundra Times

*Ray Christiansen, Bethel, member of Alaska Senate, and Carl E. Moses, Unalaska, member of Alaska House of Representatives.*

Tundra Times

*Jules Wright, Fairbanks, member of the Alaska House of Representatives, with Ralph Perdue, Fairbanks, former president of the Fairbanks Native Association.*

The growing political importance of Natives was evidenced again in November when association leaders were elected to the legislature. The three elected to the State

Tundra Times/Anchorage Daily News

*John Westdahl, St. Mary's, and Frank See, Hoonah, members of the Alaska House of Representatives.*

House were: A University of Alaska student who was president of the Tanana Chiefs, John Sackett; Jules Wright, president of the Fairbanks Native Association; and the founder of the Northwest Alaska Native Association, Willie Hensley of Kotzebue. Together with Carl E. Moses of Unalaska, Frank See of Hoonah, John Westdahl of St. Mary's — all in the House — and Ray Christiansen in the State Senate, Natives held seven of the sixty seats in the legislature.

To continue the work of the Alaska Federation of Native Associations, the name temporarily adopted for the statewide group, an Aleut from St. George, Flore Lekanof, was elected chairman. When the group met a second time (early in 1967), it emerged with a new name, The Alaska Federation of Natives, and a full-time president, Emil Notti.

# Chapter 17            Proposed Legislation

Tundra Times

*Secretary of the Interior Stewart Udall.*

Before 1966 drew to a close, one of the principal recommendations of the new Alaska Federation of Natives was realized: Interior Secretary Udall stopped the transfer of lands claimed by Natives until Congress could act upon the claims. The Interior Secretary's action of imposing a "land

**Land freeze**

117

freeze" brought an immediate and angry response from State officials. Governor Walter Hickel, who had won the governorship in the 1966 election, complained in a letter to Udall that the land freeze denied the State its right to select its land entitlement under the provisions of the Statehood Act. Udall replied that both the Statehood Act and the Organic Act of 1884 recognized the existence of Native land rights, and that he could not give the state any lands claimed by Natives until the Congress enacted a settlement. He explained:

> In the face of Federal guarantee that the Alaska Natives shall not be disturbed in the use and occupation of lands, I could not in good conscience allow title to pass into others' hands ... Moreover, to permit others to acquire title to the lands the Natives are using and occupying would create an adversary against whom the Natives would not have the means of protecting themselves ...

Arguing that Udall's action was illegal, the State of Alaska filed a lawsuit to require him to transfer lands to the State. Since the basis of the State's action was land it wanted near Nenana, the Nenana Native council joined in the lawsuit as an interested third party. More than two years would pass before a court ruling was given.

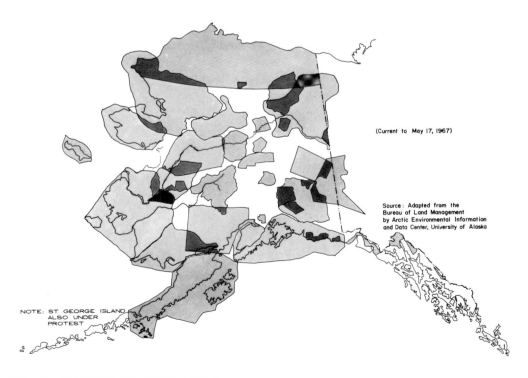

(Current to May 17, 1967)

Source: Adapted from the Bureau of Land Management by Arctic Environmental Information and Data Center, University of Alaska

NOTE: ST. GEORGE ISLAND ALSO UNDER PROTEST

MAP 9 NATIVE CLAIMS AND PROTESTS, 1967

Meanwhile, the extent of land affected by Udall's freeze was rapidly growing as additional claims or protests were filed by Native villages or organizations. By May of 1967, thirty-nine protests had been filed. They ranged in size from a 640-acre claim by the village of Chilkoot to the 58 million-acre claim of the Arctic Slope Native Association. Because many claims were overlapping, the total acreage under protest — about 380 million acres — was greater than the land area of the state.

**First bills**

The first two bills to resolve the claims were introduced in the Congress in the summer of 1967, one sponsored by the Department of the Interior, the other by the Alaska Federation of Natives (AFN). Both bills authorized a court to determine how much money should be paid to Natives for lands they had lost. The AFN bill would also have the court award title to lands with no maximum acreage specified. The Interior bill, on the other hand, would authorize a maximum of 50,000 acres per village in trust.

The Interior bill was criticized by Native spokesmen because the eight-to-ten million acres that would be granted was insufficient for traditional uses and because the land was to be in trust status.

**AFN importance**

In October of 1967 the one-year-old AFN met, resolved differences among members, and adopted a constitution. Among other things, the constitution tried to provide for a financial base for Federation operations: associations and villages were to provide funds to it according to their ability to pay.

The Federation had become the voice of Alaska's Natives in 1966. With the decisions made at its second meeting, it had become an even stronger voice.

The importance of the Federation was emphasized at the same meeting when Hickel's attorney general, Edgar Paul Boyko, proposed that the Federation and the State work together to develop a new proposal for settlement of the claims: Boyko agreed to a large land settlement, including the minerals beneath the surface. He said:

> ...we would like to provide subsurface rights, even to large grants of land ... The State needs land — the Natives need lands. The State and the Natives should go into partnership.

**Land Claims Task Force**

Following the suggestion, a Land Claims Task Force was established under State sponsorship. Its chairman was State Representative Willie Hensley; members of its legislative drafting committee were leaders of Native organizations: Emil Notti, president of the Federation; John Borbridge, Jr., Tlingit-Haida; Alice Brown, Kenaitze Natives; Richard Frank, Fairbanks; Charles Franz, Alaska Peninsula; Byron Mallott,

*Alice Brown, Kenaitze, the only woman on the State of Alaska's Land Claims Task Force.*

Yakutat; Hugh Nicholls, Arctic Slope; Harvey Samuelsen, Bristol Bay; and Donald Wright, Cook Inlet. Legal advice was furnished by Alaska attorneys Roger Conner, Clifford Groh and Barry Jackson. Also in the group were representatives of the State and the Department of the Interior.

In January of 1968, the Task Force delivered its report. Its recommendations for land, money, and instruments of settlement were:

1) Forty million acres of land to be conveyed to Native villages in fee simple; all lands currently used for fishing and hunting activities to be available for such use for up to 100 years; the Native Allotment Act to remain effective;

2) Ten percent of the income produced by the sale or lease of oil rights from certain lands to be paid to Natives; the total to be at least $65 million; and,

3) The settlement to be carried out by business corporations organized by villages, regions, and by one which would be statewide.

The Task Force also recommended passage of companion state legislation that would have provided up to $50 million to Natives from mineral revenue from certain state lands, but only if the land freeze were lifted before the end of 1968.

**Congressional hearings**

The bill recommended by the Land Claims Task Force was introduced in 1968 by Senator Ernest Gruening. He promptly arranged for hearings to be held in Anchorage by the Senate Interior and Insular Affairs Committee.

When the hearings opened, a large crowd — including many Eskimos, Indians, and Aleuts from across the state — attended.

Members of the committee heard Emil Notti and other leaders of Native organizations urge prompt action on the proposed bill. And they heard State Representative Hensley, other members of the Task Force, and their legal counsel explain the proposed settlement. They heard, too, from Natives who had long been prominent in the life of the state — William L. Paul, Sr., formerly of Wrangell, the first Native elected to the Territorial legislature; Frank Peratrovich, Klawock, twice president of the Alaska Senate; and Dr. Walter Soboleff, Juneau, a clergyman and member of the State Board of Education.

Members of the committee also listened as older villagers described from personal experience why a land settlement was needed. Among them, 62-year-old John Klashinoff of Cordova:

> ... When I was a boy my people lived by fishing, trapping, hunting. There was plenty for all ... We had a good living from the land ... There is no room any longer. We can no longer fish or hunt fox for a living. Now there is no land we can call our own ...

Tundra Times

*Peter John of Minto.*

And 64-year-old Peter John told them of the decline in fur-bearing animals in the Minto area as a result of mining:

> They used to get 12 to 15,000 muskrats in one spring. The mink was plentiful, and so was the fox, beaver, and otter . . . Today, you don't see fur signs any place; there are hardly any beaver and no muskrats. I remember last spring we were out hunting muskrats for one week; we caught only 29 rats, that's the poorest ratting I have ever seen in the Minto Flat area. The reason why is because the lakes are drying out and the creeks are full of sand from all of the mining that has been done around Fairbanks and Chatanika and over in Tolovana . . .

And they heard 70-year-old Andrew Isaac, chief of the village of Tanacross:

> I saw my first white man in 1904. He was a preacher. During the course of the years I saw more white men. In the early 1940's, a highway was built near Tanacross, and white men have come on to our land more and more . . .

Tundra Times

*Andrew Isaac, traditional chief of Tanacross.*

We made our claim in 1963 because the state came in and selected our land — everything, even our village and graveyard. This is not fair. We own our land — the white man does not . . .

The principal opposition to the bill at the hearing came from the Alaska Miners' Association. Its spokesman quoted the 1946 Indian Claims Commission Act, which required that claims either be presented before 1951 or that they not be presented at all. Except for such claims filed, he said that:

**Opposition**

. . . neither the United States, the State of Alaska, nor any of us here gathered as individuals owes the Natives one acre of ground or one cent of the taxpayers' money . . .

The Miners' Association spokesman also warned that a 40 million-acre land settlement would discourage mineral exploration and would possibly reserve the best hunting areas in the state to Natives.

The administration of Governor Hickel generally supported the AFN bill, but strongly urged the lifting of the land freeze. Because the freeze prevented the issuance of oil leases on federal lands, and because the State was to receive 90 percent of federal revenues from such lands, the State's income was declining. The Governor's representative said the freeze had already cost the State more than $400,000 and unless it were lifted, the State would soon face an economic crisis.

**State of Alaska**

Tundra Times

*"Take our land, take our life" — Margaret Nick Cooke of Bethel.*

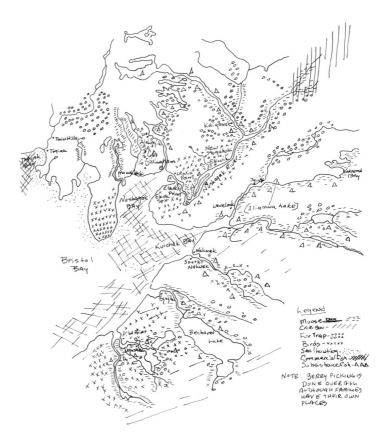

MAP 10   LAND USE MAP SUBMITTED TO CONGRESS
BY PETE PETLA OF KOLIGANEK

The subject of the land freeze was also taken up by a
second critic of the proposed legislation, the Alaska Sportsmen's Council. In a letter to the committee, the Council
complained of the bill and the freeze, but observed that the
bill could not have gotten even the qualified support of the
Hickel administration were it not for the freeze. This observa-
tion was perhaps the only point of the Council's testimony
with which many Native leaders might agree.

# A Strengthened Case                    Chapter 18

While continuation of the land freeze was not threatened
by the Congress, the election of Richard M. Nixon in 1968
did pose a possible threat to it. Once in office, the new
president would replace Interior Secretary Udall, who had
imposed the land freeze, with a person of his own choosing.

Just before the election, Udall had commented on the
importance of the freeze. "Frankly," he said, "I do not
believe we would have made any significant progress on the
Native claims issue if we had not held everyone's feet to the
fire (or perhaps I should say to the ice) with the freeze."

*Eben Hopson, aide to Governor William A. Egan and Joseph Upicksoun, president of Arctic Slope Native Association, at Congressional hearing in Barrow.*

Then, before giving up his office he changed the informal freeze into one having the force of law: he signed an executive order continuing the freeze in effect.

The man the new president nominated to replace Udall — Alaska Governor Walter Hickel — had spent the last two years trying to have the freeze lifted. Now, having been nominated to the Interior post, he said, "What Udall can do by executive order I can undo."

Cabinet nominees, however, require confirmation by the Senate. Because of the growing importance of the Alaska Federation of Natives, its endorsement was one which Hickel sought. But just as the Federation was important to Hickel, the freeze was important to Natives.

The AFN decided to withhold any formal announcement of support or opposition to Hickel until he could explain how he would protect Native land rights. To seek that explanation, a small delegation, headed by Federation president Emil Notti, set out for Washington, D. C. Federation vice-president John Borbridge, Jr. summed up the delegation's views: "... the most effective way to safeguard the Native land claims was to secure from Governor Hickel reliable assurance that, as Secretary of the Interior, he would protect the Native-claimed lands from further disposition until Congress had a chance to settle the entire Native land claims question."

**Hickel nomination**

125

*AFN Board of Directors meeting, 1968. (Left to right) Donald Wright, Frank Degnan, Willie Hensley, Emil Notti, Flore Lekanof, Al Ketzler, and Charles Franz.*

The confirmation hearings were very difficult for Hickel. Powerful conservationist groups testified in opposition to his appointment. The Native delegation had obtained support from key senators on the committee, and they sternly questioned the nominee.

**AFN victory**

Although there was much pressure to endorse, the Native delegation refused to act. Realizing that his nomination was at stake, Hickel finally gave in and promised to extend the land freeze until December of 1970. Based on that commitment, Notti and others of his delegation endorsed his nomination.

Winning Hickel's promise was an important victory for Native leaders. At the same time that the freeze protected the land rights of Natives, the freeze made a settlement a matter of concern to the State and to many persons and interests within the state. The victory was important, too, for what it told about the leadership of the AFN: it was independent, increasingly strong, and growing in its ability to influence the processes of government.

**A government study**

Although new bills had been introduced during 1968 and hearings had been held, none had been acted upon by committees of either house. The chairman of the Senate committee on Interior and Insular Affairs, Henry Jackson of Washington, had, however, requested that a program of comprehensive research be carried out as a basis for appropriate legislation. He asked that the study be performed by the Federal Field Committee for Development Planning in Alaska. This was a small federal agency headed by Joseph H. Fitzgerald, which had been established following the 1964 earthquake to bring about coordinated planning among federal and state agencies.

*Emil Notti, president of Alaska Federation of Natives and John Borbridge, Jr., vice-president, in television interview in Philadelphia.*

The document produced in response to the request, *Alaska Natives and the Land*, was made public in early 1969. Its 565 double-size pages told of present social and economic status of Natives, portrayed historic patterns of settlement and land use, and examined the many elements of land ownership and land claims.

Summarizing their findings about the economic and social circumstances of villagers, the authors said:

**Villagers**

- About three-fourths of Alaska's 53,000 Eskimos, Indians, and Aleuts live in 178 predominantly Native communities, most of which are at locations remote from the road system of the state. The median size of these places is 155 persons.

- In these villages, the few, permanent, full-time jobs at the highest rates of pay are typically held by non-Natives. State public assistance programs provide income to almost one of four households in villages; temporary relief programs provide income to about the same proportion, but usually for three months or less.

- Low cash incomes and high prices, even though supplemented by free health and educational services and food-gathering activities, have resulted in exceedingly low standards of living for villagers: dilapidated housing, absence of sewer and water facilities and electric power.

*Toksook Bay.*

- Most village adults have less than elementary school education, and large numbers have no formal education at all; for village adults speaking English, it is a second language. Nearly all Native communities have schools, but educational opportunity ends at the eighth grade in most places.

- Owing largely to socioeconomic conditions and the difficulty of providing health services to remote villages, the health status of Alaska Natives is inferior to that of the other Alaskans.

**Urban Natives**    Speaking of the Natives who live in the large cities, the authors said:

> Because adult Natives are often less well educated than other adults and lack marketable skills, their rate of joblessness in these communities is higher than among other groups, and those who are jobholders are typically in lower-paying positions. Migrants from villages to urban areas are frequently ill-equipped, by cultural as well as educational background, to make an easy transition to new patterns of life and work, but few communities have begun to provide assistance to them; and the consequences for too many are severe stresses resulting in alcohol problems and other personality disorders.

128

The research group found Natives to own little land outright: **Land ownership**

> Alaska Natives who claim two-thirds of the state own in fee simple less than 500 acres and hold in restricted title only an additional 15,000 acres. Some 900 Native families share the use of 4 million acres of land in 23 reserves established for their use and administered by the Bureau of Indian Affairs. All other rural Native families live on the public domain. And reindeer reserves account for one and a quarter million out of the four million acres of reserved lands. Without government permit, these reindeer lands may only be used for reindeer husbandry and subsistence purposes.

> Specific land legislation passed for Alaska Natives — the Alaska Native Allotment Act of 1906 and the Townsite Act of 1926 — has failed to meet the land needs of the Native people.

Of greatest importance, the researchers supported the claims of Natives to having used and occupied most of Alaska: **Valid claims**

> Aboriginal Alaska Natives made use of all the biological resources of the land, interior and contiguous waters in general balance with its sustained human carrying capacity. This use was only limited in scope and amount by technology.

And further, such claims are "valid," the researchers said, and could properly become subject to compensation.

While the report supported Native claims to most of Alaska, and suggested that 60 million acres would be required for subsistence, its accompanying recommendations for settlement included only seven to ten million acres of land that would be owned by Natives. Other lands would be available for use by Natives, however.

Recommendations of the Federal Field Committee helped to revive the idea of looking to future revenues from minerals as a means of compensating Natives for lands claimed, but not transferred to them. The AFN had proposed sharing in mineral revenues in its second bill, but because of opposition to its specific proposal, had discarded it in favor of a $500 million appropriation as compensation. **Mineral revenues**

The Field Committee's recommendations, which became the basis of a bill introduced by Senator Jackson, also raised the possible compensation to one billion dollars, the highest

*North Slope oil rig.*

of any proposal to date. Of this amount only $100 million would be appropriated. The remainder was to come from a limited share of revenues derived from minerals and other resources of federal lands.

Support of the concept of revenue-sharing by Jackson brought back unlimited revenue sharing as a feature in the AFN proposal for settlement adopted in May of 1969. The AFN board reaffirmed its position that the land settlement should be 40 million acres, the appropriation $500 million, and that Native corporations be the instruments of settlement at the village, regional and state levels. In addition, the board called for a two-percent perpetual share of the revenues produced from lands given up by Natives to the State in the settlement.

AFN president Emil Notti defended the principle of revenue-sharing by pointing out that a fair settlement of Native claims was surely related to the fair value of lands being given up. And the value of such lands was yet to be determined. With an eye on the State's upcoming North Slope oil lease sale, Notti said if the State were to get one to two billion dollars from oil companies for leases to several hundred thousand acres, too small a cash settlement for Natives would be like the sale of Manhattan Island by the Indians.

Later in the year, the value of oil to the State of Alaska —
and perhaps to Native land claimants — was made clear by
the State's oil lease sale. For the right to oil acreage in the
Prudhoe Bay region, oil companies paid over $900 million to
the State of Alaska.

One who attended the sale, *Tundra Times* staff writer
Thomas Richards, Jr., described the event:

> Inside the Sidney Laurence Auditorium, the
> governor of the State of Alaska, said, 'Let us
> manage our birthright.'

> Meanwhile [outside the auditorium], a hand-
> ful of young Natives picketed and distributed
> leaflets under the watchful eyes of police.

> Organized by Native land rights advocate
> Charlie Edwardsen, the young Eskimo and
> Indian protestors quietly proclaimed, 'We are
> once again being cheated and robbed of our
> lands.'

What the oil sale showed was that, if the State could sell
leases on small tracts of land for so much money, Natives
were not asking for too much in seeking a similar amount of
money for the surrender of millions of acres. As AFN first
vice-president John Borbridge, Jr. observed: The sale "will
clearly demonstrate that the demands of the Natives are not
out of line."

The sale also showed Congress that the State could afford
to share some of its mineral revenues with Native people by
way of compensating them for land claims surrendered.

Bruce Bedard

*Pickets at oil lease sale in Anchorage, 1969.*

131

Congressional hearings on proposed claims legislation had been held in 1969, but no bill had emerged from either committee. Natives, however, had won a continuation of the land freeze, and the oil lease sale had raised the stakes of the settlement effort. Publicity efforts of the AFN and the Association on American Indian Affairs had resulted in support from major national newspapers and publications for Native proposals for congressional settlement.

In addition, the AFN was now represented by a former Justice of the U. S. Supreme Court, Arthur J. Goldberg. His association with the AFN enhanced its national image; his distinguished reputation and prestige was to emphasize the rightness of the Native cause. Before the year ended he was joined by other counsel of national stature, including Ramsey Clark, a former U. S. Attorney General.

By early 1970 the Senate seemed prepared to move quickly on the land claims legislation. But the AFN began to worry that Senator Henry Jackson's bill with its meager land provisions would pass. And Natives were angry at opposition to the AFN land bill from Governor Keith Miller, who had succeeded to that office upon Hickel's departure for the cabinet post. Despite rising protests from Native leaders over the State's abandonment of the Task Force recommendations, Miller continued to oppose a 40 million-acre settlement and the mineral revenue-sharing provision.

Tundra Times

*AFN Board of Directors in 1970 meeting with Interior Secretary Walter Hickel (at left). Clockwise: Tim Wallis, Charlie Edwardsen, Eben Hopson, Emil Notti, Barry Jackson, Willie Hensley, Al Ketzler, Barbara Trigg, DeLois Ketzler, Larry Oskolkoff, Harvey Samuelsen, George Miller, Roy Levine, Ray Christiansen, Frank Degnan, Jerry Gray, Morris Thompson, and John Borbridge, Jr.*

Tundra Times

*Justice Arthur J. Goldberg.*

The impatience and frustration of Native leaders was dramatically emphasized in a speech AFN president Emil Notti delivered in Senator Jackson's home state of Washington in February of 1970. Notti declared that, if Congress passed a bill which did not provide a land settlement that was fair, Natives should petition for a separate nation in western Alaska. He said that an inadequate settlement bill would make the Alaska Native people as homeless as the Jewish people were before the nation of Israel was created for them. Notti said that a new nation in western Alaska could be open to American Indians as well as Alaska Natives. He said, "I will only say that it happened in Israel for a persecuted people. Why not here for a people who have lost a whole continent?" His militant stance was promptly endorsed by other Native leaders.

**Objections to bill**

In April, Senator Jackson's committee confirmed the fears of Native leaders by recommending to the Senate the adoption of Jackson's claims settlement bill.

While the bill could be applauded for the size of the total compensation awarded, one billion dollars, the revenue-sharing authorized was only for a limited number of years. But there were even more serious objections made by AFN.

The cause for strongest objection by Natives was the bill's land provisions. Land to which Natives would obtain formal title would be only slightly more than 10 million acres. One leader's reaction: "A real stunner!"

A second problem was that, instead of the 12 regional corporations sought by the AFN, only one — for the Arctic Slope — was authorized. Two statewide corporations, one for social services and another for investments, were also authorized.

Yet another major problem was what Natives called a "termination" clause. Within five years of enactment, the educational and social programs of the Bureau of Indian Affairs would cease and they would be assumed — maybe — by the State of Alaska.

Senator Ted Stevens, who had been appointed to his seat in 1968 upon the death of Senator E. L. Bartlett, urged acceptance of the Jackson bill. "I think this bill is a fair bill," he told the Tlingit-Haida Central Council. "It gives you more control and self-determination than any such bill in history."

While Stevens may have been right in his comparison, Alaska's Eskimos, Indians and Aleuts had declared they wanted land adequate to protect their ancient ways of life. Before the Senate Committee's bill was officially reported to the Senate, an AFN delegation was on its way to Washington.

When the Jackson bill reached the floor of the Senate for action in July, Senators sympathetic to the AFN position sought to amend it, but they were unsuccessful. The bill was adopted by a vote of 76-8.

It was now necessary for the AFN to look to the House of Representatives to adopt a bill more favorable to the interest of Alaska Natives.

**Other gains**

The setback suffered by AFN in the Senate was offset in some measure by other developments of 1970 which were favorable.

One was the decision of the U. S. Supreme Court which had the effect of supporting the position of Natives regarding the land freeze. By declining to review a lower court decision, the Supreme Court rejected the State's appeal that it should be free to proceed with land selections.

A second important development was AFN's success in obtaining a loan of $225,000 from the Yakima Indian Nation of the state of Washington. Until this loan was obtained, AFN had been trying to stretch an earlier $100,000 loan from Tyonek to cover its expenses as well as depending upon voluntary donations of AFN board members and church organizations.

In September of 1970, Natives won their first legislative battle of the year. The House Subcommittee on Indian Affairs agreed informally to a provision that would have granted Natives title to 40 million acres of land. Since the subcommittee would fail to report its recommendations in 1970, there was to be no further action in the House during the year. The subcommittee agreement, however, was the first taste of victory for Natives regarding the extent of land settlement.

*U. S. Senator Mike Gravel, Governor William A. Egan, U. S. Senator Ted Stevens, and U. S. Representative Nick Begich.*

The decision of the National Congress of American Indians (NCAI) to give unqualified support to the AFN and to assist in obtaining Congressional action provided a significant source of national political support. The NCAI was the largest, as well as the oldest, national organization of Indians.

Additionally, the prospects for a land settlement acceptable to AFN were improved as a result of the 1970 elections. Former governor William A. Egan, who had shown himself willing to work with the AFN, defeated the incumbent governor, Keith Miller. State Senator Nick Begich, who had said 10 million acres was an inadequate settlement, was elected as Alaska's congressman.

The upsetting withdrawal of the Arctic Slope Native Association that took place during the October meeting was also to be resolved before the year ended. The break had come about because of Arctic Slope leadership opposition to the AFN plan of distributing benefits. Distribution on the basis of a region's population as urged by a majority of AFN members, was characterized by Arctic Slope executive director Charles Edwardsen, Jr. as "welfare legislation," not a land claims settlement. Edwardsen insisted that the settlement be divided on the basis of a region's historic land area, explaining that the AFN's position would "not provide for a fair exchange between what is being taken from us and what we would receive in exchange."

**Changes to
AFN proposal**

Return of the Arctic Slope Native Association to AFN was achieved through a compromise in December at a board of directors meeting. This meeting was presided over by Donald Wright, who had been elected to the presidency in October following Emil Notti's decision not to seek a fourth term.

The new AFN proposal developed at the meeting kept the concept of 12 regions, initial compensation of $500 million, and the two-percent share in future revenues from public lands, but raised the land provision to 60 million acres. The proposal also accepted the Arctic Slope argument that the regions with the largest land area should receive the most land and money, not the regions with the largest population.

The president of the Arctic Slope Native Association, Joseph Upicksoun, had added to the justification given earlier by Edwardsen for his group's position. He told leaders of other regions:

> We realize each of you has pride in his own land. By an accident of nature, right now the eyes of the nation and the world are centered on the North Slope . . .

> Without intending to belittle your land, the real reason for the entire settlement is the oil, which by accident is on our land, not yours.

Under the proposal, apart from an initial $8 million payment to each region, the $500 million and whatever land was obtained in the settlement would be distributed on the basis of lands lost. Money from mineral developments, however, would be shared among the regions. Arctic Slope, for instance, would retain half of the revenues it received from mineral development and distribute the remainder to other regions on a population basis.

Tundra Times

*New AFN president Donald Wright (center) with Philip Guy, vice-president, and Frances Degnan, secretary.*

Tundra Times                                                    Tundra Times

*Arctic Slope President, Joe Upicksoun and Executive Director, Charles "Etok" Edwardsen, Jr.*

These two provisions, the "land loss" formula and the revenue-sharing proposal, were the foundation for a settlement acceptable to Native regions having mineral potential and those without, and those having large populations and those only lightly populated. In modified form, these two provisions would later be reflected in the legislation adopted.

# Chapter 20                    A Legislative Settlement

Soon after the 92nd Congress convened in 1971, the AFN bill was introduced in the Senate by Senators Fred Harris (Oklahoma) and Ted Kennedy (Massachusetts) and in the House of Representatives by Congressman Lloyd Meeds (Washington). Key features of this bill were full title to 60 million acres of land, an initial payment of $500 million, perpetual sharing in minerals from lands given up, and establishment of regional corporations.

**New bills**

A second bill introduced in the Senate was the bill which had passed in the Senate in 1970, Senator Henry Jackson's bill.

A third bill was introduced by the chairman of the House Committee on Interior and Insular Affairs, Wayne Aspinall of Colorado. Aspinall's bill provided for the smallest amount of land of the three — about 100,000 acres. Additional lands would be available for subsistence use on a permit basis.

It also provided that the settlement would be administered through an agency largely controlled by the Governor of Alaska. Although the agency would include four Natives, they would be appointed by the governor, not chosen by other Natives. Aspinall's opposition to Native owned and controlled corporations was reflected in an internal memorandum of his committee. This memorandum warned about the "lack of democratic controls in a large corporation, particularly with unsophisticated people."

The Aspinall bill was clearly the least acceptable to the Alaska Federation of Natives.

**Final campaign**

Against a backdrop of continuing intensive publicity efforts by AFN leaders, the Association on American Indian Affairs and others, the AFN launched what was to be its final campaign in the legislative halls for a claims settlement.

Since efforts to amend Senator Jackson's bill before its passage in 1970 had been unsuccessful, the AFN focused its energies upon winning favorable action in the House of Representatives. Even though Aspinall headed the key committee, Alaska's new congressman, Nick Begich, had won appointment to a seat on it. In addition, several other members were sympathetic to AFN's position.

Winning favorable House action was, nonetheless, expected to be difficult. While the AFN had exceptionally capable attorneys, president Don Wright was urged to hire lobbyists — persons who were engaged professionally in persuading congressmen to pass legislation favorable to his clients. The urging had come from Alaskans on the Potomac, an organization of Natives living in Washington, D. C., and others. Based upon his assessment of the difficulties ahead, Wright did employ lobbyists to assist the AFN board of directors and the AAIA representatives in their lobbying effort.

Any bill faced major problems without presidential support. President Richard M. Nixon had delivered a policy statement the preceding year that implied a favorable stance toward Alaska Native claims. But now, in 1971, there was a new militancy among interests opposing the claims, and Natives feared that his administration would introduce a bill like the earlier ones providing only a modest land settlement.

Wright sought the attention of the White House through the National Council on Indian Opportunity, a panel of presidentially appointed American Indians and Alaska Natives designed to provide Native advice on federal policies at the highest level of government. In a letter to its chairman, Vice-President Spiro T. Agnew, Wright said:

> The Native people of this country fear that your administration is about to commit the greatest betrayal of the Native people in the history of this nation. I refer to the likely proposal, by the administration for a settlement of the . . . land claims.

138

Tundra Times

*Laura Bergt of Fairbanks.*

Wright's request for a meeting was supported by Laura Bergt, an Eskimo from Fairbanks, and other Indian members of the Council. The meeting was arranged.

Joining Wright and Mrs. Bergt in the meeting with Vice-President Agnew were Al Ketzler of the Tanana Chiefs and State Senator Ray Christiansen of Bethel. Wright's presentation of Native land rights was so impressive that Mrs. Bergt reported, "He visibly moved everyone in the room, including the three Natives who were there . . ." The meeting was considered significant in moving the Administration to a new position.

The most important new factor in moving the White House and the Congress toward a settlement was the continuing delay in construction of a pipeline to carry oil from the North Slope to Valdez. Until the claims of Natives to land were settled, it was clear that no permit for the pipeline construction could be issued by the Department of Interior. Many national oil companies and many contractors had made enormous investments in anticipation of pipeline construction and were impatient to move ahead to recover their investments.

**Oil pipeline**

How support from the Nixon Administration was won was later summed up by Guy Martin, legislative assistant to Congressman Begich. Martin wrote:

> The Natives had a good cause. It was an
> election year. The Indian rights movement
> was gaining strength and acceptance. Still,

none of these factors could have been a controlling influence at the White House, or even made it possible for Native leaders to see the White House staff without other assistance. This assistance came largely from the oil industry and related business interests, and from the only Republican in Alaska's delegation, Senator Ted Stevens. This was the first of many times that the shared fates of the land claims and the trans-Alaska pipeline would produce a strange coalition of support for the Native cause.

**Nixon proposal**    The new Administration proposal was presented to the Congress in a special message from President Nixon in early April. It provided for 40 million acres of land in fee simple title, $500 million in compensation from the federal treasury, and an additional $500 million to come from mineral revenues from lands given up. On the same day the Administration's bill was introduced, Wright met with President Nixon. Wright reported that the President showed a willingness to veto any bill providing land which Natives believed inadequate to meet their needs.

The White House commitment dramatically improved the chances of winning a favorable resolution of Alaska Native land rights. No longer did the Jackson bill seem to be the "generous" proposal in which the Senate had taken so much pride one year earlier. The Administration position also changed the picture in the House. Before the announcement of White House support, the AFN had to place its hopes for favorable House action on the endorsement of key Democratic congressmen. Because of President Nixon's personal intervention, Natives could now expect aid from Republican congressmen as well. This meant that the chances for persuading Chairman Aspinall to retreat from his conservative position, which had been poor before, had now become a distinct possibility.

The prospects for favorable House action were also improved when Aspinall's committee heard the testimony of Governor William A. Egan. Except for the AFN proposal that mineral revenue sharing be in perpetuity, Egan largely supported the AFN position, stating that a 60-million-acre settlement would be acceptable. Unlike his predecessor, the governor agreed to a two-percent share of state mineral revenues with Alaska Natives.

Congressman Begich played a key role during the summer of 1971 in keeping the legislative process going. Aspinall threatened, almost weekly during that summer, to call off the subcommittee sessions which would have the effect of closing the door to a settlement. Each time the threat was made, Begich convinced Aspinall to allow the process to continue. He pleaded with congressmen of widely differing opinions to

*One of many Washington, D. C. meetings. (Left to right, seated) George Miller, Joe Upicksoun, Nels Anderson, Al Ketzler, Frances Degnan, Donald Wright, Senator Ted Stevens, Adeline Katongan, Philip Guy, Hank Eaton, and Al Nakak; (standing) John Katz, Max Gruenberg, Richard Frank, Brenda Itta, Fred Paul, Jim Wickwire, Charlie Edwardsen, Cliff Groh, Bob Willard, Iliodor Philemonof, and Frank Petersen.*

find areas of agreement so that prompt action could be taken. Begich agreed with the provisions sought by Alaska Natives, but he rarely argued for them openly within the subcommittee. Although he was frequently criticized by AFN leaders for not taking an advocacy role, Begich maintained that his most important job was to keep the subcommittee moving, and that the AFN had votes for 40 million acres in the subcommittee anyway.

With pressure upon Congressmen growing from the Native lobby, oil interests, and the Nixon administration, there was increasing agreement that a settlement had to be achieved. Begich called together AFN president Don Wright, Aspinall's staff assistant, and Alaska Attorney General John Havelock, and agreement was reached on the specific terms of settlement.

On August 3, the subcommittee reported its recommendations to the full committee. It provided for 40 million acres of land, with 18 million acres available for immediate village selection and 22 million acres to be selected after the State completed its selection authorized under the Statehood Act; $425 million in compensation to be paid from the federal treasury over a period of 10 years, and $500 million to be paid toward the settlement from the State's mineral revenues. It also incorporated the concept of regional corporations sought by the AFN. The subcommittee package was a

**House bill**

tribute to Begich's role as an architect of the House compromise. One veteran lobbyist observed, "It is the best individual achievement I have ever heard for a freshman congressman."

When the subcommittee bill cleared the full committee and was brought to the floor of the House in October, it faced a strong challenge from congressmen favorable to environmental interests. Representatives John Saylor of Pennsylvania and Morris Udall of Arizona proposed an amendment to the bill which would have extended the land freeze for another five years and provided for strict controls over the uses of lands. The Udall Amendment was opposed by the AFN, the State, the Administration, oil interests, and the House leadership. Although conservationists waged a fierce campaign, the amendment was defeated after two days of debate. On October 20, by an overwhelming vote of 334 to 63, the House of Representatives voted to accept the committee's land claims bill.

**Senate bill**

After it had become apparent that the House was going to pass a land bill, the Senate moved swiftly to act upon its own version of the claims settlement. In dealing with the House the AFN was also developing its strategy for Senate legislative action. The Senate considered itself to be more generous in dealing with Native affairs than the House, and Native leaders relied on competition between the two bodies of Congress to produce a favorable Senate bill.

The Senate Interior Committee, reporting its recommendations after a short meeting on September 15, performed as the Native leaders had expected it would. Its bill provided for $500 million to come from mineral revenue sharing and $500 million from the federal treasury — $75 million more than the House bill. Under one land option of the bill, Natives could obtain 50 million acres, but 20 million acres would be only for subsistence use, not owned outright.

The Senate bill provided for only seven regional corporations, but also one for urban Natives, another for Natives living away from Alaska, and two statewide corporations. It also provided for a land-use planning commission proposed by Senator Mike Gravel of Alaska.

In November the Senate bill reached the floor and, with but little opposition, was adopted by a vote of 76 to 5.

Since there were differences in the two bills, each house appointed senior members of its Interior committees and members of the Alaska delegation to a conference committee. Their task: to produce a bill acceptable to both the House and Senate.

**Compromise bill**

The conference committee began meeting in late November and concluded its work on December 3. Of the several dozen compromises reached in the 29-page bill, the key features were generally favorable to the AFN position. Title to 40 million acres would be confirmed. The amount of

142

*At left, AFN president Donald Wright.*

*Below, delegates attending the 1971 convention discuss provisions of the land claims legislation.*

Robert Koweluk

compensation was set midway between the Senate and House versions at $962.5 million. And there would be 12 regional corporations established to administer the settlement.

On December 14, the conference committee version of the bill was adopted by the House by a vote of 307 to 16 and by the Senate by unanimous consent. One step remained before it would become law: the President needed to sign the measure.

Before signing the bill into law, President Nixon wanted to know whether the settlement was acceptable to Alaska Natives. There were provisions in the legislation opposed by AFN, such as the tax provisions. And some things sought by AFN, such as mineral revenue sharing in perpetuity, had not become part of the legislation.

**Final approval**

On December 16, from all over Alaska and from other states more than 600 delegates assembled in Anchorage at a special convention to consider the settlement. AFN president Don Wright called upon them to study the bill and weigh its provisions. Claims of Natives to almost all of Alaska would be given up in exchange for title to about one-ninth of the state's land area plus compensation. Two days later, by a vote of 511 to 56, the Alaska Federation of Natives accepted the settlement. By special telephone arrangements, the President was advised of the acceptance. Then the delegates, standing motionless and silent, heard the President say, "I want you to be among the first to know that I have just signed the Alaska Native Claims Settlement Act."

The struggle by Alaska Natives for a claims settlement was at an end. Implementation of the act would now begin.

Tundra Times

*Delegates and others hear President Nixon announce his signing of the settlement act.*

# UNIT FIVE

**Tundra Times**

25¢

Inupiat Paitot *People's Heritage*

Don Nena Henash *Our Land Speaks*

Unangax Tunuktauq *The Aleuts Speak*

Tlingit
Ut kah neek *Informing and Reporting*

Vol. 9, No. 15     Wednesday, December 22, 1971     Fairbanks, Alaska

## NIXON PENS BILL INTO LAW

### 'I Want You to Be Among the First to Know...' Nixon Says

By MADELYN SHULMAN
Staff Writer

In a ceremony marked only by a special taped message to the convention of the Alaska Federation of Natives the President of the United States signed the Alaska Native Claims Act of 1971 into law shortly before 1 p.m.

# THE ALASKA NATIVE CLAIMS SETTLEMENT ACT: AN INTRODUCTION

*"The Settlement Act is a complex settlement of a complex situation. Some of its provisions are susceptible to differing interpretations, the more so because there are three parties-at-interest: The Natives, the State of Alaska, and the Federal government, which still has vast riches and vast responsibilities in Alaska. Many problems have arisen already and many more will arise in the implementation of the law.*

*Enactment required goodwill and broad statesmanship. Fulfillment of the spirit and letter of this historic legislation will require the same great qualities.*

*The Alaska Native Claims Settlement Act is monumental legislation of which all Americans, Native and non-Native, can be proud."*

—Stewart French, "Alaska Native
Claims Settlement Act," The
Arctic Institute of North America,
August 1972

When the Alaska Native Claims Settlement Act was signed into law on December 18, 1971, it was hailed by the *Tundra Times* as "the beginning of a great era for the Native people of Alaska."

That the Congress held a similar view is suggested by a statement of policy which was made a part of the act. In adopting the act, the Congress had declared, in part, that the settlement should be accomplished:

- in conformity with the real economic and social needs of Natives . . . ;

- with maximum participation by Natives in decisions affecting their rights and property;

- without establishing any permanent racially defined institutions, rights, privileges, or obligations; and

- without creating a reservation system or lengthy wardship or trusteeship . . .

Under the act, Alaska Natives would receive fee simple title to 40 million acres of land. Native claims based on aboriginal title to any additional lands in Alaska were extinguished. Existing reserves, except for Annette Island, were revoked. The Native Allotment Act, which had also allowed trust status, was revoked. Compensation for claims extinguished was set at $962.5 million, which would be paid over a number of years.

All United States citizens with one-fourth or more Alaska Indian, Eskimo, or Aleut blood who were living when the settlement bill was enacted were qualified to participate, unless they were members of the Annette Island Reserve community of Metlakatla. (As noted earlier, Tsimshian Indians of this community had been granted a reserve by Congress in 1891, following their emigration from Canada.)

Benefits under the settlement act would accrue to Natives not through clans, families, or other traditional groupings, but, instead, through the modern form of business organization called a corporation. All eligible Natives were to become stockholders — part owners — of such corporations.

The first step for a Native to take to become a stockholder would be to enroll — to register his name, his community and region of permanent residence, and to prove that he was an Eskimo, Indian, or Aleut as defined in the act. Based upon the region which he considered his permanent home, he would be enrolled and become a holder of 100 shares of stock in one of the 12 (or perhaps 13) regional corporations to be created under the act.

The act provided that no rights or obligations of Natives as citizens, nor rights or obligations of the government towards Natives as citizens, would be replaced or diminished. It called, however, for a study of federal programs affecting Natives to see whether changes of any kind should be considered. Within three years the Secretary of the Interior

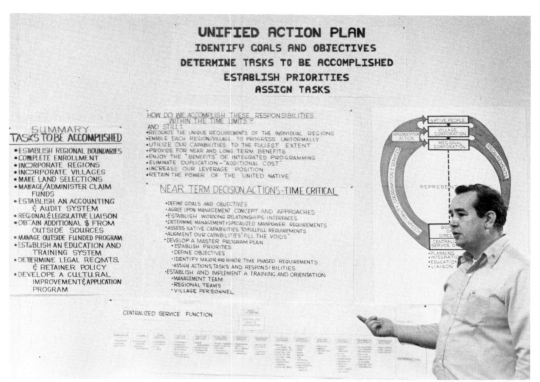

*AFN executive director Harry Carter identifying some of the tasks and decisions that lie ahead.*

was to deliver his recommendations to Congress regarding the future operation and management of these programs.

The act also authorized the Secretary of the Interior to withdraw up to 80 million acres of land in Alaska for study to determine if these lands should be added to existing national parks or forests, wildlife refuges, or wild and scenic river systems. Following the study, the Secretary would make recommendations regarding the lands to Congress.

A 10-member Joint Federal-State Land Use Planning Commission was to be established to make recommendations concerning use or disposition of lands in Alaska. Broadly told, the Commission's role would be one of developing recommendations that would take into account the interests of various groups of people, such as Natives and other residents of Alaska, and the interests of the people of the nation as a whole.

# Chapter 21        Land and Money

In terms of the land and money settlement, the Alaska Native Claims Settlement Act was clearly an historic event. With extinguishment of their aboriginal claims, Alaska Natives were to obtain fee simple title to more land than was

Tim Samuelson

*With 106 people enrolled, Kokhanok was entitled to four townships (92,106 acres).*

held in trust for all other American Indians. And compensation for lands given up was nearly four times the amount all Indian tribes had won from the Indian Claims Commission over its 25-year lifetime.

MAP 11

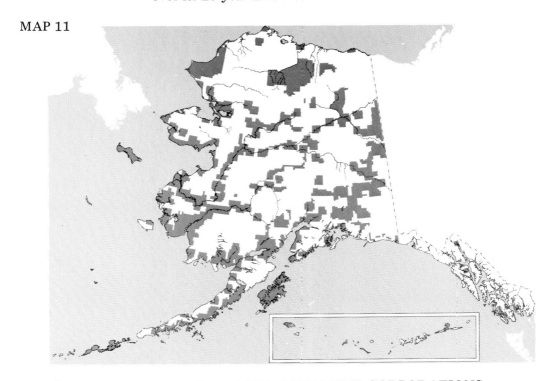

LANDS WITHDRAWN FOR SELECTION BY NATIVE CORPORATIONS

**Land**     To assure that 40 million acres would be available for selection by Natives, the Secretary of the Interior was to set aside land around villages and elsewhere before the land freeze was lifted. Such withdrawal would protect these lands over the three-year period in which village corporations could make their selections and the four-year period in which

148

reg_onal corporations could make their selections. Land already in private ownership could not be chosen. Land in national parks or lands set aside for national defense purposes could not be chosen either, except for the surface of lands in Naval Petroleum Reserve No. 4, in northwest Alaska.

Of the 40-million-acre settlement, 22 million acres were earmarked for selection by villages. As with the money distribution, the number of acres to which a village was entitled was to be determined by enrollment. With some exceptions noted below, entitlements would be determined as follows:

| Enrollment | Entitlements |
|---|---|
| 25 through 99 | 3 townships ( 69,120 acres) |
| 100 through 199 | 4 townships ( 92,160 acres) |
| 200 through 399 | 5 townships (115,200 acres) |
| 400 through 599 | 6 townships (138,240 acres) |
| 600 or more | 7 townships (161,280 acres) |

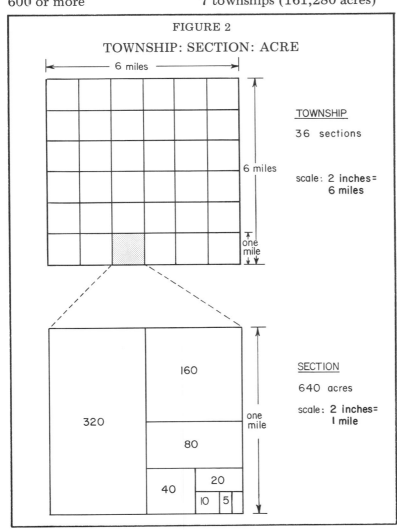

FIGURE 2

TOWNSHIP: SECTION: ACRE

Whatever their size, villages in southeastern Alaska could choose only a single township (23,040 acres), a limitation justified in the act by the earlier cash award of the Tlingit-Haida settlement. A limiting factor for other villages in the foregoing table was land which was in national forests or wildlife refuges, lands chosen by the State but not yet patented to it, and Naval Petroleum Reserve No. 4. In such areas, selections would be limited to three townships (69,120 acres), and other township entitlements, if any, would have to be made elsewhere.

U. S. Forest Service

*The surface estate of lands selected by village corporations would go to village corporations.*

The village corporations would own only the surface estate to lands they selected. Their ownership would not include the minerals below the ground. The rights to the minerals — the subsurface estate — would belong to regional corporations. This would be true for all 22 million acres selected, except for village selections made in Petroleum Reserve No. 4 or in wildlife refuges.

If villages on revoked reserves voted to acquire title to their former reserve they would obtain fee simple title not only to its surface, but also to its minerals. They would forego, however, other benefits under the act.

Once villages obtained their lands, they would transfer some tracts to individuals — Native or non-Native, some to organizations, and some to municipal, state, or federal governments, and retain the remainder.

Sixteen million acres of land would be selected by regional corporations on the basis of land area within their regions, rather than population. Under a complicated land-loss formula, these lands would be chosen by whichever of 11 regional corporations had small enrollments but large areas within their boundaries. Owing to the earlier Tlingit-Haida settlement, the southeastern region would not be among the corporations eligible for this provision.

*The subsurface estate of lands selected by village corporations would go to regional corporations.*

The remaining two million acres would be set aside for grants of title of lands to special Native corporations organized in the non-Native cities of Sitka, Kenai, Kodiak, and Juneau (which had been historic Native places); for grants to groups of Natives or to individual Natives residing away from villages; for Native allotments which were filed for before the passage of the act; and for cemeteries and historic sites.

Compensation for claims given up was to come from two sources: Congressional appropriations and mineral revenues from State and federal lands. The act established the Alaska Native Fund in the U. S. Treasury and authorized the appropriation of $462.5 million to be paid into it over an 11-year period. It also provided for the payment of $500

**Money**

151

million into the Fund from revenues obtained from certain mineral resources from federal and State lands in Alaska. Such payments (chiefly based on oil and gas), by the State and federal governments would continue until the total amount was reached. Until production of oil would begin on the North Slope, revenues from mineral resources were expected to be negligible.

Payments from the Alaska Native Fund would be made only to regional corporations. They, in turn, would retain part of the funds and pay out part to individual Natives and village corporations.

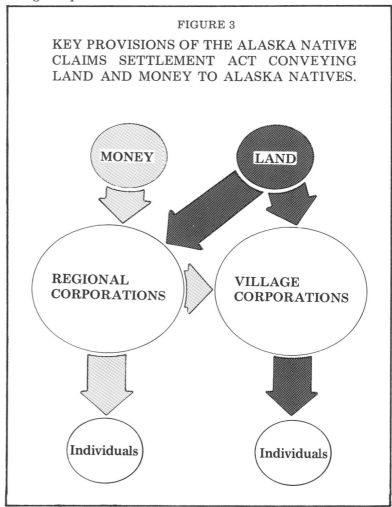

FIGURE 3

KEY PROVISIONS OF THE ALASKA NATIVE CLAIMS SETTLEMENT ACT CONVEYING LAND AND MONEY TO ALASKA NATIVES.

The amount of money each regional corporation would receive was to be based upon its proportion of enrolled Natives to the total number enrolled. During the first five years, at least 10 percent of the claims money and other income received by a regional corporation was to be distributed directly to individuals — its stockholders — and at least 45 percent of such money was to be distributed to village corporations within its boundaries.

The amount received by each village corporation was to be based upon its proportion of stockholders to the total number of stockholders in the region. Natives enrolled to regional corporations but not to villages would receive their proportionate share directly, which meant that their payments would be larger than if they were also enrolled to villages. They would not be granted land by village corporations, however, or otherwise benefit from activities these corporations carry out.

# Chapter 22                 The Corporation as Vehicle

There was no mention of corporations in the first bills introduced in 1967 to settle Alaska Native claims. These bills would have resolved claims through "tribes, bands, villages, communities, associations or other identifiable groups of Eskimos, Indians, and Aleuts." Beginning with the Governor's Task Force bill of 1968, however, business corporations were proposed as the means of carrying out the settlement, and after that time were fully accepted. Indeed, the theme of the 1971 convention of the AFN, the last held before Congress adopted the act, was "In the white man's society, we need white man's tools."

Under the settlement act all of the money and virtually all of the land goes initially to business corporations. It is through these organizations that nearly all of the benefits flow to enrolled Natives. The business corporation is the vehicle of settlement.

**The business corporation**

The business corporation is organized to earn money. By having a number of people pool their financial resources, the corporation obtains money to purchase equipment and hire persons of specialized skills to carry out money-making activities. Those who put their dollars into the enterprise become stockholders who share in the ownership of the corporation. As owners, they may expect to earn dividends — shares in the profits of the corporation.

While the corporation is a business organization, people and laws treat it, in many ways, as if it were a real person. A corporation may buy or sell goods and services. It collects money and spends it. It makes agreements and it may break them. If it violates a law, it may be charged with a crime. If it is, the corporation is charged with the offense, as though it were a real person; its stockholders are not.

**Control systems**

Most of the control systems of a corporation are provided for in the State law that allows corporations to be established and in two sets of papers which State law requires: articles of incorporation and bylaws. State law sets out what corporations may do and what they may not do. And, as noted earlier, many of the laws that apply to persons also apply to corporations.

The articles of incorporation are a kind of agreement (which has been approved by the State government) on some rules of control among the people who first set up a corporation. They establish the basic relationship between the stockholders, who are the owners of the corporation, and the company and its management. Anything that the stockholders do not want changed without their say-so should be in the articles. The articles give the stockholders the right to elect directors. All of the rest of the basic control of the corporation is left to the directors whom the majority have chosen.

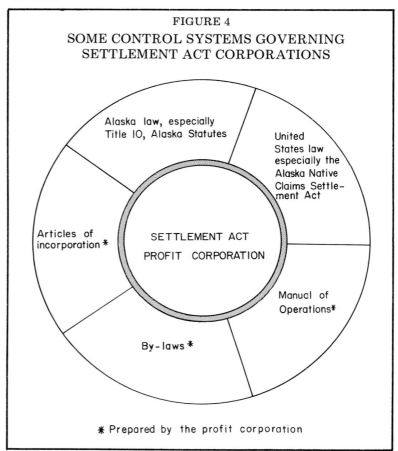

FIGURE 4

SOME CONTROL SYSTEMS GOVERNING
SETTLEMENT ACT CORPORATIONS

Alaska law, especially
Title IO, Alaska Statutes

United States law especially the Alaska Native Claims Settlement Act

Articles of incorporation *

SETTLEMENT ACT
PROFIT CORPORATION

Manual of Operations*

By-laws *

* Prepared by the profit corporation

The bylaws contain most of the rules of control between the directors, who are usually not employees of the corporation, and the officers of the corporation, who are often employees. If the officers are employees, it is they who have responsibility for its day-to-day operation, subject only to broad policy direction from the directors. The bylaws establish the titles and responsibilities of each of the principal officers of the corporation. Bylaws can be amended by the directors at any time.

Law, articles of incorporation, and bylaws define the basic control system for a corporation. Within that framework, the board of directors provides more detailed directions for the management of the corporation. These directions are recorded in the minutes of the directors' meetings.

Other rules, dividing control of the corporation among officers and employees, are contained in operations manuals and in memoranda issued by the officers to employees.

These rules of control, taken together, set out the terms under which corporations are run, and identify who gets to make decisions about what.

Another set of rules — a system of accountability — helps the people who own or manage the corporation to determine how successfully the corporation is performing.

**A system of accountability**

Since the primary purpose of most business corporations is to make profits, their systems of accountability are organized to help determine whether they are. Their books of accounts will show the flow of dollars and things having dollar values in and out of the corporation.

Calista (J. Hout)

*Tim Kaganak of Scammon Bay registers for stockholders' meeting.*

All of these books and accounts are normally available for a concerned stockholder to look at for the asking. But most stockholders are content to review the annual report of the corporation — a summary statement of how well the corporation is performing its business — which is usually distributed to all stockholders for the annual meeting.

**Role of stockholders**

Although a corporation's stockholders are its owners, the role of stockholders in the life of a typical corporation is a very limited one.

One of the stockholder's most important roles is that of participating in the election of the corporation's board of directors. It is that board, the officers it chooses, and the staff it hires which will determine the course of the corporation's activities. While an elaborate system of control exists for corporations, it is only a framework within which a corporation engages in activities expected to be of benefit to its stockholders. What the corporation sets out to do, and how effectively it accomplishes it, is dependent upon the qualities of judgment and vision brought to the enterprise by corporate leaders. '

Calista (J. Hout)

*Mary Gregory (at microphone) speaking at Calista meeting.*

Even though this role of a stockholder is an important one, a sole stockholder in a large corporation has little voting strength by himself. In order to gain some advantage in selecting directors or taking other action at a stockholders' meeting, groups of stockholders sometimes have agreements among themselves as to how they will vote. Each of several stockholders may give his proxy — his power to vote — to another stockholder for use at an annual meeting. Such a proxy would be "special," binding the holder to vote for a specific candidate for director or a list of candidates named in the proxy. Another kind of proxy is a "general" one, allowing the holder to vote for anyone he chooses to vote for. However, it should be noted that there is no substitute at the annual meeting for the eloquence of the individual stockholder in calling for the election or rejection of persons seeking seats on the board of directors.

The stockholder's right to vote also extends to extraordinary decisions relating to the corporation. One example of such a decision would be a recommendation from the officers that a large part of the assets of the corporation be sold. Another example would be a decision to dissolve the corporation.

Corporations established under the claims settlement act are governed not only by the control systems imposed by the State of Alaska upon all corporations, but also by the act itself.

The articles of incorporation and bylaws of a regional corporation require the approval of the Secretary of the Interior, not just the State. Furthermore, any proposed changes in the articles of incorporation require the Secretary's approval for a period of five years after incorporation. Financial reports of regional corporations are to be furnished to the Secretary and to the Congress.

Unlike typical business corporations formed by the voluntary purchase of stock by individuals, corporations established under the act obtain initial capital and operating monies from Congressional appropriations and mineral revenues. They obtain land under the act. They then make eligible Natives stockholders by issuing stock. Unlike stockholders in typical corporations, these stockholders cannot sell their stock or transfer any rights in it for 20 years. Over this period, with one exception, only Natives have voting rights. Depending upon the provisions of a corporation's bylaws, a non-Native custodian of a stockholder who is a minor may be allowed to vote.

Other controls imposed by the act upon corporations created under it are taken up in chapters which follow.

Henry Peck

*Arctic Slope Regional Corporation members hear James Wickwire, its attorney. Foreground, Oliver Leavitt (at left) and Eddie Hopson (at right).*

**Regional business corporations**

With the exception of members of certain revoked reserves, all enrolled Natives were to become stockholders in business corporations formed along the boundaries of 12 regional Native associations listed in the settlement act, or a special 13th corporation.

The 12 associations in Alaska whose boundaries would be the basis of the regional business corporations were the Arctic Slope Native Association, Bering Straits Native Association, Northwest Alaska Native Association, Association of Village Council Presidents, Tanana Chiefs Conference, Cook Inlet Native Association, Bristol Bay Native Association, Aleut League, Chugach Native Association, Tlingit-Haida Central Council, Kodiak Area Native Association, and the Copper River Native Association. All eligible Natives enrolling to these regions would become stockholders in the corporations formed in them, except for members of reserves revoked by the act which voted to accept full ownership of their former reserves.

Henry Peck

*Traveling to discuss the claims settlement act. From left: Brenda Itta of Barrow, Allen Soosuk and David Stone of Point Hope, and Joe Upicksoun, president of the Arctic Slope Regional Corporation, Barrow.*

The 12 regional corporations would have important roles in implementing the settlement within their geographic boundaries. Among other things, they would:

- receive payments made by the federal and State governments as compensation, disburse about half to village corporations and individuals, and retain the remainder;

- become owners of the subsurface estate — the mineral resources — of all 40 million acres selected under the act; and

- supervise the incorporation of villages, assist them in their land selection programs, and review their spending plans.

Natives residing outside of Alaska who were adults would be required to vote when they enrolled on whether they wished to establish a 13th region of their own. If a majority of those voting favored such a region, it would be established for those favoring it. Benefits for its members would be limited to sharing only in the authorized money settlement. Those opposing the 13th region would be enrolled to one of the other 12 corporations. If a majority voting opposed the formation, all nonresident Natives would become stockholders in one or another of the 12 regional corporations in Alaska.

Some eligible Natives would become stockholders only in regional corporations, because their permanent homes were away from villages certified to benefit from the act. They would be "at-large" stockholders. Other eligible Natives would be members of both regional and village corporations.

All eligible Native villages would be required to form corporations. Eligible villages were defined as communities half or more of whose population were Natives, having at least 25 Natives who were residents, and not being modern or urban in character. While more than 200 villages were listed in the act, some of them would not be eligible and others not in the list could be found eligible.

**Village Corporations**

Joyce Hooley

*Kiana, one of the 11 eligible villages within the NANA region.*

Eligible villages were given the choice of incorporating either as business corporations or as nonprofit corporations. The nonprofit corporation would not make money nor pay dividends, but would provide a service of some kind to the village.

Village corporations would not replace village councils or the governing bodies of municipal governments, but some of the same persons might serve on both.

One of the responsibilities of a village corporation would be to plan for the use of claims money received. But its plan would require the approval of its regional corporation before it could obtain its share of the claims money. The village corporation was also to select land and to plan for its transfer or management. In selecting land, the village would have the assistance of its regional corporation. Any proposed transactions in land by the village would have to be submitted to the regional corporation for its review and advice.

These illustrations of the subordinate role of the village corporation to the regional corporation, together with the regional responsibilities over its basic control systems show clearly that the village corporation was meant to be not entirely independent. How much freedom in decision-making it would have would be discovered in practice over the next few years.

**A new vocabulary**

All eligible Natives were to become stockholders in one or two corporations, and these corporations would receive, hold, and manage nearly all of the land and money from the claims settlement. But most Natives had but little familiarity with the corporation as a form of organization, the laws governing it, and how it functions.

Tundra Times

*Percy Herbert, Franklin Madros, and Stanley Jones at a Tanana Indian Conference.*

To understand the corporation and other terms of the settlement act meant acquiring a whole new vocabulary of perhaps thousands of words. Furthermore, the deadlines imposed by the law (such as establishing regional corporations within 18 months) meant that new vocabulary had to be acquired promptly.

There was yet another difficulty for thousands of beneficiaries of the act. Many villagers, particularly older persons of northern and western Alaska, could neither read nor write English, and some of them did not speak nor understand it.

Poet and musician John Angaiak of Tununak, who speaks both English and Yupik, says some explanations are reasonably manageable. A bilingual Native with a formal education certainly can understand "profit-making" and he might explain, as he translates, that "profit-making is a parent dollar that gives birth to many more little dollars." Similarly, Angaiak says he might begin moving toward a definition of corporation in Yupik with relative ease — corporation-aaq naucimalartuq pikestai akingevkararkauluki — "a corporation is made up of owners who receive money through it."

But Angaiak says that some translators might have difficulty with a lawyer's definition because the terms employed are not known to him. "The corporation is a group of people, put together by statute as a legal person, given powers to contract, to own property, to acquire and dispose of it in the name of the corporation, and otherwise act upon business within the limits of the powers granted by the articles of

Tundra Times

*A successful whaling crew.*

161

incorporation." To translate such a definition demands that substantial knowledge be possessed by the translator, in addition to his being bilingual.

Even though specific legal terms might be difficult to translate, the function of a corporation would be understandable, at least to whaling communities. This is the view of Charles Edwardsen, Jr. of Barrow, whose role in the claims struggle was portrayed by Hugh Gallagher in *Etok: A Story of Eskimo Power*. Edwardsen wrote that the Inupiat are accustomed as members of a whaling crew to working together to achieve a shared goal, just as a corporation does. "Now," he said, "the Eskimo has a new harpoon."

---

### ADDITIONAL COMPENSATION
### FOR TRESPASS BEFORE 1971?

In 1975 the possibility remained that Alaska Natives might obtain money payments in addition to the $962.5 million authorized by the claims settlement act. Such compensation, if any, would be based upon damages caused by trespassers on Native-claimed lands before the act's adoption.

The door was opened to the possibility of compensation by a decision handed down in late 1973 by a federal court in *Edwardsen v. Morton.* In that case (filed in late 1971) Charles Edwardsen, Jr. and others contended that North Slope Eskimos had suffered damages to their hunting grounds, graveyards, and other places because of oil exploration activities. Their suit was against the Department of the Interior, which had allowed the activities, and its then-Secretary Rogers C. B. Morton. The court held that the settlement act extinguished any title held by Natives, but that its passage did not prevent trespass suits for damages occurring before its adoption, December 18, 1971.

The court also ordered the U. S. Departments of Justice and the Interior to file suits on behalf of North Slope Eskimos. In September, 1975, federal attorneys sued Alyeska Pipeline Company, the State of Alaska, and 124 other organizations or persons for an unspecified amount of money.

In response, a spokesman for the State declared that if the suit were successful, it would allow Natives to bring additional suits for all instances of trespass by all non-Natives. The spokesman, Attorney General Avrum Gross, announced that the State would contend the claims cited by Edwardsen and others were extinguished by the settlement act.

# UNIT SIX

Henry Peck

# SETTLEMENT ACT ORGANIZATIONS

*"The native regions established by the act are required to be profit-making corporations; the villages may opt for profit-making and/or nonprofit-making. This means a people who have traditionally lived closely with the land, being dependent upon it and its wildlife for their subsistence, are now forced to become businessmen and to consider the land they select for its money-making potential."*

—Sierra Club Bulletin, 1974

*"Forced to become businessmen? What's wrong with that, anyway? Maybe it doesn't make sense to a conservationist sitting in comfort in San Francisco. But it certainly makes sense to a people who for all too long have lived in a sod hut."*

—Anchorage Daily Times
October 21, 1974

*"Whatever the actual situation may be, we reserve the right to speak and decide for oursleves; it is not the place for you or the Sierra Club to decide what is right or wrong for us.*

*"What we need is a sincere two-way exchange of ideas and philosophies, so that we may understand and accept the best of what different cultures have to contribute to the survival of everyone. We cannot do it if there is force or if people speak for us out of ignorance and insensitivity."*

—Larry Merculieff, St. Paul Island, in a letter to
the Anchorage Daily Times, October 25, 1974

As 1974 was drawing to a close, 12 regional Native corporations having about 76,500 stockholders were established and operating in Alaska. All had held stockholders' meetings at which permanent officers and boards of directors (ranging from 10 to 35 members) had been elected. Several of the corporations were actively engaged in profit-making enterprises.

In the last week of the year a federal court ordered the creation of a 13th regional corporation for Natives living outside of Alaska who wanted the optional corporation established. The effect of the ruling was expected to be the transfer of some 5,000 stockholders from Alaska corporations to the new 13th regional corporation once it was formed.

Across Alaska 203 villages had been certified as eligible for land and money benefits. Taken together, these village corporations had about 49,000 stockholders. While a few had already become engaged in profit-making activities, the principal activity of most village corporations had been one of choosing land to which they would obtain surface title.

But the three years that had passed since the enactment of the claims settlement had been hectic. The fundamental and far-reaching task of enrollment had to be completed within two years, but this had required Natives to file their applications within 15 months. Within the state, the Bureau of Indian Affairs had contracted with the regional corporations to carry out enrollment. To reach Natives outside Alaska, advertising in newspapers, magazines and on television was widely employed, and those responding to the notices were furnished information packages. Because the regulations governing enrollment were complicated, many applications were slow in being returned or were marred by errors. Adding to the difficulty of enrollment were uncertainties of interpretation such as, for instance, the meaning of "permanent residence."

Anchorage Daily News

*Cook Inlet Native Association enrollment program. Pete Ezi and Otto Thiele.*

Even after the roll was certified, adjustments were being made to it on the basis of errors or challenges to eligibility. There were 800 to 1,000 Natives who learned of the requirement to enroll after the deadline had passed, so their applications were rejected and they did not become enrolled.

At the same time enrollment was proceeding, there was the 29-page law to be learned and dozens of pages of regulations to be studied (and, as will be noted later, perhaps resisted). Education and training sessions were sponsored by Native organizations throughout the state. Regions and villages had begun thinking of the fast-approaching need to select land even as they moved to form their corporations.

# Chapter 24       Regional Business Corporations

About the same time enrollment was launched, each of the 12 Native associations named in the settlement act had chosen five persons to establish business corporations along association boundaries. They accomplished their work speedily, a year ahead of the deadline. Once incorporated, interim officers and boards of directors had been chosen to serve until completion of enrollment allowed the first stockholders' meetings to be held.

With advance payments from the Alaska Native Fund (the special account in the U. S. Treasury) the regional corporations had begun to function by mid-1972. They had hired persons and organizations to assist villages within their regions to become incorporated and to begin planning for lands that villages would select. They had employed geologists and other specialists to aid them in identifying the natural resources of lands they might select. And they had engaged attorneys to analyze regulations proposed by the U. S. Department of the Interior to implement the act, to file appeals for persons whose enrollments had been rejected, and to advise them on a wide range of legal issues.

Adult Natives not residing in Alaska had voted upon enrolling whether they desired a 13th corporation. Based upon the Department of the Interior's finding that a majority had rejected it — the nonresident Natives who had sought to enroll to it had become at-large stockholders in one or another of the 12 Alaska corporations. A court was later to reverse the finding.

With the September 1974 distribution from the Alaska Native Fund, the 12 regional corporations had received almost $209 million as first payments of funds due Alaska Natives under the settlement act, and had disbursed several millions of dollars to individuals and villages consistent with the act. Remaining funds (along with most of the village funds) were invested in a variety of ways or were being used for the continuing costs of administering the settlement.

Including all nonresident Natives, the regional corporations range in size from Ahtna, Inc., with almost 1,100 stockholders, to Sealaska Corporation, with nearly 16,500 stockholders. In terms of land area within their boundaries, the corporations range from Koniag, Inc., with about 7,300 square miles to Doyon, Limited, with more than 200,000 square miles.

## Figure 5
### THE 12 REGIONAL CORPORATIONS

| | Number of Stockholders (9-14-74) | Stockholders residing in region (8-28-74) | Total population within region (1970) | Number of village corporations |
|---|---|---|---|---|
| Ahtna, Inc. | 1,092 | 495 | 1,332 | 8 |
| The Aleut Corporation | 3,353 | 1,667 | 7,694 | 12 |
| Arctic Slope Regional Corporation | 3,906 | 2,886 | 3,266 | 8 |
| Bering Straits Native Corporation | 6,916 | 4,638 | 5,749 | 16 |
| Bristol Bay Native Corporation | 5,517 | 3,596 | 4,995 | 29 |
| Calista Corporation | 13,441 | 11,561 | 12,617 | 56 |
| Chugach Natives, Inc. | 2,099 | 1,062 | 6,286 | 5 |
| Cook Inlet Region, Inc. | 6,243 | 4,181 | 145,072 | 6 |
| Doyon, Limited | 9,221 | 6,683 | 57,354 | 34 |
| Koniag, Inc., Regional Native Corporation | 3,340 | 1,958 | 9,409 | 9 |
| NANA Regional Native Corporation | 4,905 | 3,643 | 4,043 | 11 |
| Sealaska Corporation | 16,493 | 9,529 | 42,565 | 9 |
| Totals | 76,526 | 51,899 | 300,382 | 203 |

Sources: Enrollment data: Enrollment Office, U. S. Bureau of Indian Affairs, Anchorage, Alaska. Population: U. S. Bureau of the Census, U. S. Census of Population, 1970, Alaska.

Note: Figures subject to change upon formation of the 13th regional corporation.

In the portrayal of the 12 corporations which follows and the accompanying chart (Figure 5), the number of stockholders includes those who might become members of the 13th corporation once established. The accompanying maps show generalized land status before village and regional selections were made.

Arctic Environment Information and Data Center (J. C. LaBelle)

*Formation of village corporations at historic village sites has led to resettlement of old sites. Above, Nuiqsut.*

*The corporate office of the Arctic Slope Regional Corporation is in Barrow, pictured below. The village corporation at Barrow is Ukpeagvik Inupiat Corporation.*

Naval Arctic Research Laboratory

O. Eugene Cote

## Ahtna, Inc.

*Robert Marshall,*
*President*

Smallest of the regional corporations in number of stockholders is Ahtna, Inc. — a name derived from the group of Athabascans historically occupying the area. About half of its nearly 1,100 stockholders live within its region. The total population of the nearly 28,000-square-mile area is only about 1,300 persons.

Ahtna's stockholders chose Robert Marshall, a regional supervisor for highway maintenance, as its first president. The corporation's office is in Copper Center, the largest community of the region.

Several of the state's highways cross the region and all of Ahtna's eight villages are on the road system. Three of the villages lie along the pipeline route.

The region is a high inland plateau, ringed by rugged mountains, and experiences colder winter temperatures and higher summer temperatures than the nearby coastal regions.

168

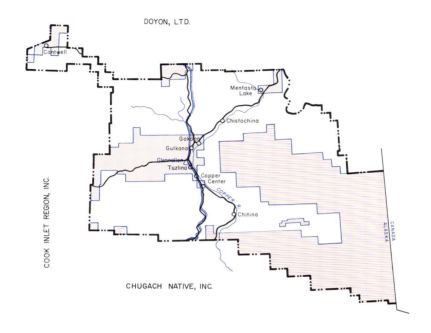

DOYON, LTD.

Cantwell

Mentasta Lake

Chistochina

Gakona
Gulkana
Glennallen
Tazlina
Copper Center

COPPER R.

Chitina

COOK INLET REGION, INC.

CHUGACH NATIVE, INC.

ALASKA
CANADA

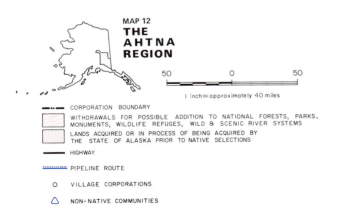

MAP 12
**THE
AHTNA
REGION**

50        0        50

1 inch = approximately 40 miles

▬▬▪ CORPORATION BOUNDARY

WITHDRAWALS FOR POSSIBLE ADDITION TO NATIONAL FORESTS, PARKS, MONUMENTS, WILDLIFE REFUGES, WILD & SCENIC RIVER SYSTEMS

LANDS ACQUIRED OR IN PROCESS OF BEING ACQUIRED BY THE STATE OF ALASKA PRIOR TO NATIVE SELECTIONS

▬▬ HIGHWAY

▪▪▪▪▪ PIPELINE ROUTE

O    VILLAGE CORPORATIONS

△    NON-NATIVE COMMUNITIES

169

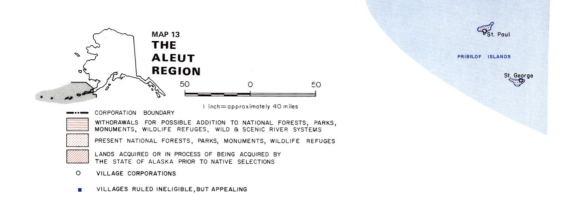

MAP 13

# THE ALEUT REGION

50    O    50

1 inch = approximately 40 miles

- - - - CORPORATION BOUNDARY

WITHDRAWALS FOR POSSIBLE ADDITION TO NATIONAL FORESTS, PARKS, MONUMENTS, WILDLIFE REFUGES, WILD & SCENIC RIVER SYSTEMS

PRESENT NATIONAL FORESTS, PARKS, MONUMENTS, WILDLIFE REFUGES

LANDS ACQUIRED OR IN PROCESS OF BEING ACQUIRED BY THE STATE OF ALASKA PRIOR TO NATIVE SELECTIONS

O    VILLAGE CORPORATIONS

■    VILLAGES RULED INELIGIBLE, BUT APPEALING

St. Paul

PRIBILOF ISLANDS

St. George

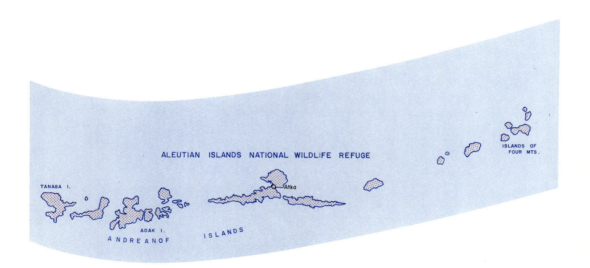

ALEUTIAN ISLANDS NATIONAL WILDLIFE REFUGE

ISLANDS OF FOUR MTS.

TANAGA I.

Atka

ADAK I.

ANDREANOF    ISLANDS

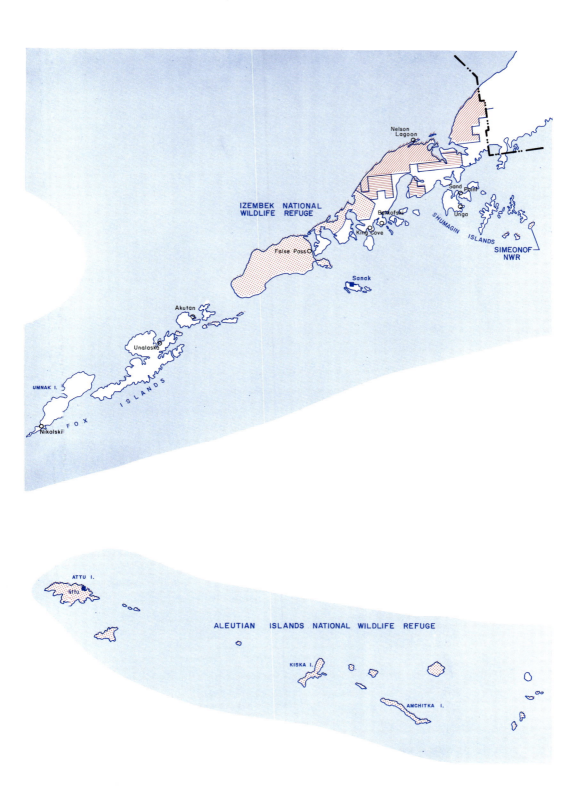

Nelson
Lagoon

IZEMBEK NATIONAL
WILDLIFE REFUGE

Sand Point

Belkofski

King Cove

Unga

SHUMAGIN ISLANDS

SIMEONOF
NWR

False Pass

Sanak

Akutan

Unalaska

UMNAK I.

FOX ISLANDS

Nikolski

ATTU I.

Attu

ALEUTIAN ISLANDS NATIONAL WILDLIFE REFUGE

KISKA I.

AMCHITKA I.

## The Aleut Corporation

*Carl Moses,*
*President*

The Aleut Corporation embraces an area of about 11,000 square miles extending southwestward from the Alaska mainland for more than one thousand miles. Apart from the lower Alaska Peninsula, all of its lands are islands — the Pribilofs, Unalaska, Umnak and others.

The corporation has more than 3,300 stockholders, about half of whom live in the 12 villages within the corporation boundaries. With 549 stockholders, the Tanadgusix Corporation (Our Land) at St. Paul is the largest village corporation. Following the Aleut Corporation's first stockholders' meeting, its board of directors chose Carl Moses as its president. Moses, a businessman in Unalaska and former state legislator, replaced Mike Swetzof, who had been interim president. The corporation office is in Anchorage.

The largest Native communities in the region are St. Paul, Sand Point, King Cove and Unalaska. Fishing and seafood processing, harvest of the Pribilof Island fur seals, government, and some cattle grazing are the principal economic activities of the region. In addition there are two large military stations (Adak and Shemya) which together account for about half of the region's population of 7,700 persons.

The region is volcanic in origin and is one of the world's most active seismic zones. The climate is relatively mild, but it is often rainy and windy.

J. C. LaBelle

## Arctic Slope Regional Corporation

The Arctic Slope Regional Corporation is the only one of the 12 whose boundaries are the same as those of a regional government, in this case, the North Slope Borough. Barrow, the most northern community in the state, is the location for the offices of the borough and the corporation. In addition to Barrow, seven other villages have incorporated pursuant to the settlement.

There are about 3,900 stockholders in the corporation, more than two-thirds of whom live in the region and over half of whom live in Barrow. A major spokesman in the Arctic Slope's case for a settlement based on lands lost, Joe Upicksoun, was elected first president of the corporation.

*Joseph Upicksoun,*
*President*

The region's more than 84,000 square miles make it second to Doyon, Ltd., in total land area. All of the region is north of the Arctic Circle. Winters are cold and windy and summers are cool. Precipitation is light. The region is underlain with permafrost which is estimated in some places to be 1,300 feet thick.

Before oil and pipeline construction began, the total population of the region was about 3,500 persons, but there were at least three times that number in 1974. The oil reserves at famed Prudhoe Bay are estimated to be the largest in the United States.

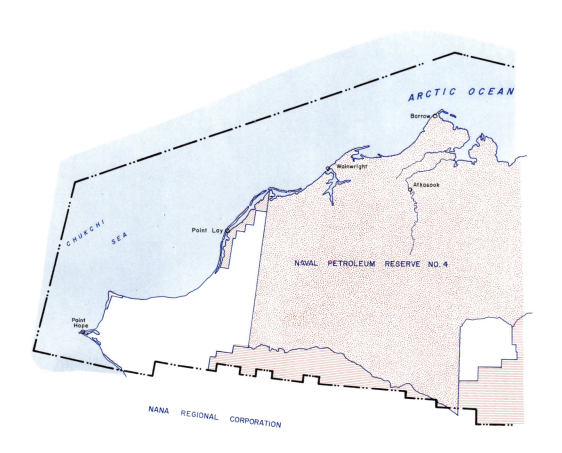

ARCTIC OCEAN

Barrow

Wainwright

Atkasook

CHUKCHI SEA

Point Lay

NAVAL PETROLEUM RESERVE NO. 4

Point Hope

NANA REGIONAL CORPORATION

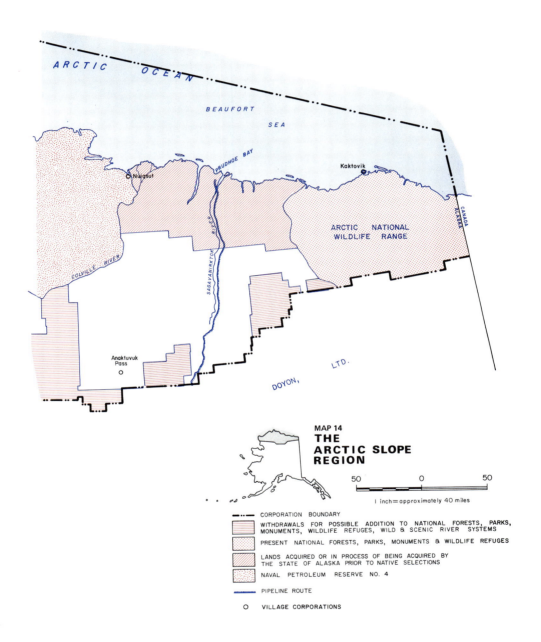

ARCTIC OCEAN

BEAUFORT SEA

PRUDHOE BAY

Kaktovik

Nuiqsut

CANADA
ALASKA

COLVILLE RIVER

SAGAVANIRKTOK RIVER

ARCTIC NATIONAL
WILDLIFE RANGE

Anaktuvuk
Pass

DOYON, LTD.

MAP 14
**THE
ARCTIC SLOPE
REGION**

50      0      50

I inch = approximately 40 miles

- - - - CORPORATION BOUNDARY

WITHDRAWALS FOR POSSIBLE ADDITION TO NATIONAL FORESTS, PARKS, MONUMENTS, WILDLIFE REFUGES, WILD & SCENIC RIVER SYSTEMS

PRESENT NATIONAL FORESTS, PARKS, MONUMENTS & WILDLIFE REFUGES

LANDS ACQUIRED OR IN PROCESS OF BEING ACQUIRED BY THE STATE OF ALASKA PRIOR TO NATIVE SELECTIONS

NAVAL PETROLEUM RESERVE NO. 4

PIPELINE ROUTE

O    VILLAGE CORPORATIONS

**Bering Straits Native Corporation**

Walt Hays

*Jerome Trigg,*
*President*

Nome, the city made famous by the gold rush, is the location of the office of the Bering Straits Native Corporation. Its first president is Jerome Trigg, former president of the Arctic Native Brotherhood and an early organizer for Native land rights.

This corporation has more than 6,900 stockholders. About half of them live either in Nome or one of the 16 other villages in the region. The remainder live outside the region's nearly 23,000 square miles. With 2,060 stockholders, Sitnasuak Native Corporation in Nome is the largest village corporation.

About 800 Eskimos of Gambell and Savoonga and 250 of Elim are not members of the corporation, since their villages chose to accept title to St. Lawrence Island and Elim, respectively, in place of money and lesser land entitlements under the act.

Principal employment in the region is to be found in Nome, where government and service industries predominate. There is some mining in the region. Food gathering activities are important in the economy of the smaller villages.

Three of the region's villages are connected by roads. There is no deep-water port anywhere along its coast.

Winter temperatures are low; summers are relatively warm. Precipitation is light. Permafrost is continuous over the area.

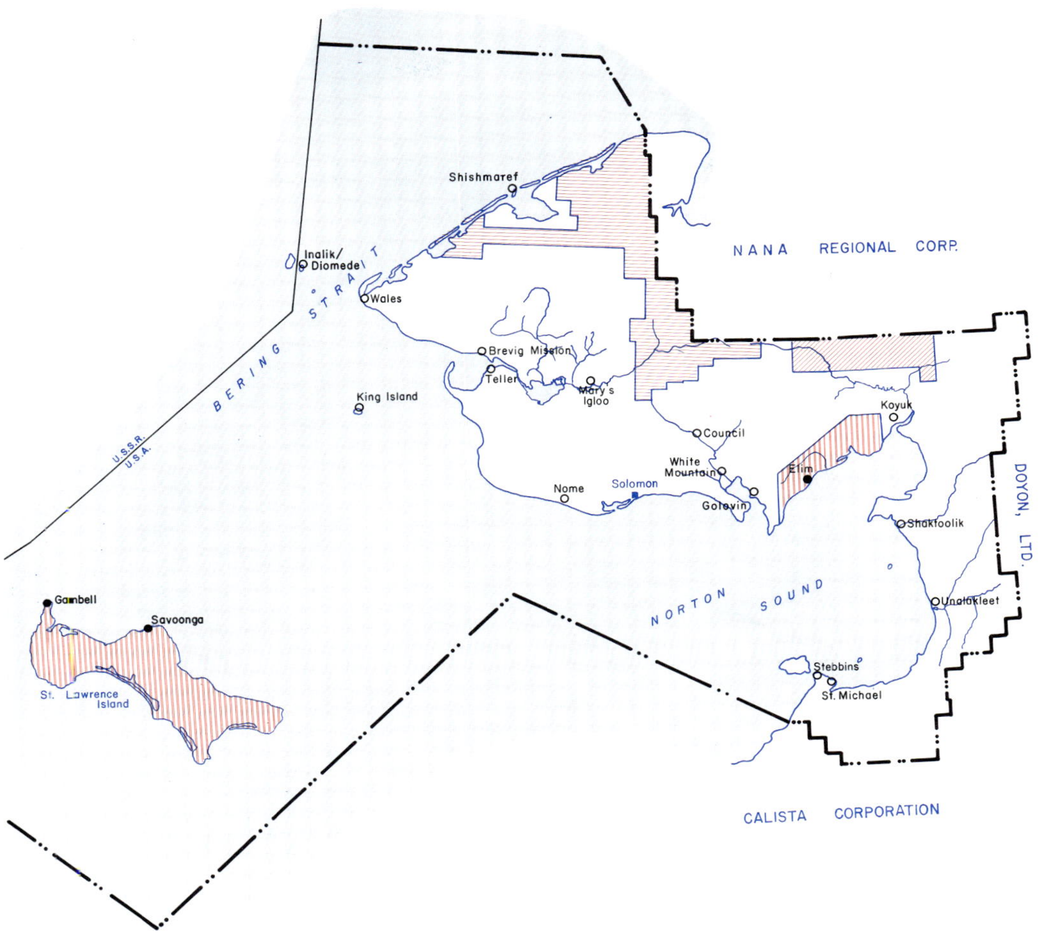

Shishmaref

Inalik/
Diomede

Wales

NANA   REGIONAL   CORP.

BERING   STRAIT

Brevig Mission

Teller

King Island

Mary's
Igloo

Koyuk

Council

White
Mountain

Elim

U.S.S.R.
U.S.A.

Nome

Solomon

Golovin

Shaktoolik

DOYON,   LTD.

NORTON   SOUND

Unalakleet

Gambell

Savoonga

St. Lawrence
Island

Stebbins

St. Michael

CALISTA   CORPORATION

MAP 15
**THE
BERING STRAITS
REGION**

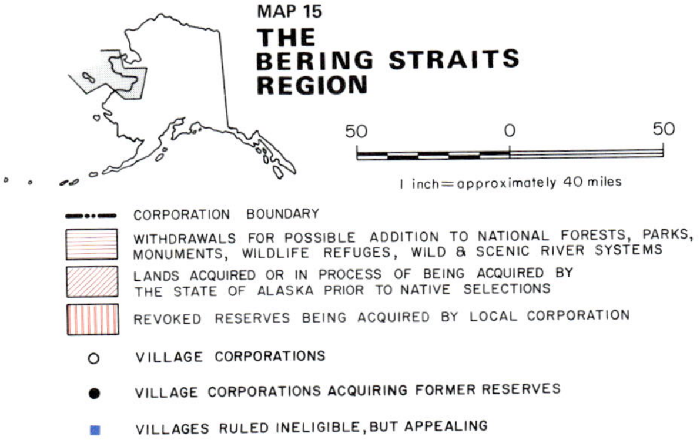

50            0            50

1 inch = approximately 40 miles

▪▪▪— CORPORATION   BOUNDARY

WITHDRAWALS FOR POSSIBLE ADDITION TO NATIONAL FORESTS, PARKS,
MONUMENTS, WILDLIFE REFUGES, WILD & SCENIC RIVER SYSTEMS

LANDS ACQUIRED OR IN PROCESS OF BEING ACQUIRED BY
THE STATE OF ALASKA PRIOR TO NATIVE SELECTIONS

REVOKED  RESERVES BEING ACQUIRED BY LOCAL CORPORATION

○    VILLAGE CORPORATIONS

●    VILLAGE CORPORATIONS ACQUIRING FORMER RESERVES

▪    VILLAGES RULED INELIGIBLE, BUT APPEALING

177

John Hale

## Bristol Bay Native Corporation

*Harvey Samuelsen, President*

The Bristol Bay Native Corporation has about 5,500 stockholders, of whom about 3,300 live in one or another of the 29 villages within the region. Total population in the 40,000-square-mile region is about 5,000.

Dillingham, which, with 925 stockholders, is the largest of the village corporations in the region, is the location of the regional corporation's office. A member of the original board of directors of AFN, Harvey Samuelsen, was elected president at the first stockholders' meeting. Its 35-member board of directors is the largest board of any of the regional corporations.

Two villages — Naknek and South Naknek — are within the Bristol Bay Borough, a small regional government.

Barred by mountains from the rest of the state, this region faces the salmon-rich Bristol Bay and Bering Sea. Since the 1880's, the economy of the area has been based upon catching and processing of salmon. There is much subsistence hunting, fishing, and food gathering. Sport fishermen also contribute to the economy of the region.

Precipitation varies within the region from 20 to 160 inches a year. Summer temperatures are moderate; minimum winter temperatures are often below zero.

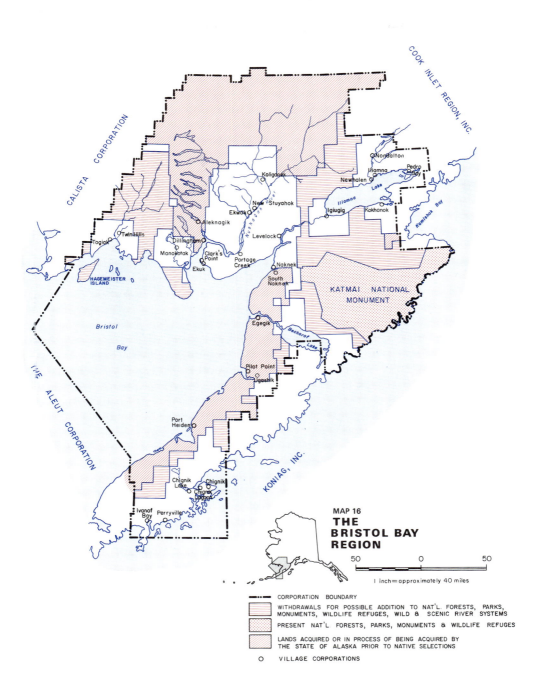

COOK INLET REGION, INC.

CALISTA CORPORATION

Nordalton

Iliamna
Pedro Bay
Newhalen

Iliamna Lake

Kamishak Bay

Koligoak

New Stuyahok
Ekwok
Igiugig
Kokhanok

Aleknagik

Togiak
Twin Hills
Levelock

Dillingham
Manokotak
Clark's Point
Portage Creek

Ekuk
Naknek

South Naknek

HAGEMEISTER ISLAND

KATMAI NATIONAL MONUMENT

Bristol

Bay

Egegik

Becharof Lake

Pilot Point
Ugashik

THE ALEUT CORPORATION

Port Heiden

KONIAG, INC.

Chignik Lake
Chignik
Chignik Lagoon

Ivanof Bay
Perryville

MAP 16
THE
BRISTOL BAY
REGION

50          0          50

1 inch = approximately 40 miles

CORPORATION  BOUNDARY

WITHDRAWALS  FOR  POSSIBLE  ADDITION  TO  NAT'L.  FORESTS,  PARKS,
MONUMENTS,  WILDLIFE  REFUGES,  WILD  &  SCENIC  RIVER  SYSTEMS

PRESENT  NAT'L.  FORESTS,  PARKS,  MONUMENTS  &  WILDLIFE  REFUGES

LANDS  ACQUIRED  OR  IN  PROCESS  OF  BEING  ACQUIRED  BY
THE  STATE  OF  ALASKA  PRIOR  TO  NATIVE  SELECTIONS

O          VILLAGE  CORPORATIONS

179

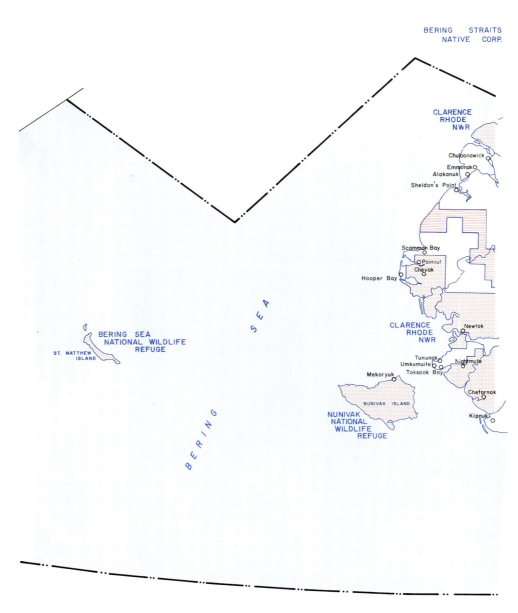

BERING    STRAITS
NATIVE   CORP.

CLARENCE
RHODE
NWR

Chuloonawick

Emmonak
Alakanuk
Sheldon's Point

Scammon Bay
Paimiut
Chevak
Hooper Bay

BERING   SEA

BERING   SEA
NATIONAL WILDLIFE
REFUGE

ST. MATTHEW
ISLAND

CLARENCE
RHODE
NWR

Newtok

Tununak
Umkumuite        Nightmute
Mekoryuk        Toksook Bay

NUNIVAK   ISLAND

Chefornak

Kipnuk

NUNIVAK
NATIONAL
WILDLIFE
REFUGE

BERING

SEA

THE    ALEUT   CORP.

180

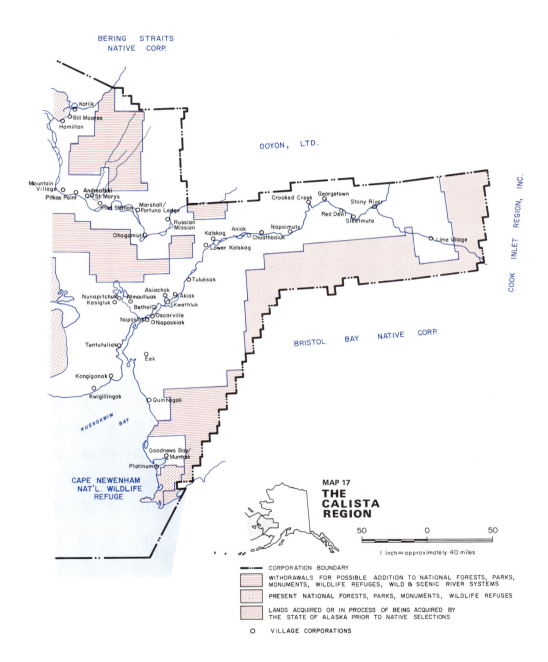

BERING STRAITS
NATIVE CORP.

Kotlik
Bill Moores
Hamilton

DOYON, LTD.

Mountain
Village
Pitkas Point    Andreafski
              St. Marys
         Pilot Station
                   Marshall/
                   Fortuna Ledge

Crooked Creek    Georgetown
                         Stony River
              Red Devil
                    Sleetmute

Russian
Mission

Ohogamiut

Kalskag    Aniak    Napaimute
       Chuathbaluk
Lower Kalskag

Lime Village

Tuluksak

Akiachok    Akiak
Nunapitchuk  Atmautluak  Kwethluk
Kasigluk   Bethel
         Oscarville
Napakiak   Napaskiak

BRISTOL    BAY    NATIVE    CORP.

Tuntutuliak

Eek

Kongiganak

Kwigillingok    Quinhagak

KUSKOKWIM    BAY

Goodnews Bay/
Mumtrak
Platinum

CAPE NEWENHAM
NAT'L. WILDLIFE
REFUGE

COOK INLET REGION, INC.

MAP 17
**THE
CALISTA
REGION**

50          0          50

1 inch = approximately 40 miles

⸺ CORPORATION BOUNDARY

WITHDRAWALS FOR POSSIBLE ADDITION TO NATIONAL FORESTS, PARKS,
MONUMENTS, WILDLIFE REFUGES, WILD & SCENIC RIVER SYSTEMS

PRESENT NATIONAL FORESTS, PARKS, MONUMENTS, WILDLIFE REFUGES

LANDS ACQUIRED OR IN PROCESS OF BEING ACQUIRED BY
THE STATE OF ALASKA PRIOR TO NATIVE SELECTIONS

O    VILLAGE CORPORATIONS

## Calista Corporation

*Robert Schenker,
President*

With an enrollment of almost 13,500, most of whom live in southwest Alaska, Calista Corporation has the largest number of resident stockholders. And, with 56 villages within its boundaries, Calista assists and guides a larger number of village corporations than any other regional corporation.

In Yupik Eskimo, Calista means "the worker" or "one who works."

Former State Senator Ray Christiansen, who was interim president of the corporation, was named chairman of the board of directors following the first stockholders' meeting. A former Anchorage businessman, Robert H. Schenker, moved from his position as manager to that of president and general manager of the corporation. The main office of the corporation is in Anchorage. A second office is in Bethel, the principal community within the region. The largest village corporation is the Bethel Native Corporation with 1,725 stockholders.

There are almost 56,000 square miles within Calista boundaries, but a total population of only about 13,000 persons.

Only two of the region's villages are joined by a road. Two major rivers, the Yukon and Kuskokwim, flow through the area to the Bering Sea.

Most of the villagers of the region depend principally upon fishing, hunting, and food gathering for subsistence.

Winter temperatures are low and summer temperatures relatively high. Precipitation is generally light. Most of the region is underlain with permafrost.

C. D. Evans

## Chugach Natives, Inc.

Chugach Natives, Inc. has about 2,100 stockholders, about half of whom live within the boundaries of the region. Five villages have incorporated to participate in the settlement. The largest is Eyak Corporation with 323 stockholders.

The corporation's office is located outside the region — in Anchorage. One of the early proponents of winning recognition for aboriginal rights to land, Cecil Barnes, was elected first president of the corporation.

The word "Chugach" is reportedly a corruption of "Chug-uk," the Sugcestun Aleut word for "hurry-up."

*Cecil Barnes,*
*President*

The region is almost 15,000 square miles in area, more than half of which is part of the Chugach National Forest. Although forests of Sitka spruce and western hemlock cover much of the area, there has been little commercial use of the timber. High oil and gas potential exists on the narrow coastal plain and on the outer continental shelf of Prince William Sound and the Gulf of Alaska.

Fishing and tourism are important to the economy of the region, but activities related to the trans-Alaska pipeline are of increasing importance. Since Valdez is the pipeline terminus, extensive construction of tanks and related facilities was taking place in 1975.

The total population of the area is about 7,000 persons, most of whom live in Valdez and Cordova.

The climate is generally mild with most areas having moderately heavy precipitation.

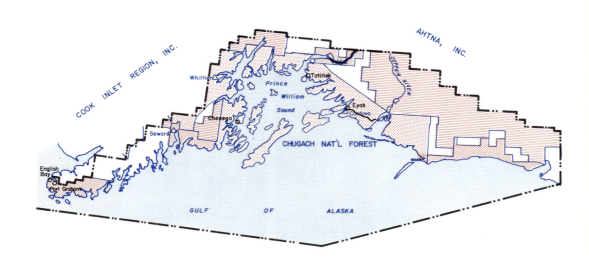

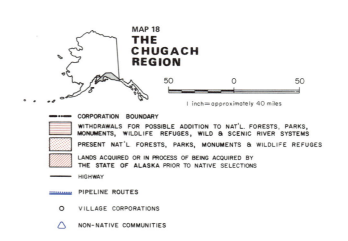

MAP 18
## THE CHUGACH REGION

50      0      50

1 inch = approximately 40 miles

━━━━ CORPORATION BOUNDARY

▨ WITHDRAWALS FOR POSSIBLE ADDITION TO NAT'L. FORESTS, PARKS, MONUMENTS, WILDLIFE REFUGES, WILD & SCENIC RIVER SYSTEMS

▨ PRESENT NAT'L. FORESTS, PARKS, MONUMENTS & WILDLIFE REFUGES

▨ LANDS ACQUIRED OR IN PROCESS OF BEING ACQUIRED BY THE STATE OF ALASKA PRIOR TO NATIVE SELECTIONS

──── HIGHWAY

┄┄┄ PIPELINE ROUTES

O VILLAGE CORPORATIONS

△ NON-NATIVE COMMUNITIES

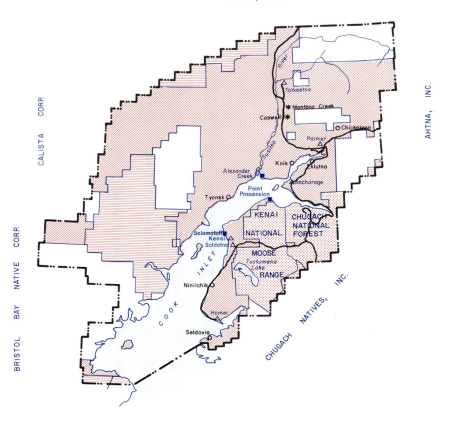

DOYON, LTD.

CALISTA CORP.

AHTNA, INC.

BRISTOL BAY NATIVE CORP.

Talkeetna

Montana Creek
Caswell
Chickaloon

Palmer

Knik
Eklutna
Alexander Creek
Anchorage
Point Possession
Tyonek

KENAI

CHUGACH NATIONAL FOREST

Salamatoff
Kenai
Soldotna
NATIONAL

COOK INLET

MOOSE
Tustumena Lake
RANGE

Ninilchik

CHUGACH NATIVES, INC.

Homer

Seldovia

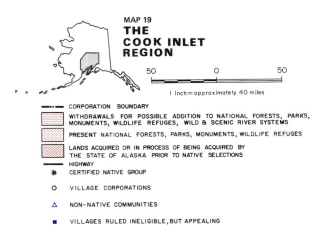

MAP 19
**THE
COOK INLET
REGION**

50     0     50

1 inch = approximately 40 miles

—•••— CORPORATION BOUNDARY

WITHDRAWALS FOR POSSIBLE ADDITION TO NATIONAL FORESTS, PARKS, MONUMENTS, WILDLIFE REFUGES, WILD & SCENIC RIVER SYSTEMS

PRESENT NATIONAL FORESTS, PARKS, MONUMENTS, WILDLIFE REFUGES

LANDS ACQUIRED OR IN PROCESS OF BEING ACQUIRED BY THE STATE OF ALASKA PRIOR TO NATIVE SELECTIONS

——— HIGHWAY

✳ CERTIFIED NATIVE GROUP

○ VILLAGE CORPORATIONS

△ NON-NATIVE COMMUNITIES

■ VILLAGES RULED INELIGIBLE, BUT APPEALING

185

## Cook Inlet Region, Inc.

*Roy Huhndorf,
President*

Cook Inlet Region, Inc. is the only regional corporation whose stockholders are, for the most part, residents of a highly developed urban area. Most of its nearly 6,500 stockholders live within the region and the largest number of them live in the Anchorage area.

In 1975 the board of directors chose Roy M. Huhndorf, of Anchorage as its president. Huhndorf (of Eskimo descent but born in Nulato) followed Ralph (Andy) Johnson of Anchorage and George Miller of Kenai in the position.

Within the nearly 38,000 square miles of the region live about 150,000 people, nearly half of the state's total population. The region reaches from Seldovia, one of the six villages in the region, almost to Mt. McKinley National Park in the north.

The village of Tyonek, the only community on the west side of Cook Inlet, has the largest number of stockholders (303) of any of the region's six village corporations.

The only oil and gas wells now in production in the state are located on the Kenai Peninsula and in Cook Inlet. The state's principal agricultural area, the Matanuska Valley, is also within the region. Government, transportation, and commercial enterprises are major employers.

There are four boroughs in the region, and all villages are located within one or another of the boroughs.

Precipitation is light. Except for the northern parts, winters are moderately cold, and summers are warm.

National Park Service (Robert Belous)

## Doyon, Limited

*John Sackett,*
*President*

With more than 200,000 square miles within its boundaries, Doyon, Limited is the largest regional Native corporation in land area. Within its boundaries live about 58,000 persons, more than half of them residents of the Fairbanks area.

Doyon, a word which means "chief" or "important person" in Koyukon Athabascan, has more than 9,200 stockholders. About two-thirds of them live within the region.

Chosen to be the first president of Doyon was John Sackett, a businessman and State legislator from Galena who, as a college student, had become engaged in the claims struggle. The principal office of the corporation is in Fairbanks, but regional offices also are located at four villages.

Three of the 37 villages within the regional boundaries — Arctic Village, Venetie, and Tetlin — voted to take title to their reserves, and hence will not participate further in the claims settlement. Of the 34 village corporations continuing to participate, the largest (with 737 stockholders) is Fort Yukon.

Government employment, transportation, and commercial activities provide the economic base for this region. Two major highways and the Alaska Railroad meet in Fairbanks. The region is to be crossed by the trans-Alaska pipeline and its service road. The Yukon River and its major tributaries — the Tanana and the Porcupine — are important waterways.

The isolated communities of the region depend heavily upon food gathering activities for subsistence.

This is an area of very cold winters and warm summers. Precipitation is relatively light. Permafrost is present throughout the region.

187

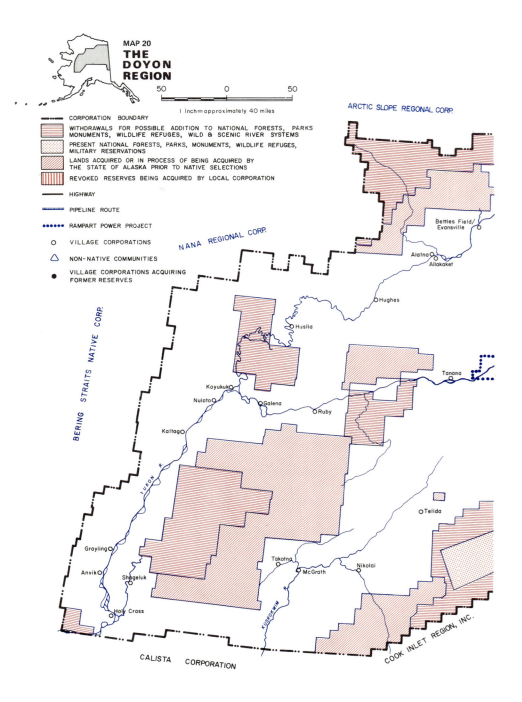

MAP 20

# THE DOYON REGION

50    0    50

1 inch = approximately 40 miles

CORPORATION BOUNDARY

WITHDRAWALS FOR POSSIBLE ADDITION TO NATIONAL FORESTS, PARKS, MONUMENTS, WILDLIFE REFUGES, WILD & SCENIC RIVER SYSTEMS

PRESENT NATIONAL FORESTS, PARKS, MONUMENTS, WILDLIFE REFUGES, MILITARY RESERVATIONS

LANDS ACQUIRED OR IN PROCESS OF BEING ACQUIRED BY THE STATE OF ALASKA PRIOR TO NATIVE SELECTIONS

REVOKED RESERVES BEING ACQUIRED BY LOCAL CORPORATION

HIGHWAY

PIPELINE ROUTE

RAMPART POWER PROJECT

○   VILLAGE CORPORATIONS

△   NON-NATIVE COMMUNITIES

●   VILLAGE CORPORATIONS ACQUIRING FORMER RESERVES

ARCTIC SLOPE REGIONAL CORP.

NANA REGIONAL CORP.

BERING STRAITS NATIVE CORP.

Bettles Field/ Evansville

Alatna
Allakaket

Hughes

Huslia

Tanana

Koyukuk
Nulato
Galena
Ruby

Kaltag

YUKON R.

Telida

Grayling

Takotna
McGrath
Nikolai

Anvik
Shageluk

KUSKOKWIM

Holy Cross

CALISTA    CORPORATION

COOK INLET REGION, INC.

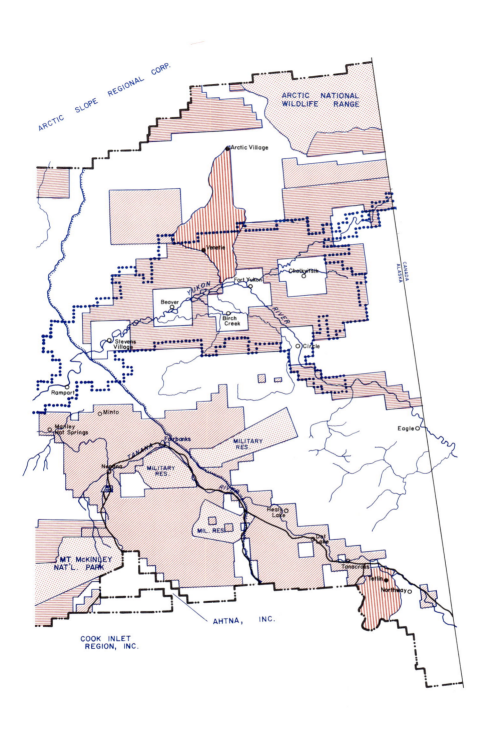

ARCTIC SLOPE REGIONAL CORP.

ARCTIC NATIONAL
WILDLIFE RANGE

Arctic Village

Venetie

Chalkyitsik

Fort Yukon

YUKON

Beaver

Birch
Creek

RIVER

Stevens
Village

Circle

Rampart

Minto

Manley
Hot Springs

Eagle

Fairbanks

MILITARY
RES.

TANANA

Nenana

MILITARY
RES.

RIVER

ALASKA

CANADA

Healy
Lake

MIL. RES.

Dot
Lake

MT. McKINLEY
NAT'L. PARK

Tanacross

Tetlin

Northway

AHTNA, INC.

COOK INLET
REGION, INC.

## Koniag, Inc., Regional Native Corporation

*Jack Wick,*
*President*

With an area of about 7,300 square miles within its boundaries, Koniag, Inc. is the smallest of the regional corporations in land area. It includes the Kodiak Island group and a portion of the upper Alaska Peninsula.

Koniag, Inc. has nearly 3,300 stockholders, of whom 1,350 live in Kodiak, the city in which the corporation's office is located. Almost one thousand others live in the nine certified villages of the region. The largest village corporation, Natives of Afognak, Inc., has 392 stockholders. Virtually all of the 9,500 persons who live in the region live within the Kodiak Island Borough, the regional government for the Kodiak Island group.

The name of the corporation is shortened from Koniagmiut, the name applied to the original inhabitants of the island.

The president of Koniag is Jack Wick, a young Larsen Bay fisherman, recently returned from the Vietnam War. He had also been interim president of the organization.

Catching and processing seafood is, by far, the major industry of the region. There is some cattle grazing.

The region is mountainous and has a rugged and indented shoreline. Temperatures are relatively mild, but precipitation is heavy. During fall and winter, storms with winds up to 100 miles per hour are common. Earth tremors are frequent.

190

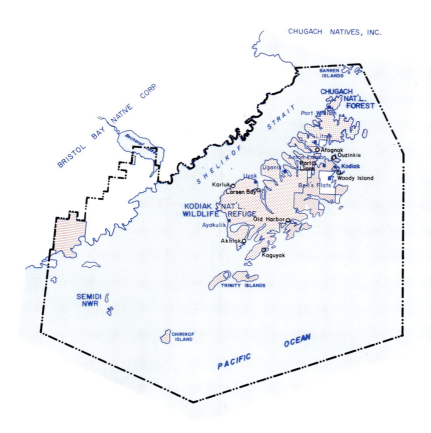

CHUGACH NATIVES, INC.

BRISTOL BAY NATIVE CORP.

BARREN
ISLANDS

CHUGACH
NAT'L.
FOREST

Port Wilson

SHELIKOF STRAIT

Litnik

Afognak

Ouzinkie

Anton Larson
Port
Lions

Kodiak

Woody Island

Uganis

Uyak

Bell's Flats

Karluk

Larsen Bay

KODIAK NAT'L.
WILDLIFE REFUGE

Old Harbor

Ayakulik

Akhiok

Kaguyak

TRINITY ISLANDS

SEMIDI
NWR

CHIRIKOF
ISLAND

PACIFIC OCEAN

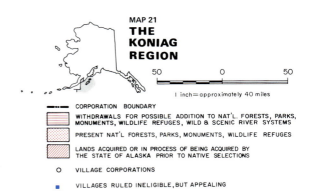

MAP 21
**THE KONIAG REGION**

50      0      50

I inch = approximately 40 miles

▄▄▄ CORPORATION BOUNDARY

WITHDRAWALS FOR POSSIBLE ADDITION TO NAT'L. FORESTS, PARKS,
MONUMENTS, WILDLIFE REFUGES, WILD & SCENIC RIVER SYSTEMS

PRESENT NAT'L FORESTS, PARKS, MONUMENTS, WILDLIFE REFUGES

LANDS ACQUIRED OR IN PROCESS OF BEING ACQUIRED BY
THE STATE OF ALASKA PRIOR TO NATIVE SELECTIONS

○   VILLAGE CORPORATIONS

■   VILLAGES RULED INELIGIBLE, BUT APPEALING

191

Margaret Bauman

## NANA Regional Corporation, Inc.

*John Schaeffer,*
*President*

NANA Regional Corporation, Inc. embraces an area of about 36,000 square miles fronting on Kotzebue Sound. The corporation's office is in Kotzebue, a traditional trading center of the northwest.

There are about 4,900 stockholders in NANA of whom about three out of four live in the region. The total population of the region is about 4,000 persons.

The regional corporation takes its name from the initials of Northwest Alaska Native Association, the organization formed in 1966 to seek a claims settlement. Robert Newlin of Noorvik, a long-time city councilman and regional leader, was elected chairman of the board of directors of the corporation. Its president and general manager is John Schaeffer, a former commanding officer of a National Guard battalion.

Kotzebue is the principal community of the region. Its corporation, Kikiktagruk Inupiat, has 1,983 stockholders, the most of any village corporation in the region. Federal and State governments are major employers. Subsistence activities are important in the economy of the entire area.

Most of the NANA region lies north of the Arctic Circle. Precipitation is light, winters are cold, and summers are moderate.

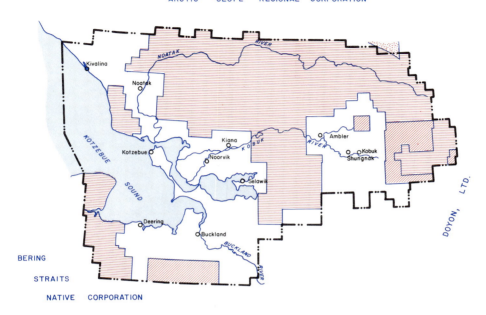

ARCTIC   SLOPE   REGIONAL   CORPORATION

NOATAK RIVER

Kivalina

Noatak

KOTZEBUE SOUND

Kiana

Kotzebue

Noorvik

KOBUK RIVER

Ambler

Kobuk
Shungnak

Selawik

Deering

Buckland

BUCKLAND RIVER

DOYON, LTD.

BERING

STRAITS

NATIVE   CORPORATION

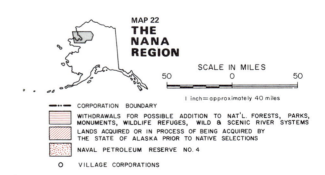

MAP 22
**THE
NANA
REGION**

SCALE IN MILES

50          0          50

1 inch = approximately 40 miles

---··--   CORPORATION  BOUNDARY

WITHDRAWALS  FOR  POSSIBLE  ADDITION  TO  NAT'L.  FORESTS,  PARKS,
MONUMENTS,  WILDLIFE  REFUGES,  WILD  &  SCENIC  RIVER  SYSTEMS

LANDS  ACQUIRED  OR  IN  PROCESS  OF  BEING  ACQUIRED  BY
THE  STATE  OF  ALASKA  PRIOR  TO  NATIVE  SELECTIONS

NAVAL  PETROLEUM  RESERVE  NO. 4

O     VILLAGE  CORPORATIONS

C. D. Evans

## Sealaska Corporation

*John Borbridge, Jr.,*
*President*

The largest of the regional corporations in number of stockholders is Sealaska Corporation. More than half of its nearly 16,500 stockholders live in southeastern Alaska. The total population of the region is about 43,000 persons.

Juneau, the state capital, is the location of the corporate office of Sealaska. At its first stockholders' meeting, John Borbridge, Jr., a prominent figure in the claims struggle, was named president.

Within the region's nearly 32,000 square miles are nine villages which have incorporated as village corporations to receive both land and money benefits of the act. The largest of these is Hoonah, which has 868 stockholders. A tenth village, Klukwan, elected to accept title to its reserve and, thereby, to remove itself from further participation in the settlement. Also within the region is Metlakatla, the reserve whose residents are not beneficiaries under the act.

There are four boroughs in the region, encompassing only a small part of the total area.

The salmon and timber industries are economic mainstays of the region. With the state's capital in Juneau, state and federal governments are major employers.

The climate is mild and precipitation is heavy.

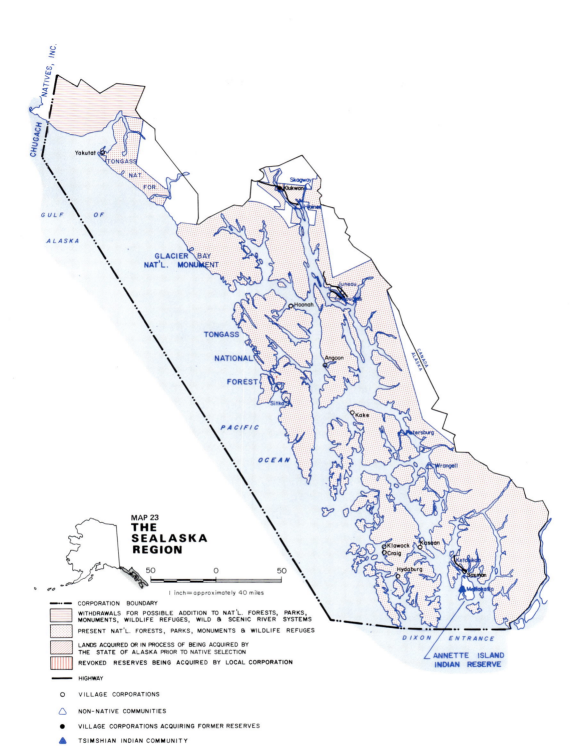

CHUGACH NATIVES, INC.

GULF OF ALASKA

Yakutat ○
TONGASS NAT FOR.

Skagway
Klukwan
Haines

GLACIER BAY
NAT'L. MONUMENT

Juneau

Hoonah ○

TONGASS

NATIONAL

FOREST

Angoon ○

Sitka ○

CANADA
ALASKA

Kake ○

Petersburg

PACIFIC

Wrangell

OCEAN

MAP 23
**THE
SEALASKA
REGION**

Klawock ○    Kasaan
○ Craig
Hydaburg ○

Ketchikan
Saxman

50    0    50

1 inch = approximately 40 miles

Mallakatla

DIXON   ENTRANCE

ANNETTE ISLAND
INDIAN RESERVE

–  –  – CORPORATION BOUNDARY

WITHDRAWALS FOR POSSIBLE ADDITION TO NAT'L. FORESTS, PARKS,
MONUMENTS, WILDLIFE REFUGES, WILD & SCENIC RIVER SYSTEMS

PRESENT NAT'L. FORESTS, PARKS, MONUMENTS & WILDLIFE REFUGES

LANDS ACQUIRED OR IN PROCESS OF BEING ACQUIRED BY
THE STATE OF ALASKA PRIOR TO NATIVE SELECTION

REVOKED RESERVES BEING ACQUIRED BY LOCAL CORPORATION

———— HIGHWAY

○    VILLAGE CORPORATIONS

△    NON-NATIVE COMMUNITIES

●    VILLAGE CORPORATIONS ACQUIRING FORMER RESERVES

▲    TSIMSHIAN INDIAN COMMUNITY

195

The settlement act had provided that Natives residing outside of Alaska could enroll to a village and one of the 12 regions, to a region only, or to a 13th region that might be established. If it were established, its members would share only in the money portion of the settlement, not the land nor money obtained from the resources of the land.

About 18,000 Natives who lived outside Alaska enrolled — the largest number of them from the state of Washington. Others lived in California, Oregon, Texas, and other states and nations. When they enrolled, those over 18 years of age voted on whether they desired the establishment of a 13th region.

About 6,000 adult enrollees voted on the question. The 13th regional corporation failed to pass by a few hundred votes. As a result, all nonresident Natives became stockholders in one or another of the 12 regional corporations within the state, and some became members of village corporations as well.

Some of the persons who wanted a 13th region filed court action on the basis that the issue was complicated and confusing to voters and that the results certified by the Department of the Interior were in error. They won their court case. Late in 1975, the Department announced establishment of a 13th region. It asked eight nonresident Native associations to nominate persons to be incorporators and scheduled an election. The first meeting of stockholders and directors was scheduled to be held before February, 1976.

With the first distribution of funds by the corporation, all nonresident Natives were to be given a final opportunity to enroll in the 13th region or in one of the others.

Because the money received by corporations is based upon their enrollments, transfer of 5,000 or so stockholders to the 13th region was expected to reduce the 12 corporations' income by as much as $25 million. Such compensation would go to the new corporation. Transfer of stockholders was also expected to affect land entitlements of some villages and regions.

# Local Business Corporations                Chapter 25

Within three years of passage of the settlement act, 216 local corporations had been organized in villages and cities, and at other locations which Natives had identified as their permanent residences:

- 203 were village corporations which were acquiring land and money benefits of the settlement;

- seven others were located on five former reserves but neither they nor their stockholders were sharing in the money benefits;

- four others — located in non-Native communities — were acquiring land, but were not receiving money payments as corporations;

- two others were certified as "groups" which were acquiring land, but were not receiving money payments as corporations.

An additional 14 village corporations were organized but were not certified to be eligible for benefits. (All of the local business corporations and their enrollments are listed in Appendices B-E).

| | Village Corporations overseen by region | Village Corporation stockholders | At-large Stockholders | Village Independent Corporations, their stockholders | |
|---|---|---|---|---|---|
| Ahtna, Inc. | 8 | 960 | 132 | | |
| The Aleut Corporation | 12 | 2,314 | 1,039 | | |
| Arctic Slope Regional Corporation | 8 | 3,521 | 385 | | |
| Bering Straits Native Corporation | 16 | 5,570 | 1,346 | 3 | 1,079* |
| Bristol Bay Native Corporation | 29 | 4,850 | 667 | | |
| Calista Corporation | 56 | 12,886 | 555 | | |
| Chugach Natives, Inc. | 5 | 867 | 1,232 | | |
| Cook Inlet Region, Inc. | 6 | 957 | 5,286 | 1 | 477** |
| | | | | 2 | 80*** |
| Doyon, Limited | 34 | 6,693 | 2,528 | 3 | 428* |
| Koniag, Inc., Regional Native Corporation | 9 | 2,003 | 1,337 | 1 | 500** |
| NANA Regional Native Corporation | 11 | 4,466 | 439 | | |
| Sealaska Corporation | 9 | 4,080 | 12,413 | 1 | 251* |
| | | | | 2 | 4,444** |
| TOTAL | 203 | 49,167 | 27,359 | | |

Figure 6
STOCKHOLDERS AND LOCAL CORPORATIONS
BY REGION
September 14, 1974

\* Enrolled to revoked reserves which chose full title to their reserves instead of participating in other provisions of the settlement act; not stockholders in regional corporations.

\*\* Enrolled in one or another of the four named cities; at-large members of their regional corporations.

\*\*\* Enrolled to two groups which incorporated and were certified by the Bureau of Indian Affairs; at-large members of their regional corporations.

Note: All stockholder figures subject to change upon formation of the 13th regional corporation.

Source: Enrollment Office, U. S. Bureau of Indian Affairs, Anchorage, Alaska.

While the act had allowed villages to organize as profit or nonprofit corporations, all villages organized profit corporations to obtain benefits under the act, for otherwise no distribution of the benefits could be made to their members. As with other such corporations, these local corporations are governed by State and federal law and operate within the framework established by their articles of incorporation and bylaws. They carry out activities expected to profit those who share in owning them — their stockholders. Boards of directors, chosen by stockholders, elect presidents and other officers to guide the activities of all paid employees and consultants.

Like the regional corporations, these local corporations are also controlled in a variety of ways by the settlement act.

**Village Corporations**

The 203 village corporations which have been certified as eligible to obtain land and money benefits under the act are in the process of obtaining title to the surface estate of more than half of the land provided for in the act. They are, in turn, the means through which most Natives will obtain individual title to parcels of land. As they receive their shares of funds distributed by their regional corporations and invest them, the village corporations are expected to produce profits over a long-term for their stockholders.

Taken together, these village corporations have over 49,000 stockholders. In size they range from Lime Village, Paimiut, Telida, and Ohogamiut, none having more than 25 stockholders, to Barrow and Nome, both of which have more than two thousand each. Most of the village corporations — three-fourths of them — have 300 or fewer stockholders. The median size is 171 stockholders.

Tim Samuelson

*Sand Point, one of 203 village corporations.*

More than one-fourth of the village corporations — 56 of them — are within the Calista region. The fewest village corporations are in the Chugach region where there are only five. All stockholders in the village corporations are, of course, also stockholders in the regional corporations.

As noted in an earlier chapter these village corporations are not entirely independent. If a village corporation desires to amend its articles of incorporation, it must obtain the approval of its regional corporation. To obtain its share of the distribution from the Alaska Native Fund it must submit its spending plan to the regional corporation. And, until December 18, 1981, it needs to seek the advice of the regional corporation before it can sell or lease lands.

Because December 18, 1974 was the deadline for land selection by villages, the most important activity of village corporations in the first three years was choosing lands to which they were entitled under the settlement act. Even though this was true, a few village corporations had launched new enterprises or purchased existing businesses before 1974 drew to an end.

With the exception of the Annette Island Reserve, all reserves and reservations in Alaska were revoked by the settlement act. Village corporations on such reserves, however, were allowed to obtain full title to their former reserve lands if they voted to give up all other benefits for themselves and their stockholders under the act. Of the 25 such village corporations, seven chose title to their former reserves.

**Local corporations on revoked reserves**

These seven are Elim, Tetlin, Klukwan, each with its own reserve; Gambell and Savoonga, which share the former St. Lawrence Island Reserve; and Arctic Village and Venetie, which share the former Venetie Reserve.

Tim Samuelson

*Tetlin, one of seven villages choosing full title to their former reserves.*

These local corporations are in the process of obtaining ownership — both surface and subsurface — to their former reserves. Except for Klukwan, whose deposits of iron ore may have dictated its choice, these local corporations will also own more land than if they had chosen to participate in both the land and money benefits of the settlement.

Unlike the village corporations which are, in several ways, subordinate to the regional corporations, these seven local profit corporations are independent. However, they do not share as corporations, nor do their 1,758 stockholders share as individuals, in any of the money distributed under the act. Furthermore, the regional corporations have no legal obligation to provide assistance of any kind to them.

*Kodiak is one of four named cities in which enrolled Natives incorporated to obtain up to one township of land.*

**Local corporations: four named cities**

Another category of local business corporations is made up of the four corporations formed by Natives in Juneau, Kenai, Kodiak and Sitka. These communities, historic Native places but now no longer villages, were the subject of a special provision of the settlement act.

Like the village corporations, these four are obtaining surface ownership of land, but no more than one township each, whatever their size. The corporation with the largest number of stockholders is Goldbelt, Inc., in Juneau, which has 2,640. Sitka's corporation, Shee Atika, Inc. ("village on the ocean side of the island") has 1,804. The corporations in Kodiak and Kenai have 500 and 477 stockholders, respectively.

Unlike the village corporations, these corporations do not receive monies distributed by the region. Their stockholders, however, do share in the distribution as at-large stockholders in the three regional corporations in which they are members.

By the end of 1974 two local corporations had been certified as "groups" by the Bureau of Indian Affairs. The two are Caswell Native Corporation, with 35 stockholders, and Montana Creek Native Corporation, with 45 stockholders. Both communities are within the Cook Inlet region.

Under the act, Native groups which do not qualify as villages may incorporate and obtain the surface estate in no more than 7,680 acres of land. As with villages, the subsurface estate goes to the regional corporation.

Groups which incorporate do not receive funds from their regional corporation, but their stockholders are also stockholders in the regional corporation and, as such, share in the compensation provided for by the act.

**Local corporations: groups**

# Chapter 26        Other Organizations

Implementation of the settlement act saw two new governmental organizations established to perform tasks required by terms of the act. Existing organizations saw their roles changing to meet new demands.

Regional Native associations, freed from activities aimed at obtaining a settlement, turned their attention largely to social and educational programs. Most of these associations became nonprofit arms of the regional corporations.

The two newly-established governmental organizations were the Joint Federal-State Land Use Planning Commission and the Alaska Native Claims Appeal Board.

The Joint Federal-State Land Use Planning Commission was provided for in the settlement act to carry out a process of planning for land use in Alaska and to make recommendations to the State and federal governments regarding such use.

This 10-member commission, half of whose members are appointed by the Governor of Alaska and half by the President, has its office in Anchorage. A former executive director of AFN and founder of the Kodiak Area Native Association, Harry Carter, was a member of the original commission. Upon his resignation, he was replaced by John Schaeffer, the president and executive director of NANA Regional corporation.

During its first years, the Commission undertook to assemble information about lands and resources and to review federal withdrawals.

**Joint Federal-State Land Use Planning Commission**

Information that could aid in evaluating land values existed but was widely scattered. The Commission's resource planning team conducted inventories of factors such as timber or minerals that could be expected to establish land values; the Commission then made this information available to villages and regions. It did not, however, make specific selection recommendations to any region or village.

Federal-State Land Use Planning Commission

*Walter Sampson, Land Planner of NANA, addressing the Federal-State Land Use Planning Commission. He is accompanied by Robert Newlin, Chairman of the Board, NANA Regional Corporation. Behind them is Frank Ferguson, a State Senator and NANA Director.*

Over the years, federal agencies had withdrawn a vast amount of land in the state for specified purposes. Some of this land was being used for the purpose for which it was withdrawn but much of it was not. In many instances, these withdrawn lands were close to villages and could interfere with their land selections. It became the Commission's responsibility to review these withdrawals and make recommendations for modifications in their sizes when it became evident that they were not being used for their original purposes.

**Alaska Native Claims Appeal Board**

The Alaska Native Claims Appeal Board was organized as part of the U. S. Department of the Interior in early 1974 to review questions of village eligibility and disputes over land selection and to make recommendations for final action to the Secretary of the Interior.

The four-member board — all Alaska residents — has its office in Anchorage. It is often referred to as the Ad Hoc Appeal Board.

*The Federal-State Land Use Planning Commission in 1972. From left: James Hurley, Charles Herbert, Joseph H. Fitzgerald, Co-Chairmen Jack Horton and Joe P. Josephson, Max Brewer, Celia Hunter, Dick Cooley, and Harry Carter.*

Although a list of villages expected to benefit under the settlement was contained in the act, the eligibility of some of them was uncertain. Further, some communities which were claimed as villages by enrolling Natives were not on the list.

The initial determination of eligibility was made by the Bureau of Indian Affairs. Protests against some of the Bureau's findings then were filed by State or federal agencies, Native groups, private firms, and others. By mid-1974, 109 appeals were before the Board regarding 38 villages, but final action was completed on all of them by the end of the year.

The Board is expected to have a life of five to seven years. The first of what was expected to be many land selection appeals was filed early in 1975.

Even though provision for a statewide Native organization was discarded in the final shaping of the claims settlement act, the organization which had been the vehicle for winning the settlement was not discarded by Natives. Three years after the victory, the Alaska Federation of Natives was, instead, firmly established as an organization of continuing significant influence in the state.

**Alaska Federation of Natives, Inc.**

Immediately after the achievement of the settlement, the AFN's future had looked very bleak. The principal binding force for Natives across the state had been the struggle for a settlement act and that goal had been realized. None of the act's benefits would go to AFN, but they would go to corporations formed in regions and villages. And the organization was in debt.

During this period, State Senator Willie Hensley, who had succeeded Don Wright as president, served for six months without a salary. There was no money with which to pay him.

203

While the Native community seemed to want AFN to continue, its leaders were deeply involved in organizing at regional and local levels to carry out the settlement.

However, issues common to regions in the implementation of the settlement pumped new life into AFN, now incorporated as a nonprofit organization. One of the first of many such issues was the wholly unacceptable regulation drawn up in the Department of the Interior in 1972 regarding village eligibility and land selection.

There were numerous problems in the proposed regulations. To illustrate, the word "urban" was defined in them in such a way that none of the larger Native communities would have been able to select land. Furthermore, the settlement act had provided for "maximum participation by Natives in decisions affecting their rights and property," but the regulations had been developed without any participation of Natives. Following several meetings between the Department of the Interior, regional representatives, and AFN, Inc., more nearly acceptable regulations were adopted.

*Integrity*
*Pride in Heritage*
*Progress*

*Alaska Federation of Natives symbol.*

Although the AFN had once again proven a suitable vehicle for statewide Native action, it was still hampered by financial problems. Then, in December of 1973, at a meeting of the AFN board of directors, the regional corporations agreed to a program of financial support. Under terms of this agreement, each region was to contribute $8,000 plus $1 for each of its members annually toward the cost of operating the AFN.

The emerging role of the statewide organization had been clarified six months earlier when board members voted to separate the educational and service functions of the Federation from its role as land claims spokesmen. In 1974, its Division of Human Resources administered a budget of about $10 million for educational, health, employment, and other social programs. With funds from federal agencies, the division was contracting with Native organizations, school districts, and others for, among other things, cultural heritage education projects, health aide training, and support services in colleges for Native students.

In mid-1975, Roger Lang, a Tsimshian from Sitka, resigned to enter private business. He was replaced by Sam Kito, a Tlingit from Petersburg, who moved to the AFN presidency from the position of executive vice-president of Doyon, Ltd.

With the return of the Arctic Slope Regional Corporation to the AFN in October, 1975, all 12 regional corporations were members of the AFN.

Tundra Times

*Roger Lang, AFN president, 1974-1975.*

Anchorage Daily News

*Sam Kito, AFN president, 1975-*

The Alaska Native Foundation (ANF) was established in 1968 with financial assistance of the Ford Foundation to help plan for the claims settlement once it was achieved. When first organized, it was the AFN Charitable Trust, but it now has no formal association with AFN.

The Foundation offers a variety of services to regions and villages in the fields of financial and organizational management, land selection, and other areas by means of training sessions, preparation of research papers, and through the "Alaska Native Management Report," a twice-monthly newsletter.

**Alaska Native Foundation**

*Alaska Native Foundation president Emil Notti in land claims training session.*

Financial support for Foundation activities comes from grants and contracts. The president emeritus of AFN, Emil Notti, was in his sixth year as president of the Foundation in 1974.

**Regional nonprofit corporations**

While the role of regional corporations was clearly defined in the settlement act, the act contained no provision for the regional Native associations from which they had sprung. In addition to waging the battle for a claims settlement, most of the associations had carried on a variety of social programs with grants or contracts from government agencies or foundations.

Even with the claims settlement, the need for such programs still existed and could not be met by corporations whose main responsibility was to earn a profit. There was still a vital role for the nonprofit organizations. These corporations, some with new names, are: the Aleut League; the Arctic Slope Native Association; Kawerak (Bering Straits region); Bristol Bay Native Association; Yupiktak Bista — "servant of the people," (Calista region); North Pacific Rim Native Corporation (Chugach), Cook Inlet Native Association, Tanana Chiefs Conference (Doyon region); Kodiak Area Native Association; Mauneluk — "no money," (NANA region), and the Tlingit-Haida Central Council.

The activities of the nonprofit corporations are tailored to meet the needs of Natives within each region. Broadly told, these activities most often fall within the areas of health, education, housing, and employment assistance.

The Cook Inlet Native Association, for instance, operates a Native Assistance Center in Anchorage. Many Natives come to Alaska's largest city from rural areas and some need help in an unfamiliar environment. This the Center attempts to provide. The Tanana Survival School, which began operation in late 1973, is designed to give Athabascan students a renewed sense of identity and cultural ties to their past. The school is operated by the Tanana Chiefs Conference.

The regional nonprofit corporations also play important advocacy roles for the people of their areas. Kawerak, for instance, urged the airlines serving northwest Alaska to give safety instructions to passengers in Inupiat, not just in English. The Bristol Bay Native Association's efforts in 1974, following a disastrous salmon run, led to designation of the area as a "disaster area" which resulted in special programs of assistance. And Yupiktak Bista has worked consistently at trying to bring about improved transportation for the people of southwest Alaska.

U. S. Department of the Interior

*Senior officials of the U. S. Bureau of Indian Affairs Flore Lekanof, St. Paul, and Morris Thompson, Tanana. Thompson was named Commissioner in 1974.*

**Alaska Tribal
Association**

Eleven village corporations which are receiving land but no money under the settlement act organized as a nonprofit corporation, the Alaska Tribal Association, in late 1974. The corporations are from the four cities named in the act (Juneau, Kenai, Kodiak, and Sitka) and the seven located on former reserves (Arctic Village, Elim, Gambell, Klukwan, Savoonga, Tetlin, and Venetie).

The purposes of the organization are to secure funding, to distribute information, and to otherwise advance their interests. Village corporation presidents make up the board of directors. George Miller, Jr., of Kenai was elected president of the Association.

If a bill introduced in Congress in 1975 becomes law, the problem of these corporations having no money would be remedied. The bill provides for a one-time appropriation of $100,000 for each village on former reserves and of $250,000 for each of the four-named cities. Such an appropriation would be in addition to appropriations scheduled for the Alaska Native Fund.

# UNIT SEVEN

# THE MONEY SETTLEMENT

*"So many bankers are taking me to lunch these days, I'm getting fat."*

—A Native regional corporation
leader, *Anchorage Daily News*,
December 24, 1972

*"The money we get is going for our kids — for their education."*

—Daisy Demientieff, Anchorage
*Anchorage Daily News*,
December 16, 1973

*"What is the village going to do with its money? Don't really know, not yet."*

—Bob Hawley, Kivalina
*Anchorage Daily News*
August 21, 1973

*"We'll probably just invest our money, at least for the time being while we plan."*

—Roy Ewan, Executive Director,
Ahtna, Inc., *Anchorage Daily News*
August 21, 1973

As 1975 opened, nearly one-fourth of the compensation for land rights extinguished had been paid. Of the nearly $212 million which had gone into the Alaska Native Fund, about $209 million in checks had been distributed to the 12 regional Native corporations.

Consistent with the act, regional corporations had kept 45 percent or about $94 million. They had distributed or were scheduled to transfer checks ranging from a few thousand dollars to over two million dollars to village corporations within their regions. Taken together, the 203 village corporations were entitled to receive about $60.5 million through 1974.

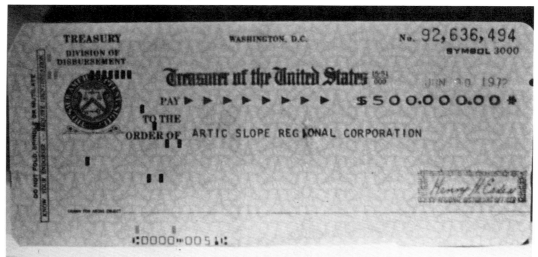

Tundra Times

*Payment of $500,000 accepted by the Arctic Slope Regional Corporation, despite error in spelling.*

Regional corporations had also mailed checks totaling about $54.5 million to the more than 76,500 Natives enrolled to them. About 27,000 persons, who were enrolled only to regional corporations had received about $1,500 each; more than 49,000 persons, who were enrolled also to village corporations, had received about $275 each.

About $2.6 million remained in the Alaska Native Fund for payment of lawyers, consultants, and Native organizations for their expenses in obtaining a claims settlement. Although the amount of money appropriated for this purpose seemed large, it still fell far short of the more than $7 million filed for by lawyers and consultants.

The source for most of the money received through 1974 was appropriations by Congress. Payments of substantial size from the mineral resources of State and federal lands awaited the completion of the pipeline from the North Slope.

Funds received by corporations were being spent to implement the settlement, and they were being invested in a variety of ways.

The $962.5 million which Natives and their corporations are to receive under the settlement act is to be paid from the special account in the U. S. Treasury called the Alaska Native Fund. As established by the act, the Fund receives money from two sources: (1) appropriations made by Congress, and (2) a two-percent share of mineral revenues obtained from certain federal and State lands in Alaska. All money in the fund, except for the $2.6 million set aside for expenses of obtaining a settlement, is to be paid out on a quarterly basis to regional Native corporations.

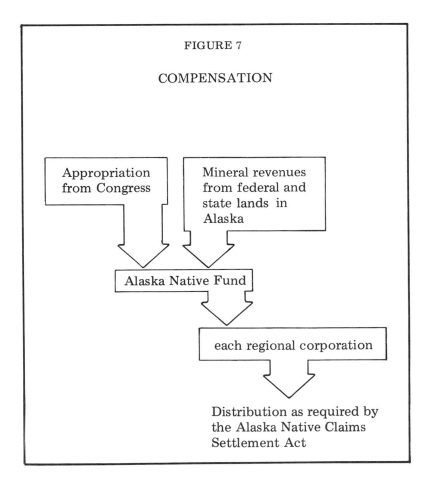

FIGURE 7

COMPENSATION

Appropriation from Congress

Mineral revenues from federal and state lands in Alaska

Alaska Native Fund

each regional corporation

Distribution as required by the Alaska Native Claims Settlement Act

Of the total compensation, $462.5 million was to be appropriated by the Congress over an 11-year period. Through 1974, nearly all of the deposits made to the Alaska Native Fund were from this source. These appropriations, made in the first four fiscal years, totaled $202.5 million.

**Congressional appropriations**

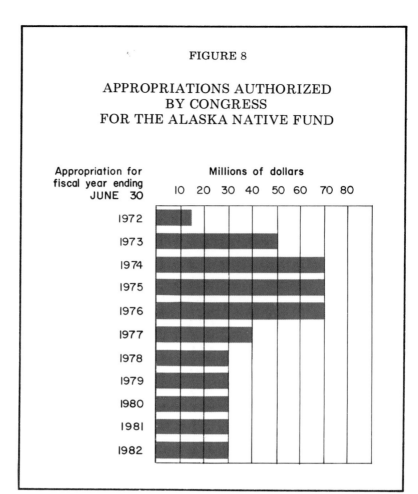

FIGURE 8

APPROPRIATIONS AUTHORIZED
BY CONGRESS
FOR THE ALASKA NATIVE FUND

In fiscal year 1976 (July 1, 1975 — June 30, 1976), the schedule provided for $70 million. In the following fiscal year, it provided for $40 million. During the next five fiscal years, it provided for $30 million annually. These authorized payments are not deposited to the Alaska Native Fund until Congress passes a specific appropriation for the purpose each year.

The eleventh and final appropriation by Congress will be made before June 30, 1982.

**Revenue sharing**

Unlike the Congressional appropriations to be paid on a fixed schedule over an 11-year period, the $500 million in compensation to come from revenue sharing has no time-table, and it may be as long as 15 years before the total is reached.

Since the most significant revenues to be shared are those from North Slope oil, and production wasn't expected to begin until 1977, mineral revenue sharing was of very little importance as a source of compensation during the first years. Only $3.3 million was deposited to the Alaska Native Fund from this source in the three years following passage of the act.

Generally, the two percent share of revenues being paid to Natives as compensation is based upon bonuses, rentals, and royalties paid by companies for mineral rights on State and federal lands in Alaska. Of the minerals covered by this provision, only oil, gas and coal, were of likely importance.

Although most minerals, most lands, and most revenues are subject to this revenue sharing plan, there are important exceptions. These exceptions include:

- metallic minerals, such as gold and silver;
- lands acquired by the State at statehood, such as tidelands, submerged lands, or lands under navigable waters;
- the Outer Continental Shelf; and
- bonuses and rentals received by the State at its September 1969 North Slope oil sale.

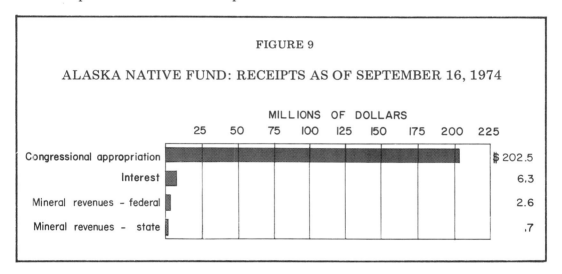

FIGURE 9

ALASKA NATIVE FUND: RECEIPTS AS OF SEPTEMBER 16, 1974

MILLIONS OF DOLLARS

| | | | | | | | | | |
|---|---|---|---|---|---|---|---|---|---|
| | 25 | 50 | 75 | 100 | 125 | 150 | 175 | 200 | 225 |

Congressional appropriation — $202.5
Interest — 6.3
Mineral revenues – federal — 2.6
Mineral revenues – state — .7

It was estimated in 1973 that once the trans-Alaska pipeline was completed and maximum flow of oil through it was achieved that the two-percent share for Natives and their corporations would be about $55 million a year. However, the rising price of oil and the rising cost of the pipeline (which reduces the value of the oil) made that estimate very uncertain. Annual payments to the Alaska Native Fund may be as much as twice that amount.

Completion of the pipeline in 1977 promised at least this: as compensation from Congressional appropriations declines, compensation from revenue sharing will begin to grow.

Even though payments are made by both the State and federal government, the $500 million to come from revenue sharing is largely the State's contribution to the settlement. North Slope oil is on State land and the two percent of the revenues to be paid Natives would otherwise go to the State. Secondly, 90 percent of mineral revenues from federal lands went to the State in the past. Under the act, two percent goes to Natives, and 90 percent of the remainder goes into the State Treasury.

The justification for the State's contribution to a federal claims settlement was that Natives had prior rights to lands granted the State, but their rights had not been recognized.

When the $500 million is reached — perhaps some time between 1982 and 1987 — all payments from State and federal governments will end. By terms of the act, Natives of Alaska will have been compensated for land claims extinguished by it.

Interest

About $6 million of the monies distributed by the Alaska Native Fund in the first three years was interest earned on deposits. This interest was earned on the appropriations made to the Fund before enrollment was completed, and therefore, before any distribution could be made. Deposits in the Alaska Native Fund no longer earn interest.

Other sources of cash

Even though compensation for lands given up is fixed in total amount and payment will come to an end, the total cash Native corporations will have as a result of the settlement is not so limited. Two other important sources of cash income are investments they make and natural resources of their lands which they develop.

Part of the money corporations receive is being invested in a variety of ways to produce cash. These include depositing cash in a bank or purchasing securities to earn interest. Another kind of investment being made is purchasing existing stores, fuel distributorships, hotels, or other businesses or establishing such enterprises.

A second additional source of income is the cash obtainable from the natural resources of the lands to which Native corporations are obtaining title. In a forested area, for instance, a village corporation might sell timber from its land and obtain cash income for itself. Regional corporations might likewise sell timber from their lands or lease rights to minerals and obtain cash. If regional corporations sell timber or rights to subsurface minerals, however, they are required to share the proceeds with other regions.

This sharing of income by a regional corporation from sale of its natural resources is limited to the 12 in-state corporations. Under the act, the corporation obtaining cash from such resources keeps 30 percent of it, and divides the remainder among all 12 (including itself). This division is made on the basis of the proportionate number enrolled to each. To illustrate: if the Bering Straits Corporation is required to distribute $100,000 from mineral development, it would retain $30,000 (30 percent); as it divided the remaining 70 percent among the regions it would allot itself another $6,300, because it has about 9 percent of the total enrollment.

FIGURE 10

SOURCES OF CASH
FOR THE TWELVE REGIONAL CORPORATIONS IN ALASKA

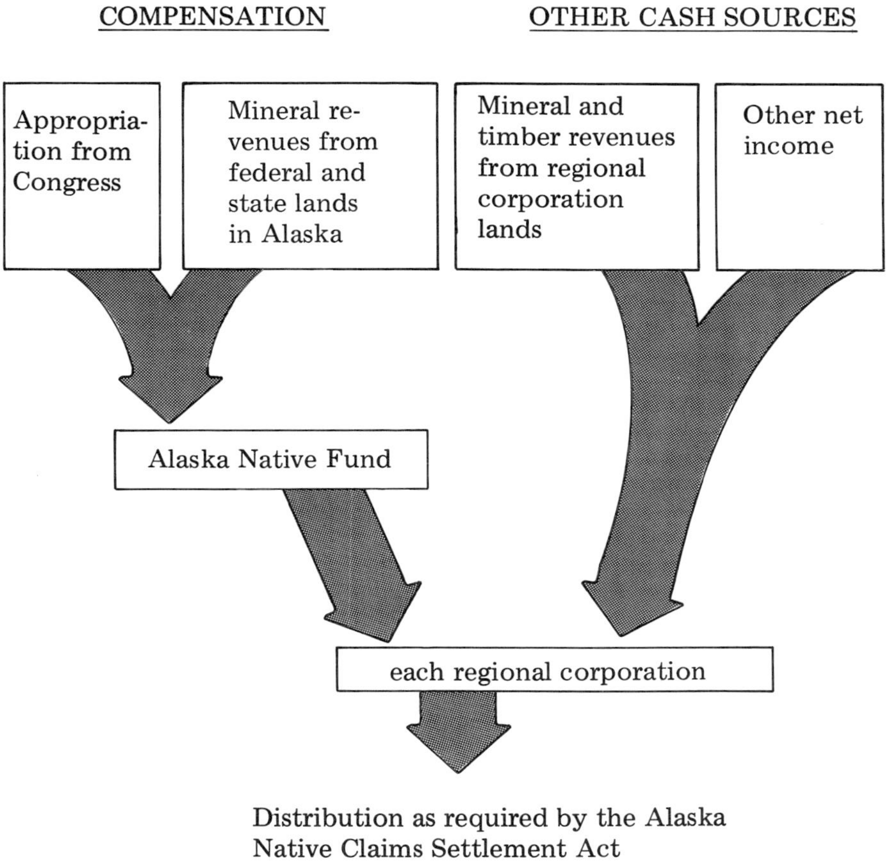

COMPENSATION                    OTHER CASH SOURCES

| Appropria-tion from Congress | Mineral re-venues from federal and state lands in Alaska | Mineral and timber revenues from regional corporation lands | Other net income |

Alaska Native Fund

each regional corporation

Distribution as required by the Alaska
Native Claims Settlement Act

Note: Only sources of cash from "Compensation" apply
to a 13th corporation under terms of the act.

This provision for sharing among regions, apparently intended to make up for the possibility that some regions might be resource-poor, is posing a number of difficult problems of interpretation. What costs of selling the resource, for instance, may be deducted in order to determine the total that should be distributed? Or, if a region uses its timber to manufacture something it then sells, how much of the income is to be distributed? These and many other questions have yet to be resolved.

These two additional sources of cash — investment and development of natural resources — may be pursued during the period in which compensation is being paid. Once compensation comes to an end, they are the only sources for generating a continuing cash flow.

# Payments to Individuals                                         Chapter 28

All money paid out from the Alaska Native Fund, except for the reserve described in the last chapter, goes directly to the 12 regional Native corporations. It is divided among them on the basis of their enrollments. Each corporation's share is determined on a per-capita basis; stated another way, a corporation's share is established by the ratio of its enrollment to the total number of Natives enrolled.

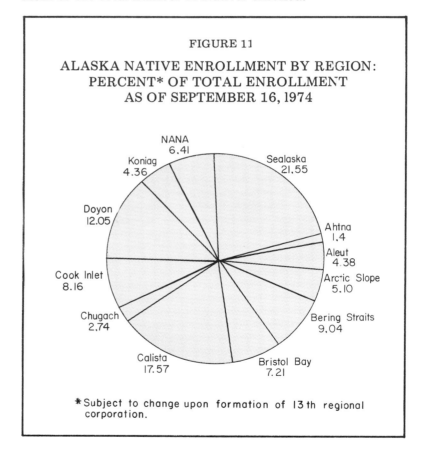

FIGURE 11

ALASKA NATIVE ENROLLMENT BY REGION:
PERCENT* OF TOTAL ENROLLMENT
AS OF SEPTEMBER 16, 1974

NANA 6.41
Koniag 4.36
Sealaska 21.55
Doyon 12.05
Ahtna 1.4
Aleut 4.38
Arctic Slope 5.10
Cook Inlet 8.16
Chugach 2.74
Bering Straits 9.04
Calista 17.57
Bristol Bay 7.21

*Subject to change upon formation of 13th regional corporation.

The percentage distribution established with the final roll does not change with deaths of stockholders and inheritance of stock by others. It does not change if stockholders move from one region to another. It remains constant unless corrections are made to the final roll or a 13th corporation is established. In the latter case, percentages of the existing corporations would decline as enrollees transferred to the 13th corporation.

Among the present 12 corporations, Ahtna, Inc. receives the smallest portion — about 1.4 percent — and Sealaska the largest — about 21.5 percent. Through the end of 1974 Ahtna had received — for itself, its village corporations, and its stockholders — almost $3 million and Sealaska had received more than $45 million. If no revisions to enrollments were made, Ahtna would receive a total of about $18.5 million from the Alaska Native Fund and Sealaska would receive a total of $206.5 million.

Once a regional corporation receives its check, it is required to distribute part of the amount received to village corporations within its boundaries (again on a per-capita basis) and part of it to individual stockholders.

Immediate cash benefits from the Alaska Native Fund are not the same for all enrolled Natives. The amount of compensation that must be paid an individual depends upon whether he is a stockholder in both a village corporation and its regional corporation, or a stockholder only in the regional corporation. The duration over which compensation must be paid is similarly determined.

**Differing direct payments**

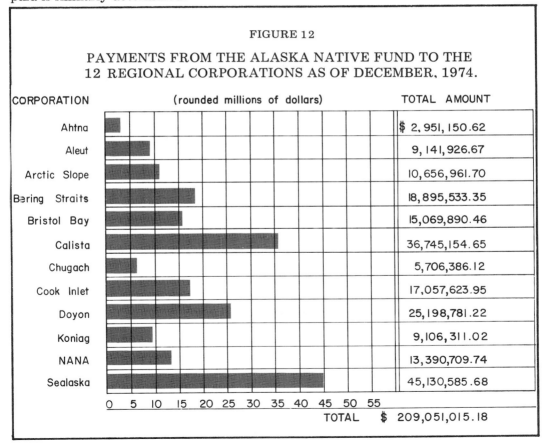

FIGURE 12

PAYMENTS FROM THE ALASKA NATIVE FUND TO THE
12 REGIONAL CORPORATIONS AS OF DECEMBER, 1974.

| CORPORATION | (rounded millions of dollars) | TOTAL AMOUNT |
|---|---|---|
| Ahtna | | $ 2,951,150.62 |
| Aleut | | 9,141,926.67 |
| Arctic Slope | | 10,656,961.70 |
| Bering Straits | | 18,895,533.35 |
| Bristol Bay | | 15,069,890.46 |
| Calista | | 36,745,154.65 |
| Chugach | | 5,706,386.12 |
| Cook Inlet | | 17,057,623.95 |
| Doyon | | 25,198,781.22 |
| Koniag | | 9,106,311.02 |
| NANA | | 13,390,709.74 |
| Sealaska | | 45,130,585.68 |

0  5  10  15  20  25  30  35  40  45  50  55

TOTAL    $ 209,051,015.18

**First five years**   During the first five years following the settlement act, the 12 regional corporations are required to distribute to their stockholders and village corporations no less than 55 percent of the funds received: (1) from the Alaska Native Fund; (2) from mineral and timber revenues shared among all regions; and (3) from investments as net income.

In this period only the first category was of substantial importance because lands (with minerals and timber) were only in the process of being selected, and because implementation costs were so great that there was little net income.

**All stockholders**   Of the required distribution, 10 percent must go to stockholders — that is, to all Natives who are enrolled in regional corporations. With $209.9 million available from the Alaska Native Fund through December of 1974, this 10 percent was almost $21 million. Given a total enrollment of about 76,500, all enrolled Natives received no less than $275 each. Before the mandatory distribution to individuals would end in fiscal year 1976, all were to receive about $100 more.

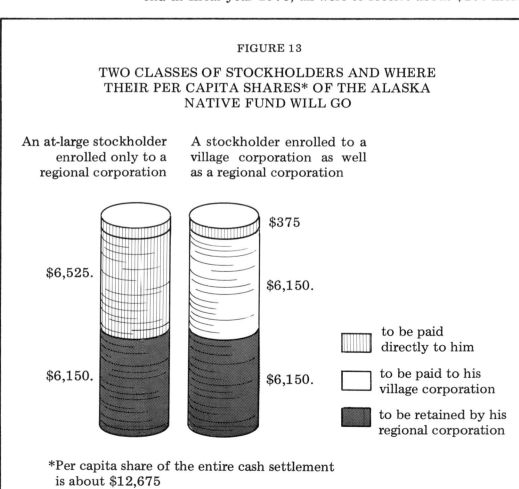

FIGURE 13

TWO CLASSES OF STOCKHOLDERS AND WHERE
THEIR PER CAPITA SHARES* OF THE ALASKA
NATIVE FUND WILL GO

An at-large stockholder enrolled only to a regional corporation

A stockholder enrolled to a village corporation as well as a regional corporation

$375

$6,525.

$6,150.

$6,150.

$6,150.

|||||| to be paid directly to him

☐ to be paid to his village corporation

■ to be retained by his regional corporation

*Per capita share of the entire cash settlement is about $12,675

The amount of this payment assumes that 100 shares of stock are owned, the situation of most stockholders. If, however, a stockholder held additional shares through inheritance, his payment would be correspondingly greater.

This $375 payment is all that must be made to about two-thirds of all Natives who are enrolled. They are stockholders in village corporations as well as regional corporations. Their village corporations were to be the recipients of their per capita shares in the other 45 percent that regional corporations were required to distribute.

**At-large stockholders**

At-large stockholders — the other one-third enrolled — receive their shares of the 45 percent directly as individuals, since they are not members of village corporations. Over the first three years these at-large stockholders (holding 100 shares of stock) received payments of about $1,500 each. Of this amount $275 was based upon the 10 percent distribution. The $1,225 was based upon the per-capita value of the 45 percent distribution, as follows: 45 percent of nearly $210 million is about $94 million; with some 76,500 persons enrolled, the per-capita value was about $1,225. When payments were made for fiscal year 1976, each of these at-large stockholders was to receive about $525 more.

Arctic Environmental Information and Data Center (J. C. LaBelle)

*Stockholders whose permanent residences are in villages, such as Point Hope, are stockholders in two settlement act corporations — the village and the region.*

**Summary: first five years**

In summary, cash benefits that regional corporations were required to distribute to individuals depended upon whether they were at-large stockholders or whether they were also members of village corporations. During the first five years, at-large stockholders were to be paid their per capita shares of 55 percent of the funds received by the regional corporation, and stockholders who are also in village corporations were to be paid their per-capita shares of 10 percent.

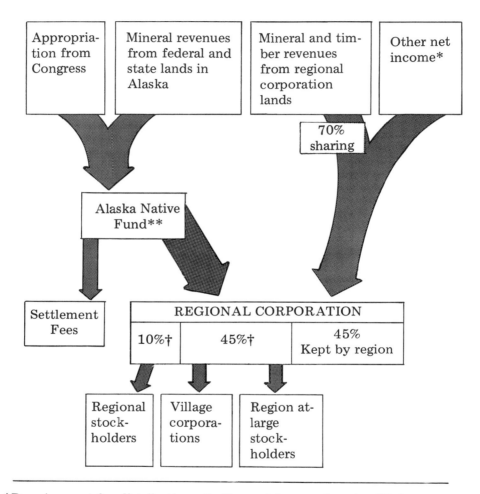

FIGURE 14

FIRST FIVE YEARS

MANDATORY DISTRIBUTION OF CASH APPLICABLE
TO THE 12 REGIONAL CORPORATIONS IN ALASKA

COMPENSATION                    OTHER CASH SOURCES

| Appropria-tion from Congress | Mineral revenues from federal and state lands in Alaska | Mineral and tim-ber revenues from regional corporation lands | Other net income* |

70% sharing

Alaska Native Fund**

| Settlement Fees | REGIONAL CORPORATION | | |
| | 10%† | 45%† | 45% Kept by region |

| Regional stock-holders | Village corpora-tions | Region at-large stock-holders |

*Requirement for distribution of other net income is not settled.

**Some interest on monies in the Fund were distributed in the first two payments (only) to the regions.

†Not less than. . . .

NOTE: Congressional appropriations extend over an 11-year period; federal and state resource revenues cease after $500 million is reached.

After the fifth year, the mandatory distribution of 10 percent to individuals comes to an end. The act does not require further payments by regional corporations to stockholders in village corporations. Individual payments must continue, however, for those who are not members of village corporations. These at-large stockholders must be paid their per capita shares directly as long as their regional corporations are receiving funds from the sources listed earlier.

Beginning with the sixth year, at-large stockholders must be paid their per capita shares (along with village corporations) of 50 percent of the regional corporation's income. From the Alaska Native Fund alone, each at-large stockholder (holding 100 shares) should receive an additional $4,500 over what may be as much as a 15-year period. How much each will actually receive will depend upon the return on investments made by the regional corporations and the extent to which they develop their natural resources.

Even though distribution of cash by a region to its village stockholders is not required, such stockholders may expect to receive individual cash benefits in the form of dividends from their regional and village corporations. Such cash payments will be decided upon by the boards of directors of corporations on the basis of their profits.

In summary, after 1976 the only group of stockholders who must be paid directly by the 12 regional corporations are their at-large stockholders. They must receive their per capita shares (based upon the total number of enrolled Natives) of half of the income of the regional corporations. The per capita shares of village corporation stockholders will go to their village corporations. Although these stockholders may expect to receive individual cash benefits after 1976, none are required by the act.

There are no restrictions upon the use to which individuals may put their land claims compensation. The first checks went for an endless variety of purposes. Savings accounts were opened by many parents for children who received claims checks. In Shageluk, for instance, Zho-tse, Incorporated (the village corporation) reported that such accounts had been opened for all children.

Money received by individuals as their share of compensation for land claims extinguished is not subject to income tax. If it were, the payments made to them would be partially regained by federal and State governments and rob the cash settlement of any real meaning. Money received by individuals as their shares in profits of corporations, however, is taxable.

FIGURE 15

MANDATORY DISTRIBUTION OF CASH
APPLICABLE TO THE 12 REGIONS IN ALASKA

AFTER FIVE YEARS

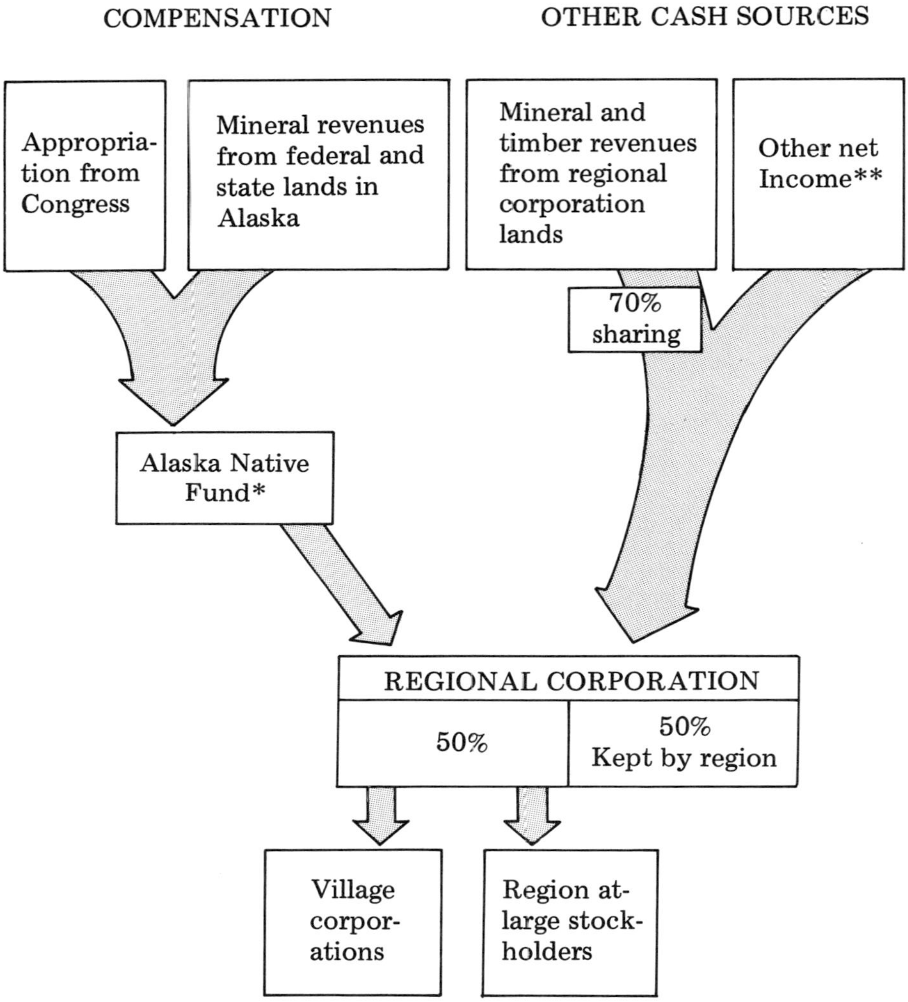

COMPENSATION                    OTHER CASH SOURCES

Appropria-tion from Congress

Mineral revenues from federal and state lands in Alaska

Mineral and timber revenues from regional corporation lands

Other net Income**

70% sharing

Alaska Native Fund*

REGIONAL CORPORATION

50%        50% Kept by region

Village corpor-ations

Region at-large stock-holders

*The fund will cease to exist after a total of $962.5 million (plus interest) is reached.

**Requirement for distribution of other net income is not settled.

222

If a 13th corporation is formed, it would be required to distribute half of its revenues to its stockholders from the beginning. Since it would have no villages, it would not be required to have more than one category of stockholders. And, since it would have no land nor share in the resources of regional lands, its only revenues would be from the Alaska Native Fund and from the investments it makes.

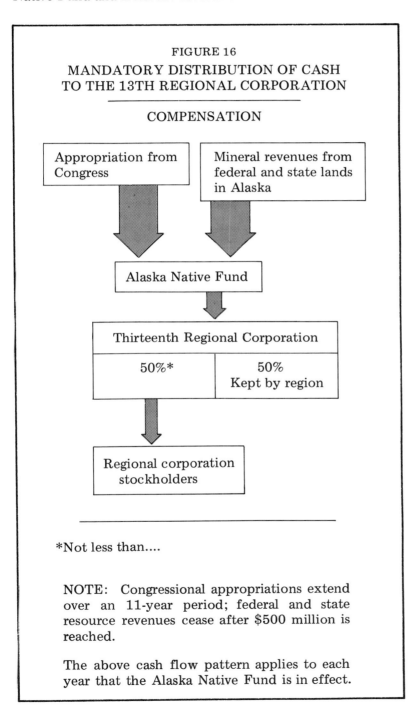

FIGURE 16
MANDATORY DISTRIBUTION OF CASH
TO THE 13TH REGIONAL CORPORATION

COMPENSATION

Appropriation from Congress

Mineral revenues from federal and state lands in Alaska

Alaska Native Fund

Thirteenth Regional Corporation

| 50%* | 50% Kept by region |

Regional corporation stockholders

*Not less than....

NOTE: Congressional appropriations extend over an 11-year period; federal and state resource revenues cease after $500 million is reached.

The above cash flow pattern applies to each year that the Alaska Native Fund is in effect.

As noted earlier, there are three groups of Natives presently living who receive no part of the compensation: those born after the settlement act became law, those 1,758 Natives who chose title to their revoked reserves, and those who failed to become enrolled before the deadline. The third group may yet benefit, if legislation introduced in the Congress to allow late enrollment becomes law.

# Funding for Village Corporations        Chapter 29

As with the regional corporations, village corporations receive compensation and other cash on the basis of their enrollments. The larger their final enrollments, the greater their cash entitlements.

Margaret Bauman

*Young Selawik stockholders listen to Wells Fargo banker from San Francisco.*

Through 1976, village corporations are to receive their proportionate shares of 45 percent of the compensation and other income of their regional corporations. During the first four fiscal years that percentage amounted to about $94 million. Given an enrollment of about 76,500 persons, this was about $1,225 per person. This amount, which was paid directly to at-large stockholders, was to be distributed to each village corporation for each person enrolled to it.

On this basis, cash entitlements for the 203 certified village corporations ranged from a low of about $27,000 to a high of about $2.5 million through 1974. Approximate amounts which village corporations were entitled to receive through this period are suggested in the table which follows:

Cash entitlements

| Number of corporations | Range in enrollment | Approximate range of cash entitlement through December, 1974 |
| --- | --- | --- |
| 114 | 22 to 192 | $ 27,000 to $ 235,000 |
| 62 | 200 to 392 | $ 245,000 to $ 480,000 |
| 17 | 400 to 595 | $ 490,000 to $ 730,000 |
| 3 | 620 to 737 | $ 760,000 to $ 905,000 |
| 3 | 839 to 925 | $1,030,000 to $1,130,000 |
| 4 | 1,725 to 2,060 | $2,115,000 to $2,525,000 |

In fiscal year 1976, the 45 percent distribution was expected to have a per capita value of about $425. On this basis, village corporations were to receive amounts ranging from about $9,500 to about $875,000.

After 1976, village corporations (along with at-large stockholders) will receive 50 percent of the income of their regional corporations. This distribution — to be made over an indefinite period of years — will have a per capita value of about $4,500 from the Alaska Native Fund. On this basis, village corporations will receive from $99,000 to $9,270,000 before the Alaska Native Fund is exhausted.

As with individual recipients of compensation, village corporations pay no taxes on funds they receive from the Alaska Native Fund. Profits from their investments or sales of resources they own are, however, subject to taxation.

Taxation

Cash payments are to be made only to village corporations certified as eligible to obtain land and money benefits of the act. This excludes corporations which: (1) have chosen full title to their former reserves; (2) have been formed to obtain land in the four named cities; and (3) have been certified as "Native groups" to obtain land.

Exceptions to distribution

To obtain its share of the compensation, an eligible village corporation is required to submit a plan for the use of the money that is satisfactory to its regional corporation. If the region finds the plan unsatisfactory, it may withhold

Obtaining funds

funds. Only a few instances of such temporary withholding are reported to have occurred through 1974.

The region also may require village corporations to carry out joint projects with other villages or with the regional corporation itself. No instances of such a requirement being imposed have been reported.

If there is disagreement between a village and its regional corporation, the act requires arbitration as provided for in the region's articles of incorporation. Such a provision typically calls for the village to appoint a person, the region to appoint a person, and these two to name a third person. This panel of arbitrators reviews the matter over which there is disagreement and makes a decision based upon a majority vote. Its decision is final and binding upon both parties.

**Uses of funds**

Within the first three years after the act's adoption many village corporations had hired staffs to carry out obligations imposed upon them under the settlement act. Land selection had to be completed by them within this period. Plans had to be drawn for the issuance of stock to all enrollees. Planning for the investment of corporate funds had to proceed. And all of these had to be accompanied by appropriate record-keeping.

Tundra Times

*Interior of apartment complex, an investment of Bethel Native Corporation.*

Even with these many duties, a number of village corporations had also purchased existing businesses or launched new enterprises. The Togotthele Corporation of Nenana, for instance, invested in a sawmill and log-home building business in that community. Its intention, according to the president, Al Ketzler, was to make profits, provide jobs, and have a use for the village corporation's timber resources. Sitnasuak Corporation purchased a grocery and general merchandise store in Nome. Many smaller corporations also purchased village stores. Perhaps the largest investment for a new business was made by Bethel Native Corporation, which constructed a million-dollar hotel and apartment building in that Kuskokwim River community.

While these efforts at generating profits — future income for their stockholders — are more dramatic than investments for interest, not all village corporations have equal opportunities open to them for new businesses. If but a few travelers pass through a village, there is little need for a hotel, for instance. Many village corporate leaders, therefore, chose to invest through bank deposits or to purchase securities to assure future dividends.

---

### THE FUTURE OF VILLAGE CORPORATIONS: ONE VIEW

Harold Napoleon, the president of Yupiktak Bista, the regional nonprofit corporation in southwestern Alaska, was interviewed by the *Tundra Drums* in mid-1975. Among other things, he was asked to "peek into the future." He commented:

> Well, just looking back a few years, we see we could have made better decisions. Village corporations, for example — money making institutions in the villages where there are no economic potentials — any economic realist will tell you that out of every one hundred, ten corporations may succeed. In some cases, rather than have a village money making corporation, a community center or a community library would have been more practical, and might have proven more valuable in 20 years when the village corporation has gone broke.

---

**Too little money**

Apart from an absence of local profit-making opportunities, there was another reason for many village corporations to simply earn interest on their share of the money: they weren't going to get very much. Furthermore, the cost to a village corporation of carrying out the tasks imposed upon it by the settlement act could equal or exceed the dollars available.

In an analysis prepared for the Alaska Native Foundation, consultant Lee Gorsuch calculated the minimum cost to a village corporation of carrying out its corporate duties at about $70,000 a year. This would provide a full-time manager, secretary-bookkeeper, limited legal fees, and some travel and office expense. He showed that even that modest budget couldn't be supported by most villages, and suggested how the problem of too little money might be solved. In addition to urging careful planning and budgeting by village corporations, he suggested that they consider management agreements with their regional corporations. Under such agreements, the village would purchase services from its region at less cost than if it hired its own staff. He also suggested two other possibilities: management corporations formed by several village corporations (a pooling of part of their money) or mergers of corporations (combining all of their money and other assets).

**Approaches being taken**

Numerous villages now have agreements with their regional corporations for the purchase of services. They include such things as the purchase of accounting and legal services and the purchase of professional advice on land and natural resources.

Management corporations — a second approach — have also been formed by groups of villages to pool part of their cash resources to employ the staff they need. By the end of 1974, three such management corporations had been organized, all within the Calista region. They are Yuqtak, made up of nine villages near Bethel; Kuskokwim Management Corporation, seven villages along the Upper Kuskokwim; and Nunivak Kaluiat Native Corporation, the eight villages of Nunivak and Nelson islands.

A third approach to the problem was being taken in 1975 in the NANA region. There, following several months of study, directors of village corporations and the regional corporation agreed to seek a merger of some village corporations with the NANA Regional Corporation. The decision whether to join the merged corporation would be made by each village. The advantages anticipated included economy of operation and improved opportunities for the management of money and land. Such a merger would require the amendment of State law and the settlement act, and the approval of the Secretary of the Interior and stockholders.

# Funding for Regional Corporations          Chapter 30

The 45 percent of the compensation retained by the 12 regional corporations through the end of 1974 amounted to about $94 million. Because the distribution among the regions is enrollment-based, there was a wide range in the number of dollars available to each corporation.

Approximate amounts available through 1974 to regional

corporations ranged from $1.3 million to $20.3 million, as follows:

| | |
|---|---|
| Sealaska | $20.3 million |
| Calista | 15.5 million |
| Doyon | 11.3 million |
| Bering Straits | 8.5 million |
| Cook Inlet | 7.7 million |
| Bristol Bay | 6.8 million |
| NANA | 6.0 million |
| Arctic Slope | 4.8 million |
| Aleut Corp. | 4.1 million |
| Koniag | 4.1 million |
| Chugach | 2.5 million |
| Ahtna | 1.3 million |

After the mandatory distribution in 1976, regions will begin retaining 50 percent of the compensation and other income they receive. Before the Alaska Native Fund is exhausted, an additional $375 million will be available from this source for the use of regional corporations.

Ahtna, Inc.

*Reviewing plans for Ahtna's motel. Ahtna Deputy Director Nick Jackson, Dean Olson, Executive Director, and Emery Clark, Project Engineer for the motel.*

A major use of claims money by regional corporations during the first three years was dictated by the role the settlement act gave them. As the vehicles of settlement, the corporations had to bear much of the costly task of implementing it.

They needed to become organized, hire staffs, and begin planning for the use of funds to be received. They needed to help villages become incorporated, to select land, and to plan

**Uses: administration**

229

for the use of their funds. And, almost at the same time they were learning the settlement act, they needed to be teaching it to others.

Opening of offices meant renting space, purchasing furniture and equipment, and hiring of staff. Carrying out planning for the use of funds meant engaging financial consultants, and planning for land selection meant hiring other experts on natural resources. Analyzing and urging changes to regulations issued by the Department of the Interior meant spending for the services of attorneys. And, working with villages to help them learn the act, to incorporate, and to plan for land selection meant substantial expenditures for travel.

One of the larger regional corporations reported spending about one-half million dollars for operations in fiscal year 1973 and about three times that amount in fiscal year 1974. The activities carried out with such funds were those required by the act or expected to be of long-term benefit to the corporation and stockholders of the region.

*Architect's drawing of the Doyon Building, Fairbanks.*

**Uses: investment**

Most of the funds retained by regional corporations are invested in bank deposits or securities, although some investment is also taking place in new enterprises.

Since the regional corporations are profit organizations, decisions on investment of their funds take into account how safe a proposed investment would be, how readily an investment can be sold or otherwise converted to cash, and the amount of interest that can be realized. As Calista explained, in its annual report to its stockholders:

> Your Board of Directors chose the following ideas as important steps so that your wealth will grow:
>
> (1) Safety. To lend money to people who have a record of always paying their debts. In our case they are strong companies, large banks, and even the government.

(2) Easy to get at. You can get back as much money as you need whenever you need it. In this case, your Board of Directors decides very carefully how much money it needs to make your corporation work.

(3) Growth (Income). After thinking about safety and making sure that we can easily take money out from the main pot, we see that this portion of the money will be able to grow and earn what is called interest income. It is no different from lending fish to a man you can trust. Let's say you loaned him 100 fish out of the extra fish that you have. Because you have helped him he pays you back 108. You have now made what is called profit or interest or income. The 100 fish you loaned out is what is called an investment, and you have earned an interest of 8 fish.

Margaret Bauman

*Nulukvik Hotel, an investment of NANA Regional Corporation.*

Earning profits for stockholders can be pursued in a variety of ways, in addition to simply earning interest. The NANA Regional Corporation purchased a hotel in Kotzebue and constructed a second one. A subsidiary — a business corporation — owned by the Arctic Slope Regional Corporation joined with Ukpeagvik Inupiat Village Corporation of Barrow to establish a hotel and restaurant in that northern community. Both Sealaska and Calista announced plans to construct multimillion-dollar buildings — Sealaska, an office building in Juneau, and Calista, a high-rise hotel in Anchorage. The Aleut Corporation purchased two 120-foot crabbing and fishing boats. In a joint venture with an experienced road building firm, the Bering Straits Regional Corporation accepted a contract for road construction in the southeastern part of the state. Ahtna, Inc. established a subsidiary to build access roads in that region for the Alyeska Service Company. Also under contract to Alyeska Pipeline was Chugach Natives, Inc. for a tug and barge service in Prince William Sound.

Many subsidiaries were being established for specific profit-making enterprises to protect the regional corporation's assets — its property and money. Even though the regional corporation was the sole owner of the subsidiary, the liability of the corporation was limited to the subsidiary's assets. In effect, the larger assets of the regional corporation were protected.

An ambitious joint venture of four regional corporations — Doyon, Ltd., Bristol Bay, NANA, and Cook Inlet Region, Inc. — is establishment of the United Bank of Alaska. Approval of the group's charter was expected by mid-1975.

Funds being invested by regional corporations in their early years were largely from compensation paid for land claims extinguished. A number of corporations, however, had already received some income from oil companies for exploration rights to lands which they would soon own. These lands and resources — in the opinion of most observers — will make up the real wealth of regional corporations and their stockholders.

As with individuals and village corporations, regional corporations pay no taxes on funds they receive as compensation but they do pay taxes on their profits.

# UNIT EIGHT

Atlantic Richfield Company

# THE LAND SETTLEMENT

*"The billion dollars is nothing; it's the land
that's the real settlement."*

—Hank Eaton, Kodiak
Anchorage Daily News
September 22, 1973

Several thousand pages of testimony from Congressional hearings carry the theme of the importance of land to Natives of Alaska. "Our whole life is lived on the land," Neal Charlie, a Minto villager, had told the Congress, "and we would not know what to do without it."

The settlement act promised full ownership of 40 million acres, almost one-ninth of the total acreage of the state. It was less than Native spokesmen had sought — given their solid claim of aboriginal title to virtually the whole state. But it was more than most observers believed could be won.

Once the land itself was acquired, Natives would become the third largest owner of land in Alaska. Only the federal government and the State would be holders of more land. Unlike government holdings, Native lands would be private, not public. Through their corporations, Natives would be, by far, the single largest group of private land owners in the state.

Three years after the settlement act village corporations had completed their selection of land that would total not more than 22 million acres. Regional corporations were proceeding to select their scheduled 16 million acres. Regions, the four named communities, and others were also proceeding to acquire the remaining 2 million acres.

Seven local corporations on five revoked reserves had voted to accept full title to their former reserves and to forego other benefits of the settlement act. By their decisions to obtain title to 3.7 million acres, the total land being conveyed to Natives under the act rose to almost 44 million acres.

Bureau of Land Management, U.S. Department of the Interior

*Filing for land as deadline nears: Erik Hansen, consultant; Andy Kamkoff, Knik; Kurt Rein, Cook Inlet Regional Corporation; and Victor Sanders, Salamatoff.*

Over 83 million acres had been withdrawn by the federal government for possible inclusion of 80 million acres in its systems of wild and scenic rivers, forests, parks, and wildlife refuges. Action by Congress on the withdrawals was still awaited in 1975.

# Chapter 31        Village Corporation Selections

All Native village corporations required to choose their lands by December 18, 1974 made the deadline. Because there were more than 200 villages which needed to select land and because the selection process was complex, there had been wide concern that the job couldn't be done.

The last of 217 village corporations filed its bulky application with the U. S. Bureau of Land Management just before closing hours on the last day. Together, the corporations had filed for nearly 24 million acres. Of those filing, 203 were certified as eligible corporations; the other 14 had been denied eligibility, but were planning court appeals or looking to legislative remedies.

Calista Corporation

*Preparing land selection applications.*

The determination of which specific lands would be selected was made by each village corporation. In most places, a special committee was formed to make choices based upon what was important to be owned by the people of the village. Across the state, villages selected lands used for subsistence — trapping, fishing, hunting, berry-picking. They also selected lands having present or future economic values — timber or mineral resources, fisheries, recreation, and tourism. Their selections were limited to designated lands and, as will be described in the next chapter, by numerous other factors.

When the applications are processed each of the 203 corporations will own the surface estate in one to seven townships, most of which will be near their villages. Entitlements of these corporations were:

| Number of Village Corporations | Number of Townships | Stated in Acres |
|---|---|---|
| 9 | 1 | 23,040 |
| 54 | 3 | 69,120 |
| 58 | 4 | 92,160 |
| 60 | 5 | 115,200 |
| 14 | 6 | 138,240 |
| 8 | 7 | 161,280 |

The number of townships to which the villages are entitled is based upon their enrollment, except for the southeastern villages. Since these nine shared in the earlier Tlingit-Haida court settlement, they are entitled to only one township each.

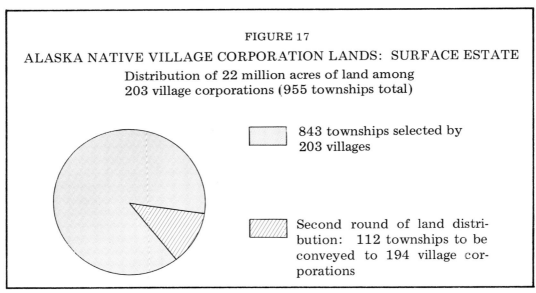

FIGURE 17

ALASKA NATIVE VILLAGE CORPORATION LANDS: SURFACE ESTATE

Distribution of 22 million acres of land among
203 village corporations (955 townships total)

843 townships selected by
203 villages

Second round of land distribution: 112 townships to be conveyed to 194 village corporations

Together the 203 village corporations are entitled on this basis to 843 townships or about 19.4 million acres. Since this is less than the acreage earmarked for villages, they will share (except for the nine southeastern villages) in an additional 2.6 million acres or 112 townships. Allocation of these lands among the 11 regions is to be based upon enrollment. Distribution of the 112 townships by the regional corporations to the villages is to be based upon their populations, subsistence needs, and historic uses (Barrow Selection, Map 24). Once that second round of selection takes place, village corporations will own the surface estate of 22 million acres.

# MAP 24  BARROW

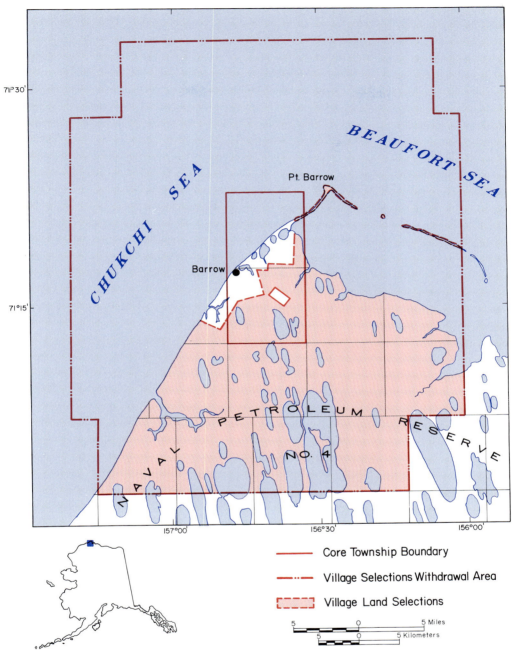

Core Township Boundary

Village Selections Withdrawal Area

Village Land Selections

The Ukpeagvik Inupiat Corporation, one of the three largest village corporations, is located at Barrow, the northernmost city in the United States. Its enrollment of 2,041 entitled it to 161,280 acres or seven townships.

The land immediately surrounding Barrow village could not be selected because it was a townsite patented to the Bureau of Land Management as trustee or held by others such as the Navy's Arctic Research Laboratory. In addition, a Navy gas well could not be selected. Apart from these situations of prior rights, the village corporation filed for all of the land within its withdrawal area. Although this is likely greater than its initial entitlement, it shows its regional corporation, the Arctic Slope, what it desires when the second round of land is made available to villages.

Since the Barrow selection is entirely within Naval Petroleum Reserve No. 4, the Arctic Slope Native Corporation will not acquire the subsurface estate. It must choose an equivalent acreage from lands designated for that purpose.

**Top-filing and overselection**

The amount of land filed for by the village corporations was substantially greater than they will obtain because there were uncertainties about ownership of parcels of land within the areas selected (Eklutna Selection, Map 25). Because of these uncertainties, the corporations overselected and top-filed. They overselected in case some of the lands they chose were already owned by others. They top-filed — applied for land which might be owned by another — in the event it was not.

**Surface estate only**

Village corporations will own only the surface estate of the land they select. The minerals below the ground — all of the subsurface estate — will belong to their regional corporations.

The surface is valuable, however. Once a village corporation conveys parcels of land to individuals and organizations as required by the act, it may sell the surface to others or it may allow its use for a fee. It may sell the timber on the land.

If its region desires to obtain the oil or mineral below the surface, it needs the consent of the village. Since the surface estate was granted to villages to protect lands used for subsistence, the village might withhold consent when subsistence activities were threatened. If consent is given, the village would be entitled to reasonable compensation from the region for damages caused to the surface.

**Land title**

Issuance of final patents to village corporations is believed to be many years away. The reason for this is that land must be surveyed before it is patented. And most of the land being selected is not yet surveyed.

There is provision, accordingly, for what is called "interim conveyance." Such a document will transfer title from the Bureau of Land Management (BLM) to the village corporation. Except for the precise description of the patent (obtainable only by surveying), the interim conveyance will be like a patent. It will allow village corporations to transfer title to individuals and organizations as required by the act, and to lease or sell land.

To obtain even the interim conveyance from the BLM will take much time. Each village corporation's application needs to be reviewed to determine with certainty that the land to be conveyed is clear of any claims by others. It will be examined to see that it meets all the requirements of the settlement act. While this process is continuing, another part of the BLM will be identifying easements — routes for public access or use — within the area selected. Once these steps have been completed, the interim conveyance is prepared, reserving the easements.

It was expected that all village corporations would receive interim conveyance to some of the acreage they selected within a year of filing their applications. As they do, similar title would go for the subsurface estate (except for wildlife refuges and Petroleum Reserve No. 4 selections) to their regional corporations.

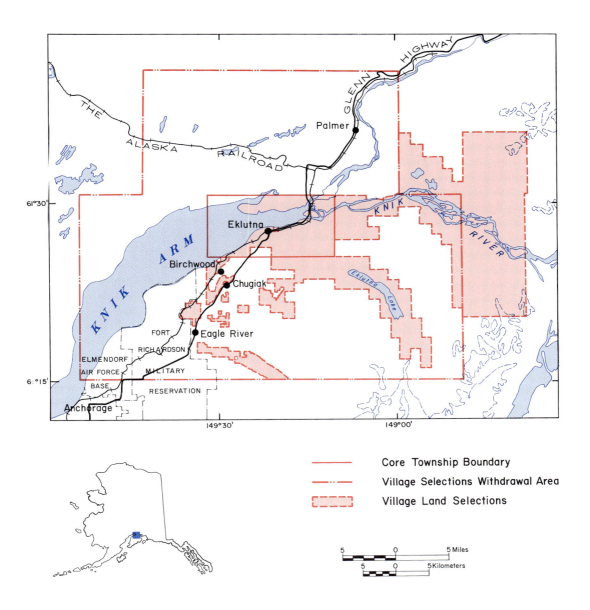

## MAP 25

### EKLUTNA

Located on Knik Arm in the highly urbanized Anchorage area, Eklutna faced land selection problems unlike any other village. Its corporation, Eklutna, Inc., enrolled 126 persons, so it was entitled to four townships or 92,160 acres.

Although a reservation had been proposed many years before, and a withdrawal made for the purpose, the reservation was never established. By the time of the settlement act, state and federal agencies had whittled down the once-large withdrawal to only two thousand acres.

Eklutna, Inc. filed generally for land at lower elevations which was not already patented to others or validly held by the state or federal governments. Large tracts were unavailable because they belonged to the Alaska Railroad, the military bases, or the federal Eklutna Power Project.

Because of the many uncertainties about land ownership in the area, Eklutna, Inc. overselected (even outside its withdrawal area) to assure that it would receive its whole entitlement.

**Other local corporations**

The three-year deadline for selecting land did not apply to local corporations in the four named cities nor to Native groups certified as eligible to receive the surface estate of land. Land selected by those other local corporations is not subtracted from the 22 million acres earmarked for villages. For these local corporations the deadline was December 18, 1975 and the land was to come from the 2 million acres withdrawn for several specified purposes.

Native corporations in the four named cities — Juneau, Kenai, Kodiak, and Sitka — were entitled to one township (23,040 acres) each. They were to choose from lands withdrawn for that purpose within 50 miles of their cities.

Certified Native groups were to select up to 7,680 acres. The amount of acreage was not to exceed 320 acres per person, and the land selected was to be in the locality of the group's residence. Only two such groups were certified during 1974, Caswell and Montana Creek, both in the Cook Inlet region. Until the selection deadline in 1975, it remained possible for additional groups to be certified.

The seven corporations which chose full title to their former reserves, instead of selecting land and obtaining money benefits, are acquiring 3.7 million acres of land. They will hold not only surface patent, but the subsurface as well. Their lands range in size from 977 acres (Klukwan) to 1,408,000 acres (Arctic Village and Venetie).

**Taxation**

Village corporations pay no property taxes on lands they acquire until 1992, except on those tracts which are developed or leased. After 1992, all land owned is subject to taxation. In the meantime, if land is sold or leased for a profit, the profit is taxable.

These provisions also apply to local corporations formed in the four named cities, to Native groups, and to former reserves.

# Limitations on Selections                    Chapter 32

Villages were not free to select any lands they desired anywhere in the state. There were numerous requirements for selection set out in the act which had the effect of limiting the choices open to villages. In addition to these requirements, villages were limited by a lack of knowledge that would assist them in making choices. And there was yet another kind of limitation: the deadline by which selections were to be completed.

**Village withdrawal areas**

Villages were required to choose their lands from land withdrawn by the act for this purpose. By being withdrawn from the public domain, these lands were made unavailable to the State or others.

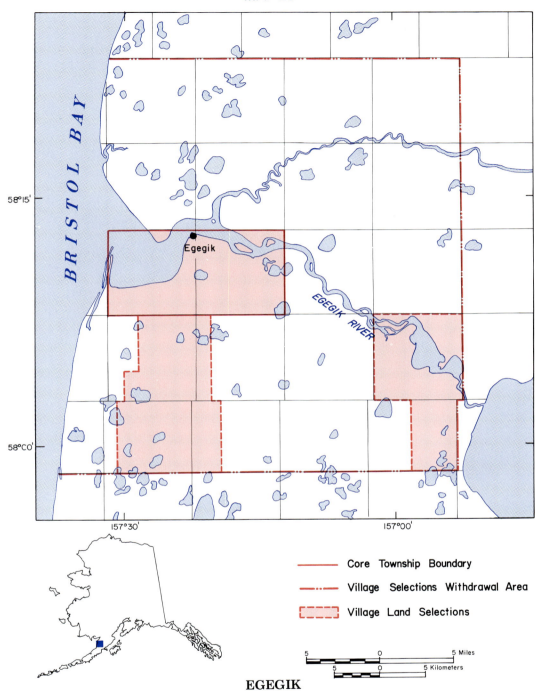

## MAP 26

58°15'

58°00'

BRISTOL BAY

Egegik

EGEGIK RIVER

157°30'    157°00'

——— Core Township Boundary

—·—·— Village Selections Withdrawal Area

▨ Village Land Selections

5    0    5 Miles

5    0    5 Kilometers

## EGEGIK

Egegik is a small fishing community on Bristol Bay. With 166 persons enrolled, its village corporation (the Becharof Corporation) was entitled to select the surface estate of four townships or 92,160 acres.

Subsistence activities were the most important consideration in the Becharof Corporation's selection. While all the nearby lands were used for subsistence, the areas of greatest importance were within the two core townships and the area south of them. These were selected.

Since Egegik and its immediate area were on state-selected lands, the village corporation could select only three townships there. For its remaining entitlement it had to go beyond such lands. There it selected other lands important to subsistence activities.

241

# MAP 27

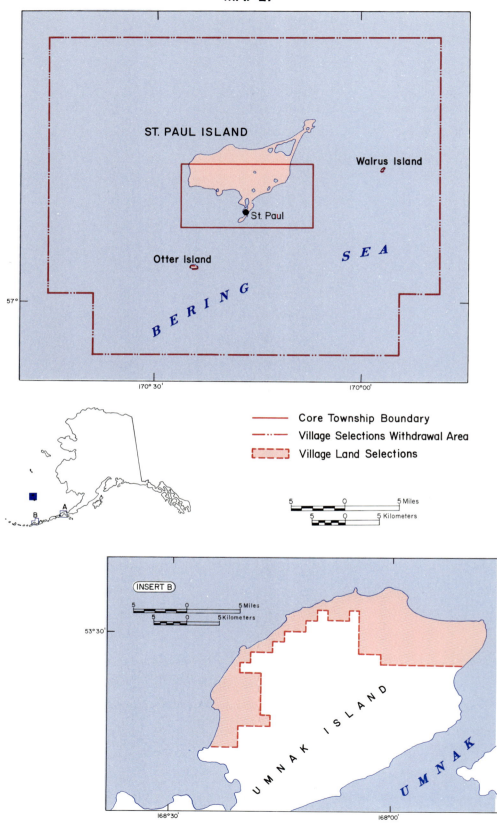

ST. PAUL ISLAND

Walrus Island

St. Paul

Otter Island

BERING SEA

57°

170° 30'          170°00'

──────   Core Township Boundary
─·─·─   Village Selections Withdrawal Area
▨▨▨   Village Land Selections

5  0  5 Miles
5  0  5 Kilometers

INSERT B

5  0  5 Miles
5  0  5 Kilometers

53°30'

UMNAK ISLAND

UMNAK

168°30'          168°00'

242

# ST. PAUL

More than 300 miles of water separates the village of St. Paul from most of the land it selected.

St. Paul, the larger of the two Pribilof Islands, has an enrollment of 549 persons. Its corporation, Tanadgusix Corporation, was entitled to select six townships (138,240 acres).

Tanadgusix Corporation selected all of St. Paul Island, except for the fur seal rookeries which are held by the U. S. Fish and Wildlife Service, and a buffer zone between the rookeries and the corporation's land. For the remainder of its entitlement, the corporation selected lands on Umnak and Unalaska islands and on the Alaska Peninsula from deficiency withdrawals.

Selections were made to assure subsistence and obtain harbor sites. They were coordinated with St. George, Sand Point, and Atka by way of planning for future management of the lands.

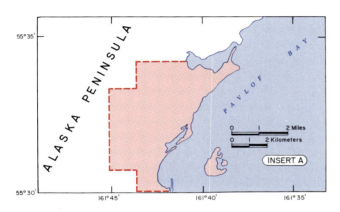

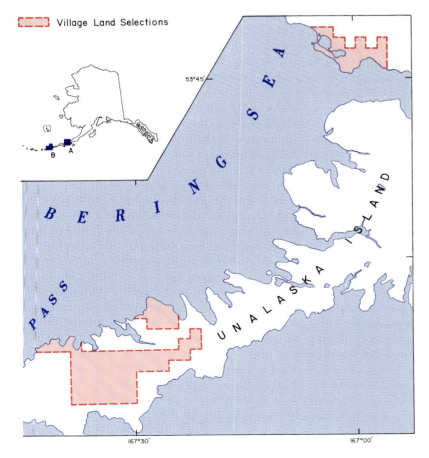

Village Land Selections

Each withdrawal consisted of the core township — an area of six miles by six miles — within which the village was located and additional townships surrounding it to satisfy each village's expected entitlement. Generally, but not always, this amounted to 25 townships.

Withdrawals were also made for village (and regional) selections at some distances from the core townships. These withdrawals were called "deficiency lands" because they were intended to make up for the fact that there was not enough public land adjoining the villages to satisfy their entitlements (St. Paul Selection, Map 27). Deficiency lands withdrawn were to be as close to the villages as possible and of similar character.

No lands patented to the State or owned by private parties were available for selection by villages. Villages could choose, however, as much as three townships in lands selected by the State but not yet patented to it (See Egegik selection, Map 26). Certain federal lands were not available.

**Prior rights**

Even within the areas withdrawn for village selection there were parcels of land which might be unavailable to the villages. These parcels could not be selected because of "prior existing rights."

There are several categories of rights established prior to passage of the settlement act. They include lands patented to others, federal holdings, valid mining claims, and lands under navigable waters.

Title to small parcels of land throughout Alaska had already been conveyed before the settlement act was passed. Under the Homestead Act, the Native Allotment Act, and other land laws, many hundreds of tracts were in individual ownership. About half of the villages had either obtained townsites or had applied for them; none of these lands could be selected, unless (in the case of those not patented), villages withdrew their applications.

Many hundreds of tracts were also held for use by federal agencies — the Coast Guard, the Bureau of Indian Affairs, the Alaska Railroad, and others. Although the act required them to review their holdings and reduce them in size if possible, the holdings they said they required could not be transferred to villages.

Another category of prior rights is that of mining claims. At the time of passage of the act many thousands of such claims existed. Those patented could not be selected. Thousands of other claims were valid under the law and the miner had possession of the surface. Only claims which had been abandoned, in effect, could be selected by the villages.

Another limitation deriving from prior rights was State ownership of tidelands and the beds of inland navigable waters. The problem was the absence of definition of "navigable waters." If the old "highway of commerce" definition prevails, the Yukon and Kuskokwim rivers would

MAP 28   CRAIG AND KLAWOCK '

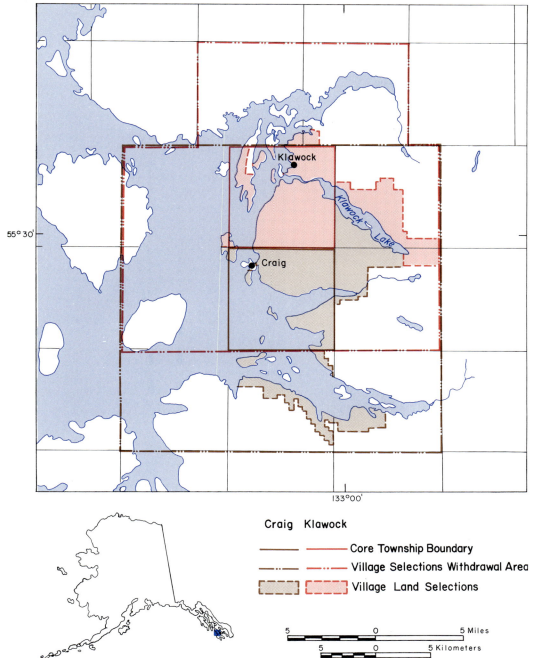

Craig   Klawock

—————— ————— Core Township Boundary
—— ·—· — ·—· ·— Village Selections Withdrawal Area
▨▨▨ ▨▨▨ Village Land Selections

5          0          5 Miles
5          0          5 Kilometers

Two communities a few miles apart on heavily forested Prince of Wales Island faced not only the problem of overlapping withdrawals, but uncertainties about the navigability of a lake as well.

Although both Craig and Klawock are large villages (with enrollments of 317 and 507 respectively), as beneficiaries of the Tlingit-Haida settlement they were entitled to only one township each. Each village corporation chose all of the land not patented within its core township as required.

The shores of Klawock Lake were desired by both village corporations. Their representatives agreed that Shaan-Seet (Craig) would select the north side of the lake and Klawock Heenya (Klawock) the south.

Both corporations overselected on the basis of a Bureau of Land Management ruling that Klawock Lake was not navigable. If that ruling prevails, the 3,000 acres of land beneath the water would be charged against the corporation's entitlements. If that ruling fails, 3,000 acres of timber land purposely overselected would go to the two corporations.

245

## MAP 29 EYAK

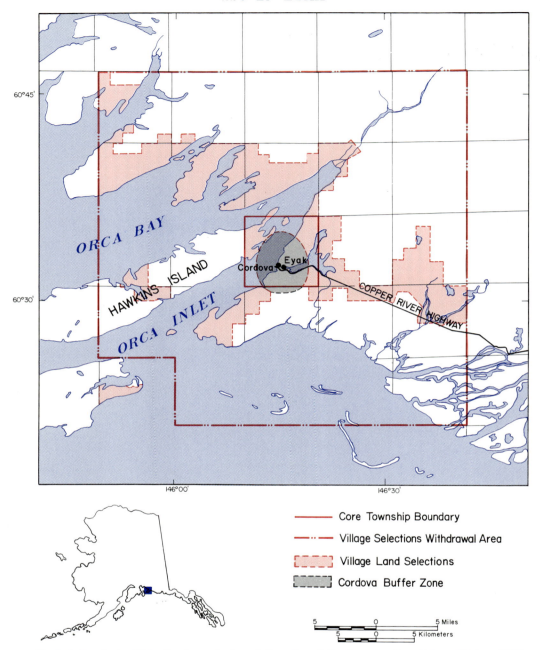

Core Township Boundary
Village Selections Withdrawal Area
Village Land Selections
Cordova Buffer Zone

5        0        5 Miles
5        0        5 Kilometers

Eyak is located within the boundaries of the city of Cordova on Orca Inlet of Prince William Sound. With an enrollment of 353 persons, Eyak Corporation was entitled to select five townships or 115,200 acres.

Since the act provides for a buffer zone between a city of this class and Native lands (to allow growth of the city), Eyak Corporation had to select two miles away from the city's boundaries. Outside this zone, it chose all land available to it within the core township, as it was required to do.

In making its remaining selections within the withdrawal area, the village corporation stressed subsistence, timber, and mineral resources. Generally, it chose lower elevation lands along the water, and avoided glaciers and glacial outwash. Land it chose along the highway was largely selected to obtain desirable timber land further out in the withdrawal area.

Because Eyak is within the Chugach National Forest, it had to choose two of its townships from deficiency lands near Miles Lake, beyond the boundary of the forest.

MAP 30

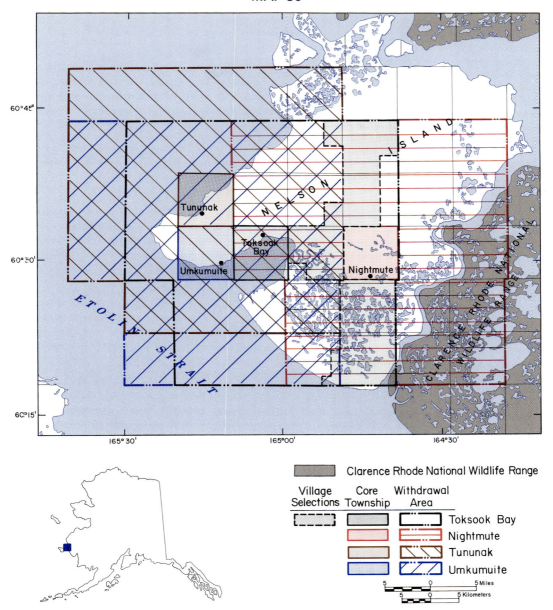

**Clarence Rhode National Wildlife Range**

| Village Selections | Core Township | Withdrawal Area | |
|---|---|---|---|
| | | | Toksook Bay |
| | | | Nightmute |
| | | | Tununak |
| | | | Umkumuite |

5 Miles
5 Kilometers

## TOKSOOK BAY

Toksook Bay is one of four villages on Nelson Island off southwestern Alaska. Its Nunakauiak Yupik Corporation's enrollment of 280 entitled it to 115,200 acres or five townships.

Nunakauiak Yupik Corporation selected its lands on the basis of subsistence values, but there were two limiting factors. One of these was one of overlapping withdrawals made necessary by the close proximity of the villages to one another. Toksook Bay, Tununak, and Umkumuite are in neighboring core townships; Nightmute is only a township away. The overlapping withdrawals required the four village corporations to agree among themselves how to divide their selection rights.

The other factor was the Clarence Rhode National Wildlife Refuge which, with Etolin Strait, surrounds Nelson Island. Since the four villages together were entitled to 16 townships, it was necessary to go outside the immediate withdrawal area. No lands were withdrawn for deficiencies within wildlife refuges. As a result, Toksook Bay chose its remaining entitlement about 50 miles east, beyond the wildlife refuge, on Baird Inlet.

be navigable for they were long used for transportation of goods; but what about thousands of lakes and streams used less extensively for noncommercial purposes by boat or by snowmachine? If the waters within a village's selection are navigable the land beneath is owned by the State; if the waters are nonnavigable, the land beneath is charged against the village's entitlement (Craig-Klawock selection, Map 28). Disagreement over the definition of "navigable waters" was expected to lead to court action.

**Other limitations**

Three other limitations on village choice were requirements that selections be compact, contiguous, and, wherever possible, not fall below a specified minimum size.

Requiring that selections be compact meant that, generally speaking, villages could not choose long, narrow tracts along a stream, for instance. One test of compactness was whether lands similar to the village site were passed over in favor of more distant lands. Requiring that selections be contiguous meant that selections needed to be joined to one another, unless separated by land not available for selection or by a navigable waterway. Scattered parcels of desirable land could not be chosen.

Although entitlements were stated in townships, the only township that had to be chosen was the core — the one in which a village was located (Eyak selection, Map 29). The other requirement regarding size was that lands selected be in whole sections, and wherever feasible, in two-section parcels. A section is one square mile or 640 acres; 36 sections make up a township.

**Special cases**

There was an additional limitation upon villages located in a National Forest, part of the National Wildlife Refuge System, or on lands chosen by the State but not yet patented to it. These villages could select only 69,120 acres (three townships) within such areas. If they were entitled to more land, it had to be selected from deficiency lands (See Toksook Bay selection, Map 30).

**Inadequate knowledge**

While villagers knew better than any other persons what lands were needed for subsistence activities, food gathering was only one of several values important in land selection. They wanted to choose lands that would protect an existing way of life for themselves and their children, but they also wanted to assure that their choices would be best for their children's futures.

To choose wisely, villagers needed the expertise of geologists, foresters, wildlife managers, lawyers, recreation planners, economists, and many other disciplines. Apart from subsistence lands, villagers had many questions to answer. Which lands will increase in value over time? Which lands should be owned to protect other lands? What value do these stands of timber have? Will there be a port or other means to allow the shipment of the timber or other resources?

To varying degrees, village corporations were able to obtain some of the expert advice they needed. Probably none of them had as much knowledge as they wanted. And, even with expert advice, the burden of weighing and deciding still fell to villagers themselves.

As villagers learned the provisions of the settlement act from regional corporations or consultants, they felt the pressures of time. All village corporations had three years in which to learn an extensive vocabulary, to gather an enormous amount of information, and to file for their lands. Furthermore, if lands chosen were to serve the goals of the village, lengthy discussions were needed to define village goals.

**Time**

The time available for training villagers in the process of land selection was very short, given the complexity of the act and the large number of villages eligible to select land. Carrying out resource and economic studies, even with expert assistance, took time. Analyzing the results of studies performed and considering their implications for village lifeways took time. But the deadline was inflexible.

National Park Service (Robert Belous)

*Ice fishing on the Kobuk River near Ambler.*

Owing to the significance of the choices represented in land selection, it was generally held that there was too little time to carry out the task well. One participant expressed concern that limitations of time, in too many instances, prevented adequate definition of village goals as a guide to land selection. Now he worries that the land selections may end up determining those goals.

# Individuals and Some Others                    Chapter 33

Although most of the land that is conveyed to Natives under the settlement act goes to corporations they own, perhaps 10,000 Natives are entitled by the act to become property owners as individuals. There are three ways in which this can take place: (1) by reconveyance by a village; (2) by individual application from those living at isolated locations; and (3) by obtaining an allotment filed for prior to passage of the act.

Natives whose permanent residences are in non-Native communities or outside the state are not entitled to obtain individual tracts of land.

**Reconveyance: individuals**

Most Natives who become individual landowners will receive their land by reconveyance from their village corporations.

Once village corporations receive title (patent or interim conveyance) to lands they have selected, they are, among other things, to reconvey parcels of land to individual occupants of such parcels. Specifically, they are required to give surface title at no cost to Natives and non-Natives who are using such parcels as:

- a primary place of residence;
- a primary place of business;
- a subsistence campsite, or
- a headquarters for reindeer husbandry.

Although there were about 49,000 Natives who considered their place of residence to be one of the 203 village corporations, it is not clear that all of them will receive tracts of village land. The act does not specify a date of occupancy which would entitle a person to an individual parcel. Some eligible corporations (such as Chenega) were formed at sites abandoned in 1964 following the earthquake. Furthermore, there is no definition of "primary" place of residence.

Persons who receive land from their village corporations may immediately sell or lease it. There is no restriction (as there is with stock ownership) against the sale of land. Individually held lands are subject to property taxes if they are developed or leased. If they are not, they are not subject to property taxes until 1992.

Margaret Bauman

*At Bering Straits Corporation stockholders' meeting, Emma Willoya asks the Bureau of Land Management to explain its work on allotments so that stockholders not fluent in English can understand.*

Individuals receiving title do not obtain the subsurface estate. Except for the wildlife refuges and Naval Petroleum Reserve No. 4, the subsurface belongs to the regional corporation. In the case of those exceptions, it is retained by the federal government.

Transfer of title to individuals is but one task of reconveyance imposed on a village corporation. It is also required to convey surface title to nonprofit organizations (such as churches) for tracts they occupy, either without cost to the organization or for what the land was worth when it was first occupied. It must also convey to the municipal, state, or federal governments surface title to lands where airports or air navigation aids are located. And it must convey to its municipal government no less than 1,280 acres of the remaining improved lands in the village; if there is no city government, this acreage is to be conveyed to the State where it would be held in trust.

As with individuals, there are many uncertainties surrounding these additional tasks of reconveyance. There is no deadline established. Which lands need to be conveyed to municipalities is not clear. Lawyers and land planners were urging early in 1975 that a set of uniform standards be developed to guide planning for reconveyance.

**Reconveyance: others**

**Other problem areas**    Some land planners are concerned about the effect of reconveyance upon historic communal uses of land in villages. As Aleut Corporation land director Larry Merculieff, for instance, has written:

> Everyone recognizes that [the settlement act] institutes the new concept of property ownership on a mass scale. In most villages, there is recognition of the right of its citizens to their homes. Use of all other land within the community is recognized as a right of every citizen ... This communal concept of land use within the village setting will be completely eliminated [with reconveyance] because the land within the village will be owned by individuals, not the community as a whole.

Fearing the impact, Merculieff has urged an evaluation of the impact of reconveyance upon cultures and lifestyles before any reconveyance takes place.

Another persisting concern is that village corporations are immediately free to sell the lands they own, after reconveyance, even though stockholders may not sell their stock in the corporation. If the potentially most important asset of the corporation — its land — is sold, the stock could become virtually valueless by the time it could be sold.

*Simon Paneak of Anaktuvuk Pass discussing land use.*

Only a small number of Natives will receive title under the act to tracts of land away from villages. Of 41 applications filed for such tracts by the deadline, 11 had been rejected by the end of 1974.

The act provided — in what was dubbed the "hermit clause" — that a Native whose primary place of residence was away from villages (or cities) could obtain up to 160 acres. He would own the surface estate and the subsurface would be owned by the region.

A Native could not acquire land under the Native Allotment Act and also under the "hermit clause." The problem for thousands of Natives was that delays in the processing of their allotments made them unsure whether to apply for isolated tracts under the act or not.

Nearly 7,500 applications were pending in 1974 for allotments of up to 160 acres filed for under the Native Allotment Act of 1906. The settlement act had revoked this earlier law, but had provided that applications for allotments made before its revocation would be honored.

Unlike lands acquired under the settlement act, Native allotments will be in a trust status. The Native obtaining the land will receive "restricted" title, rather than fee title. He may not sell or lease it without the approval of the Department of the Interior's Bureau of Indian Affairs. As long as it is so held, it may not be taxed. If the title is modified to "unrestricted" (at the allotment holder's request), the land becomes taxable.

The subsurface estate of all Native allotments to be granted will belong to the federal government.

Even though applied for under the 1906 law, lands granted as allotments would be charged to the 40 million-acre settlement. If all applications are approved, more than one million acres will be transferred to individuals as allotments. (While only 400,000 acres are earmarked for allotments, that acreage does not constitute a ceiling.) It is expected that it may be five years or more before all applications are reviewed and allotments approved or disapproved.

# Chapter 34                    Regional Corporations

The 12 regional corporations will obtain title to the subsurface estate of 22 million acres on the basis of village selections. They may obtain the subsurface estate to perhaps another million acres on the basis of the special purpose grant. In addition, six of the corporations are entitled to select 16 million acres to which they will obtain title to both the surface and subsurface estate. No lands at all will go to a 13th regional corporation.

**All 12 corporations: village subsurface**

As title to the surface estate is transferred to village corporations, title to the subsurface of the same lands, generally speaking, goes to the appropriate regional corporations. Taken together, the regional corporations will own the subsurface of 22 million acres.

On the basis of village selections, Calista will obtain the most subsurface estate, and Sealaska, the least. Calista will

FIGURE 18

ALASKA NATIVE LANDS: PROJECTED OWNERSHIP
STATUS OF 43.7 MILLION ACRES*

SURFACE ESTATE

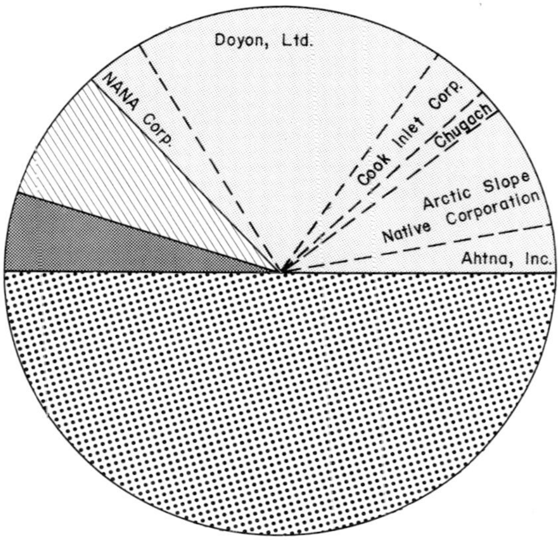

- 22 MILLION ACRES (50.3%) 203 village corporations
- 3.7 MILLION ACRES (8.5%) 7 villages on revoked reserves
- 16 MILLION ACRES (36.6%) six regional corporations
- 2 MILLION ACRES (4.6%) Special purposes**

*Subject to change upon formation of the 13th regional corporation.

**Includes one township to each special named city (Juneau, Sitka, Kodiak and Kenai); allotments; Alaska Native groups; and land designated as cemeteries and historic sites which goes to each of the 12 regional corporations. After these special purposes are met, the remainder will be divided among the 12 corporations.

Source: Land Distribution Chart, "Alaska Native Management Report," March 31, 1975.

have title to more than six million acres, because it has 56 village corporations and an enrollment of almost 13,500. Sealaska will have title to less than 208,000 acres, because its nine villages were limited to a single township each.

Although the total subsurface estate for regions equals village selections, it is not always beneath the specific lands selected by villages. The two exceptions are selections made in wildlife refuges or in Naval Petroleum Reserve No. 4. In those cases, the regional corporations will select an equivalent acreage from other lands designated for that purpose.

The 12 corporations will also obtain the subsurface estate in lands whose surface is acquired (1) by groups, (2) by individuals under the "hermit clause," (3) by local corporations in the four named cities, and (4) by the regions themselves as they select historical places or cemetery sites. Almost 600,000 acres were earmarked for these purposes.

**Subsurface rights**

As noted earlier, the regional corporation's development and removal of minerals from village lands is subject to the consent of the village corporation. This requirement is a departure from traditional property law, in that the owner of minerals, generally speaking, has the right to remove minerals as long as he pays compensation for damages to the surface.

One subject of considerable uncertainty is whether sand and gravel are part of the surface or subsurface estate. Court decisions have held that, depending upon the specific situation, they sometimes are and sometimes they are not.

U. S. Geological Survey (Charles Sloan)

*Looking for subsurface resources: test well on the Sagavanirktok River.*

**All 12: surface**        All 12 corporations will obtain title to some surface estate as well as subsurface. This is provided for as part of the two million-acre special purpose grant. These special purposes, it will be recalled, are as follows:

500,000 acres — Native groups, individual Natives at isolated locations, cemetery sites and historic places;

92,160 acres — One township each for Native corporations at Juneau, Kenai, Kodiak and Sitka;

400,000 acres — Native allotments filed for before passage of the settlement act.

One way all regional corporations will acquire the surface estate to land is in their selection of cemetery sites and places of historical or cultural significance. For this purpose (and for the other two cited above) the 500,000 acres is allocated among the regions, part of it divided equally among the 12 and part of it on the basis of population. The maximum acreages available to regions range from Ahtna's 27,800 acres to Sealaska's 65,000 acres.

The second way in which all regional corporations will acquire surface estate in lands is also through the special purposes grant. The total acreage for the preceding purposes will be subtracted from two million acres, and whatever remains is to be divided among the regions on the basis of their enrollments.

*Point Hope Cemetery.*                    Arctic Environmental Information and Data Center

## FIGURE 19

### VILLAGE LAND ENTITLEMENTS BY REGION
### 22 MILLION ACRES

Surface estate to villages
Subsurface estate to regions

| REGION | VILLAGE SELECTIONS | | SECOND ROUND | TOTAL |
|---|---|---|---|---|
| | Number of villages | Their township entitlements based on their enrollments | Additional townships based upon region's percentage of total enrollment | Entitlement for villages |
| Ahtna, Inc. | 8 | 30 | 2.0 | 32 |
| Aleut Corp. | 12 | 50 | 6.3 | 56.3 |
| Arctic Slope Native Corp. | 8 | 37 | 7.3 | 44.3 |
| Bering Straits Native Corp. | 16 | 76 | 12.9 | 89.9 |
| Bristol Bay Native Corp. | 29 | 118 | 10.0 | 128.3 |
| Calista Corp. | 56 | 245 | 25.1 | 270.1 |
| Chugach Native Corp. | 5 | 20 | 3.9 | 23.9 |
| Cook Inlet Corp. | 6 | 25 | 11.9 | 36.6 |
| Doyon, Ltd. | 34 | 140 | 17.1 | 157.1 |
| Koniag, Inc. | 9 | 40 | 6.3 | 46.3 |
| NANA Corp. | 11 | 52 | 9.2 | 61.2 |
| Sealaska | 9 | 9 | 0 | 9.0 |
| Totals | 203 | 843 | 112.0 | 955.0 |

Source: Land Distribution Chart, "Alaska Native Management Report," March 31, 1975.

Note: Figures subject to change upon formation of the 13th regional corporation.

**Six regional corporations**

The 16 million acres earmarked for selection by regional corporations will go to only half of them. The reason for this is that these regional allocations are to be principally based upon how large a land area was claimed rather than how large a Native population lived within the claimed area.

Provision for regional land selection on the basis of land rights given up had been made at the urging of regional associations (especially the Arctic Slope), which claimed use and occupancy of enormous areas of land but whose populations were small. They had successfully argued that a land claims settlement should not be based simply upon the number of people involved or their subsistence needs, but should be based upon the amount of land claimed by the region. If the provision had not been made a part of the act, some of the largest regions would have received title to the smallest amounts of land.

# MAP 31   CHITINA

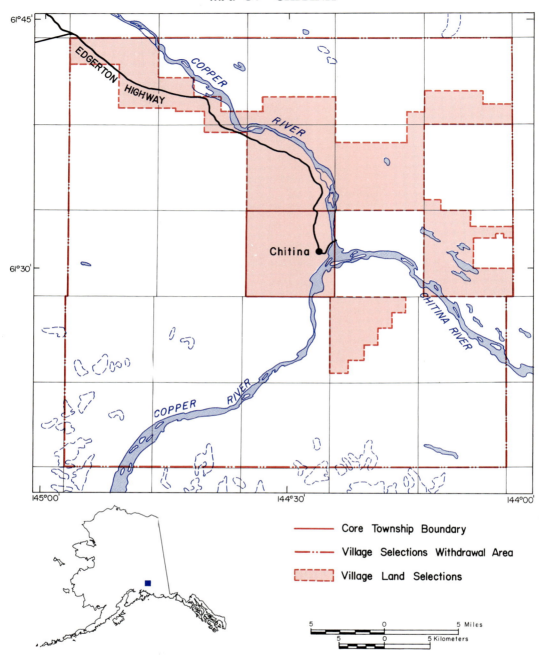

61°45'

EDGERTON HIGHWAY

COPPER    RIVER

Chitina

61°30'

CHITINA RIVER

COPPER    RIVER

145°00'                    144°30'                    144°00'

—————  Core  Township  Boundary

—·—·—  Village  Selections  Withdrawal  Area

▨  Village  Land  Selections

5        0        5 Miles

5        0        5 Kilometers

The village of Chitina is located at the junction of the Copper and Chitina rivers. Its corporation, the Chitina Native Corporation, was entitled to select five townships (115,200 acres) on the basis of its enrollment of 237 persons.

A major interest of the Chitina Native Corporation was in acquiring timber lands and access to the timber. To achieve this, the corporation selected wooded lands at low elevations (except for the core township) and along the Edgerton Highway. Some of the lands selected also are high in recreational values or are prospective agricultural lands.

Townships having the highest mineral potential were left for Chitina's regional corporation, Ahtna, which will own the subsurface estate. The checkerboard pattern of these townships is consistent with the requirement that Ahtna choose alternating townships.

The Chitina Native Corporation overselected because, in part, the whole area is dotted with mining claims, some of which may prove to be valid.

Broadly told, the complex "land loss" provision allocates the 16 million acres to specific regional corporations the difference between what each would have gotten on the basis of its land area as related to the state land area, and what its villages are getting on the basis of their populations. Five corporations with small areas but large populations are thereby excluded from sharing in the "land loss" grant. Sealaska was excluded because of its earlier Court of Claims settlement.

The six corporations entitled to share in the 16 million acres are Arctic Slope, NANA, Doyon, Ahtna, Chugach and Cook Inlet. Their estimated entitlements range from about 336,000 acres for Chugach to about 8.5 million acres for Doyon.

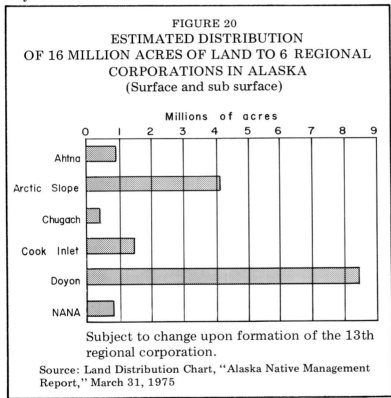

FIGURE 20
ESTIMATED DISTRIBUTION
OF 16 MILLION ACRES OF LAND TO 6 REGIONAL
CORPORATIONS IN ALASKA
(Surface and sub surface)

Subject to change upon formation of the 13th regional corporation.

Source: Land Distribution Chart, "Alaska Native Management Report," March 31, 1975

Selections made by the six corporations are to be made from the village withdrawal areas in a checkerboard pattern of townships. Knowing this, their villages often selected in a similar pattern to allow regional selections in between (Chitina selection, Map 31). If sufficient land is not available in the village withdrawal areas, regional corporations may choose any arrangement of townships in designated deficiency areas.

Regions may not acquire land already patented to others or having other valid claims upon it. An additional limitation is that regions may not select lands which the State is in the process of acquiring.

U. S. Bureau of Land Management

*Maserculiq, Inc. (Marshall/Fortuna Ledge) was the first Calista village corporation filing for land. From left: Leslie Hunter, Marshall; Lew Lively, Calista; Curtis V. McVee, Bureau of Land Management; Robert Schenker, President of Calista; and Ray Christiansen, Chairman of the Board, Calista.*

Both the surface and subsurface of these 16 million acres will be owned by the six corporations. Their selections are to be completed by December 18, 1975. Once they have title, they are free to lease or sell just as any other owner of land is.

As with lands acquired by Native individuals and village corporations, property taxes may not be levied until 1992, except for tracts which are developed or leased. Taxes may be levied before then upon profits from sales or leases of land.

# Corporations as Land Owners                    Chapter 35

As land is conveyed to village and regional corporations, a range of responsibilities falls to the new landowners — the regional and village corporations. The responsibility of land selection had been a heavy one. But, as Richard Atuk, land director for the Bering Straits Regional Corporation, told the 1974 AFN convention, "The biggest job is coming up — land management."

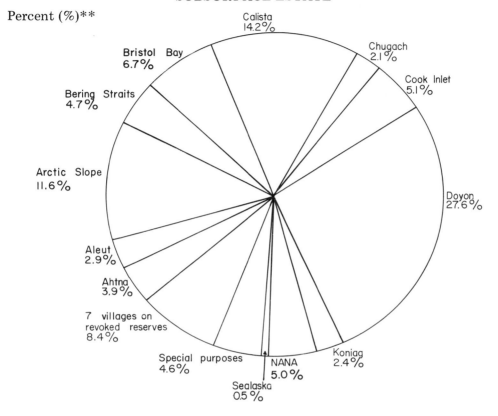

FIGURE 21
ALASKA NATIVE LANDS: PROJECTED OWNERSHIP
STATUS OF 43.7 MILLION ACRES
SUBSURFACE ESTATE

Percent (%)**

Calista 14.2%
Chugach 2.1%
Cook Inlet 5.1%
Bristol Bay 6.7%
Bering Straits 4.7%
Arctic Slope 11.6%
Doyon 27.6%
Aleut 2.9%
Ahtna 3.9%
7 villages on revoked reserves 8.4%
Special purposes 4.6%
NANA 5.0%
Sealaska 0.5%
Koniag 2.4%

*Subject to change upon formation of the 13th regional corporation.

**Based upon "Land Distribution" chart, "Alaska Native Management Report," March 31, 1975.

Twelve regional corporations will hold title to the subsurface estate of each special city, Alaska Native groups, cemeteries and historic sites. Title to the subsurface estate of allotments will be held by the federal government.

One responsibility of a village corporation once it obtains its land has already been described: it must reconvey tracts of land to individuals, organizations, and government. Village corporations also have other responsibilities which are a follow-on to their land selection activities — recording title to land, determining the value of lands for accounting purposes, planning for the second round of land selection, and other activities. Further, all Native corporations are required to pay property taxes (where property taxes exist) on lands which are developed.

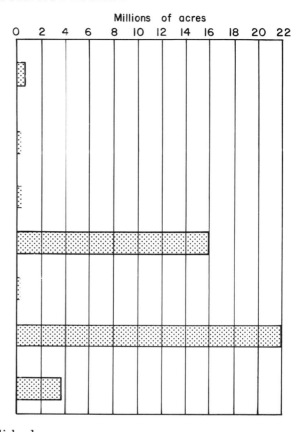

FIGURE 22
PROJECTED OWNERSHIP OF PRIVATE LANDS IN ALASKA*
SURFACE ESTATE

Millions of acres

Existing private lands patented before settlement act; Annette Island Reservation

Native groups* and Native corporations in four named cities

Native allotment holders*

Six Native regional corporations **

Six other Native regional corporations**

203 Native village corporations

Seven Native village corporations on five revoked reserves

*Total acreage not established.

**Acreage subject to change upon formation of the 13th regional corporation.

These and other land management activities are required by the settlement act or by general law. But land management goes much beyond meeting legal requirements; it is concerned with what is done with land at what locations and under what controls. While this book is not the place to treat the complex issues of land management, it is possible to suggest some of the issues involved.

Apart from requirements imposed by law, the task of land management is to direct or control events to achieve the goals of a corporation regarding its land. If a corporation wants to sell its lands, for instance, the land manager will try to do so; if it wants to keep its lands, he will plan for their retention. The choices are, of course, far more numerous than these two.

Although Native corporations are free to sell part or all of their lands, none were declaring the sale of land to be a goal by 1975. Instead, corporations were emphasizing the desirability of retaining their lands. If the land is to be retained, issues will arise over the uses of the land.

Possible uses may be seen by looking at a few goals of one corporation affecting land. These are from the Calista annual report for 1974:

- Establish within Calista Corporation land department a permanent Renewable Resource Division to continuously research and develop means and ways to protect to the maximum the subsistence lifestyle of Calista people.

- Investigate recreational development in prime geographic areas of the region.

- Establish long-range planning for development of subsurface resources of the Calista Region bearing in mind constantly that the first priority of consideration is to maintain the natural state of the land.

- To provide full support for revitalization of the reindeer industry in our region.

Pursuit of goals like these involves not only land issues, but questions of costs and calculations of profits discussed earlier.

One kind of use of Native lands that did not require any policy action by a corporation was food-gathering by Natives for subsistence. But, as will be shown, even this use requires a land management approach.

---

### NOTICE

"We are once again reminding all persons (excluding persons who are enrolled in the Bethel Native Corporation) that no fish camps or buildings of any sort may be built on any land claimed by Bethel Native Corporation, unless said person or persons first get Native people permission. This includes cutting of brush, alder, or cottonwood for purpose of smoking of fish or otherwise. Any person wishing to build as above mentioned will have to appear before the Bethel Native Corporation Board of Directors where written permission may be obtained. Edward Hoffman, Sr., President and Lucy Crow, Secretary."

Source: Legal notice from the *Tundra Drums*, June 7, 1975.

---

Fishing, hunting, harvesting plants and berries, and other gathering activities are heavily relied upon by most rural Natives for their subsistence. Living off the land is not only traditional, but — owing to the scarcity of cash income — it is required.

But preservation of subsistence opportunities may be threatened by other uses of Native lands. Any large-scale development tends to cause a migration of birds and animals away from the development. Further, public use lands neighboring Native lands may become unavailable for subsistence hunting and fishing.

Development of lands is a second kind of use which corporations are considering. Such development might mean the sale of timber for lumber and construction of a mill. It might mean drilling for oil, finding it, and building a pipeline to take it out. Or it might mean building a hotel or wilderness camps to encourage tourism.

As these illustrations suggest, any proposed use of land has implications for other possible uses. If tourists are encouraged to come to an area to fish and hunt, there will be less fish and game for local people. If coal or oil is sold by a regional corporation, it is likely to mean substantial disruption of the surface.

Although corporations have much freedom in deciding what to do with their lands, there are limitations. First, all village corporations need to submit their plans to their regional corporations for review. Second, federal or State laws may limit uses indirectly, as they do with requirements

*Caribou crossing river on the Arctic Slope.*

Thayer

264

Arctic Environmental Information and Data Center

*Laurie Kingik, Point Hope, speaking to North Slope elders, 1974.*

that stream water quality be preserved. Third, lands of corporations which are in boroughs or in cities with zoning powers are subject to governmental controls over use. Such powers of zoning give the local government the authority to designate some areas for industrial use, for instance, and other areas for residential use.

Finally, Native corporations need to concern themselves with the uses of neighboring lands, and their neighbors need to care about uses planned by corporations. Cooperative agreements regarding land use may be employed to benefit

Ahtna, Inc. (Frank Flavin)

*Tazlina village corporation president, Robert Marshall, accepts title to 150 acres from Daryll Fish of the Bureau of Land Management. At left is Robert M. Goldberg, attorney for Ahtna, Inc.*

neighboring landowners. Because most land uses have impact beyond single owner property lines, it was expected in 1975 that State control over land use might be substantially expanded.

In 1964 Alaska's Congressman had doubted the necessity of conveying land as part of a settlement, saying, "It would just lie there." What was clear in 1975 was that even letting the land "just lie there" would require land management.

# The Public                                    Chapter 36

U. S. National Park Service (John Kauffman)

*Arrigetch Peaks of the Brooks Range are within the proposed Gates of the Arctic National Park.*

Although the title of the settlement act makes plain that its subject is land for Natives, it also provides for land or rights to land to a much larger group of people — the public.

First, the act provides for selection of national interest lands and classification of others on behalf of the public. Second, it provides a means — easements — for assuring rights of limited access for the public across Native lands. Third, it requires village corporations to convey some of their land to municipalities for growth and expansion.

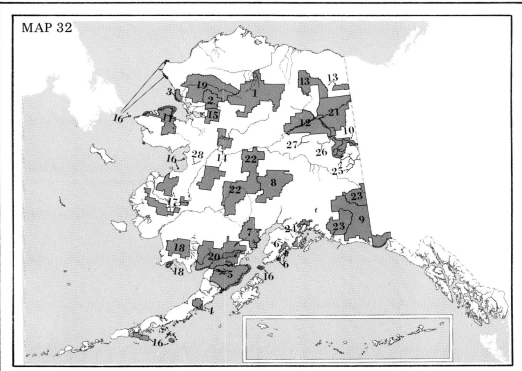

MAP 32

## INTERIOR DEPARTMENT RECOMMENDATIONS FOR ADDITIONS TO NATIONAL INTEREST LANDS

| | PROPOSAL NAME | MILLIONS OF ACRES |
|---|---|---|
| 1 | Gates of the Arctic National Park | 8.36 |
| 2 | Kobuk Valley National Monument | 1.85 |
| 3 | Cape Krusenstern National Monument | 0.35 |
| 4 | Aniakchak Caldera National Monument | 0.44 |
| 5 | Katmai National Park | 1.87 |
| 6 | Harding Icefield-Kenai Fjords National Monument | 0.30 |
| 7 | Lake Clark National Park | 2.61 |
| 8 | Mt. McKinley National Park Additions | 3.18 |
| 9 | Wrangell-St. Elias National Park | 8.64 |
| 10 | Yukon-Charley National Rivers | 1.97 |
| 11 | Chukchi Imuruk National Reserve | 2.69 |
| 12 | Yukon Flats National Wildlife Refuge | 3.59 |
| 13 | Arctic National Wildlife Refuge Additions | 3.76 |
| 14 | Koyukuk National Wildlife Refuge | 4.43 |
| 15 | Selawik National Wildlife Refuge | 1.40 |
| 16 | Coastal National Wildlife Refuge | 0.07 |
| 17 | Yukon Delta National Wildlife Refuge | 5.16 |
| 18 | Togiak National Wildlife Refuge | 2.74 |
| 19 | Noatak National Arctic Range | 7.59 |
| 20 | Iliamna National Resource Range | 2.85 |
| 21 | Porcupine National Forest | 5.50 |
| 22 | Yukon-Kuskokwim National Forest | 7.30 |
| 23 | Wrangell Mountains National Forest | 5.50 |
| 24 | Chugach National Forest Additions | 0.50 |
| 25 | Fortymile National Wild and Scenic River | 0.32 |
| 26 | Birch Creek National Wild River | 0.20 |
| 27 | Beaver Creek National Wild River | 0.20 |
| 28 | Unalakleet National Wild River | 0.10 |
| | Total | 83.47 |

National
interest lands

About 83 million acres has been withdrawn by the Department of the Interior for possible designation as National Parks, Forests, Wildlife Refuges, and Wild and Scenic Rivers. The Congress, which received the recommendations of Interior in December, 1973, must act upon them before December, 1978.

Because the withdrawals were made under Section 17(d)(2) of the settlement act, they are usually referred as the "(d)(2) lands."

The recommendations consist of 28 separate proposals ranging in size from 70,000 acres to over eight million acres. Among other things, they include proposals for three new National Forests, three National Parks, six Wildlife Refuges, four National Monuments, and additions to existing systems.

Management policies for different parts of these national systems vary, but they do place restrictions upon the activities which may be carried out within. For instance, mining and hunting are not generally permitted in National Parks.

In part because of such restrictions, the State of Alaska and private development interests complained that too much land would be removed from possible development by the national interest withdrawals. Of greater concern to village Alaskans, however, was the possible impact of the establishment of the national systems upon subsistence.

Subsistence

Concern over subsistence is greatest with regard to the nearly 63 million acres proposed as additions to the National Park and Wildlife Refuge systems. These proposals provide for continuation of subsistence activities, but also for their possible curtailment. They say, in part:

> ... existing traditional subsistence uses of renewable resources will be permitted until it is demonstrated by the Secretary [of the Interior] that utilization of these resources is neither economically or physically necessary to maintain human life nor necessary to provide opportunities for the survival of Alaskan cultures centering on subsistence as a way of life.

The conditions which might bring an end to food-gathering activities raise as many questions for Natives as they answer. At what point, for instance, are the lands' resources no longer "economically or physically necessary to maintain human life"?

Further, the proposals allow the restriction of subsistence uses if they threaten "a progressive reduction of animal or plant resources which could lead to long-range alterations of ecosystems." This was likewise a worrisome provision to Natives who continue to rely upon the land for subsistence.

In 1971 when the settlement act was passed about 48 million acres were devoted to National Parks, Forests, and Wildlife Refuges. Approval of the pending recommendations

## IMPORTANCE OF SUBSISTENCE: THREE COMMUNITIES

In 1972 representatives of the Northwest Alaska Native Association surveyed households in Kotzebue, Kivalina, and Noatak regarding their harvest of resources for subsistence. The numbers are annual averages. Although the survey collected data on the specific food or furbearer resources village-by-village, they are summarized here.

| Resources Harvested | Kivalina, Kotzebue, and Noatak |
|---|---|
| Caribou | 6,727 |
| Muskrat | 1,459 |
| Other animals | 664 |
| Bowhead whale (lbs.) | 2,144 |
| Hair seal (ringed and harbor) | 600 |
| Other sea mammals | 476 |
| Salmon | 54,444 |
| Sheefish | 138,300 |
| Trout | 179,150 |
| Whitefish | 22,167 |
| Tomcod and other fish | 15,072 |
| Ducks and ptarmigan | 3,573 |
| Other birds | 380 |
| Harvest eggs | 3,000 |
| Berries (lbs.) | 20,211 |
| Sourdock | 1,985 |
| Eskimo potato, spinach, other plants | 1,594 |

would raise the total land area set aside to about 130 million acres, more than one-third of the state's total land area of about 374 million acres.

Another withdrawal made in the name of the public interest consists of the 60 million acres set aside for study and classification. These lands, dubbed "(d)(1)" on the basis of their location in Section 17 of the settlement act, are made up of all lands in Alaska not withdrawn for other purposes or transferred to others. The effect of the "(d)(1)" withdrawal was expected to be protection of the public interest by preventing entrance by homesteaders or others until the lands were classified for specific uses.

A second way in which the settlement act provides for land rights for the public is through its requirement that easements be reserved on Native lands. Such easements would allow limited public uses of specific parts of lands conveyed to Natives.

Under the act easements were to be identified (1) across lands selected by Native corporations, and (2) at periodic

Easements

points along the courses of major waterways. They would have to be "reasonably necessary" to guarantee, among other things, a full right of public use and access for recreation, hunting, transportation, utilities, and docks.

As the Federal-State Land Use Planning Commission (established by the act) began its task of recommending standards for the identification of easements, it became clear that there was much room for disagreement. How wide should such easements be? What are "major waterways"? How many easements are "reasonably necessary"?

When, in early 1975, the Bureau of Land Management issued its preliminary system for transportation and utility corridors — a form of easements — Natives were shocked. For corridors alone the federal agency was proposing more than 11,000 miles of easements, many crossing Native lands. At hearings called on the subject, Roger Lang, then president of AFN, charged that the burden of proving the necessity of easements was on those proposing them. Natives should not have to prove, he said, that they were unnecessary. He pointedly asserted that:

> Congress clearly did not intend in the Act to grant Natives a right to select lands from the public domain and then permit federal agencies to take the land back by calling their uses 'easements.'

U. S. Fish and Wildlife Service

*Seabird nesting area near Deering.*

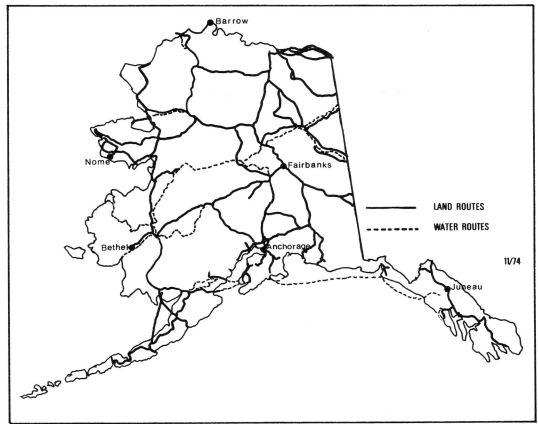

LAND ROUTES

WATER ROUTES

11/74

MAP 33   BUREAU OF LAND MANAGEMENT PROPOSED CORRIDOR SYSTEM

Since conveyance of land to Natives requires identification of easements by an Easement Task Force within the Bureau of Land Management, land would not be conveyed until a number of questions were settled. They were very much unsettled as 1974 drew to a close.

**Municipalities**

The third way in which land is to be transferred to the public is the requirement that each village corporation convey title to 1,280 acres of its land to its municipality for growth and expansion.

Unlike the village corporation which is organized for profit for its stockholders, municipal corporations exist to perform governmental services for all who live within its boundaries. These local governments may adopt rules governing conduct of their citizens, operate schools, provide police and fire protection, and carry out a host of other activities.

Only those who are stockholders are expected to benefit from village corporation activities, and it is only they who chose the board of directors. Until 1992, only Natives have such power in their corporations. City councilmen who guide municipal governments, on the other hand, are chosen by Natives and non-Natives alike who reside in the community.

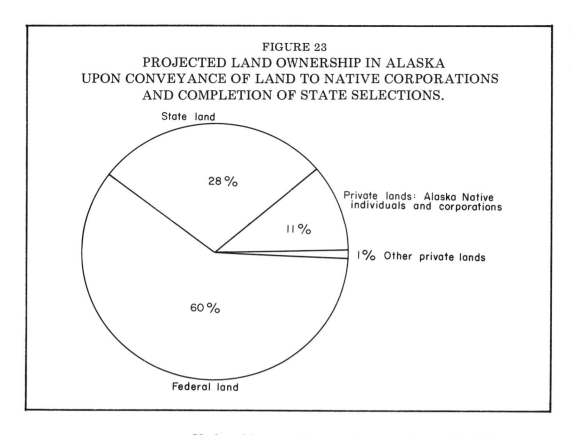

FIGURE 23

PROJECTED LAND OWNERSHIP IN ALASKA
UPON CONVEYANCE OF LAND TO NATIVE CORPORATIONS
AND COMPLETION OF STATE SELECTIONS.

State land

28 %

Private lands: Alaska Native
individuals and corporations

11 %

1 % Other private lands

60 %

Federal land

Under this provision of the act about 260,000 acres of Native land is to be transferred to the ownership of municipalities. If city governments do not exist, the acreage is to be transferred to the State to hold until such time as they are established.

**State land selections**  While the settlement act did not provide for lands to go to the State, its passage allowed the State to resume the selection of land which had been halted by the land freeze.

Before the freeze had been imposed, the State had acquired or was in the process of acquiring patent to 26 million acres. This was about one-fourth the land acreage assured Alaska by the Statehood Act. By the end of 1974, State lands selected, tentatively approved, or patented totaled over 66 million acres.

Future selections of land by the State will be made from lands not chosen by Native corporations, from lands withdrawn to serve national interests ("d-2"), but not established by Congress as conservation areas, and from lands which have been withdrawn for classification ("d-1"). If the State selects all land to which it is entitled it will hold over 103 million acres.

# UNIT NINE

Arctic Slope Regional Corporation

# SHAPING THE FUTURE

*"Many of the people I know don't understand [the act] and are fearful that actions will be taken to make money instead of doing what is right and just."*

—Bella Hammond
*Native News, May/June, 1975*

*Willie Hensley, president of NANA Environmental Systems, Inc., a subsidiary of NANA Regional Corporation.*

In adopting the settlement act the Congress rejected reservations and other institutions or requirements that would suggest that Natives were wards. Under this settlement, there would be no government direction or supervision of the uses of land and money. What the settlement would mean in the lives of Alaska Natives would depend upon the meaning given it by Natives themselves.

When the Senate committee had reported its settlement bill in 1970, it had identified the controls over land and money to be one of the principal departures from earlier Indian settlements. Although a modified bill became law, this feature was retained: the assets transferred to Natives would be managed and disposed of by them, either as individuals or through their corporations.

Natives had sought self-determination and, in the act, had largely won it. Through their corporations, Natives would decide what their goals would be and how they would be achieved. Self-determination was accompanied, however, by what some observers saw as the threat of termination — the ending of the historic relationship between Natives and the federal government.

The burden of the leadership of corporations is one of giving meaning to the settlement act. And in that task of shaping the future, a share is borne by all stockholders.

# Chapter 37 Self-determination

During Congressional debate on the proposed claims settlement in December of 1971, Representative Nick Begich pointed out that its provisions emphasize Native self-determination. He forecast that the act would permit "the social, economic, and cultural choices of Alaska's Natives to be made as independently . . . as possible."

---

### CHANGES SO FAR?

"The land claims act has done older people no good at all and [it] hasn't inspired young people . . ."

—Carl Smith, Haines

"People are more vocal now. People are standing up and saying, 'I want a better life.' People are not going to take the poor health, not being employed. They want a right to live. People are moving back. At least for Rampart [the act], has generated an interest in the village, in going back to revitalize the town and there is a lot more interest in NOT moving to the cities."

—Clara Carroll, Fairbanks

"There will be mistakes, you can be sure of that. But, in a sense, that's all right. The traditional filters and traditional buffers protecting the Native people are no longer there. The possibility of making mistakes presents a real and continuing danger, but it also presents an opportunity to realistically learn the management of our own affairs."

Dennis Demmert of Klawock
Assistant Professor, University of Alaska

In the Senate on the same day, Senator Mike Gravel expressed a similar view. Noting the economic resources that would go to Natives under the act, he said:

> This will not insure dramatic improvements in their way of life, but it will give the Native people an opportunity to build and create on their own, with their own leadership, in their own way, for the first time not dictated to by a non-Native bureaucracy thousands of miles away.

The theme was not new. Nearly four years earlier, Emil Notti, the president of the Alaska Federation of Natives had told a Senate Committee that, "Control by federal agencies over the resources and lives of Native people in Alaska has not met with any success." Notti had cited failures of canneries where managers had been chosen by the Bureau of Indian Affairs and said:

> I point these things out because there is a strong feeling among the Native people in Alaska that they want to have control of their own destiny. And if there are going to be mistakes made, we want to make them, not let the bad decisions be made in Juneau, or even farther away, in Washington, D. C. I stand here before you to state in the strongest terms possible that the representatives here today . . . do not want paternal guidance from Washington, D. C.

**Extent**     The principle of Native self-determination — freedom from governmental control over decision-making — is a basic principle of the settlement act. Although there are some limits upon self-determination, they are fewer or of slighter consequence than in other settlements with Indian groups.

The vehicle of settlement itself — the corporation — is meant to be means of assuring self-determination by Natives. They choose their leaders — the directors — to make corporate decisions. Periodic elections are meant to allow them to reject those they believe to have served them poorly, and to replace them with others.

Fee simple title to land is being conveyed to corporations and individuals. It is not "restricted title" nor "trust land" which would require Natives to obtain approval from the Bureau of Indian Affairs for its sale or lease. Native owners of these lands, like any other owners of land, may decide independently whether to sell or lease.

Native corporations are likewise free to decide how to use the money received as a result of the settlement act. They do not have to submit a plan to the Secretary of the Interior for the use of funds before they obtain them, as did the Tlingit-Haida for compensation they were awarded by the court. Neither are the corporations required to obtain governmental consent before they spend or invest their money.

Although there is no federal guardianship over the exercise of self-determination on land and money matters by Native corporations, it should be recalled that regional corporations have a guardian-like role with respect to village corporations. A regional corporation may withhold funds from a village corporation until it submits a satisfactory plan. A regional corporation may require village corporations to undertake projects of benefit to the region. The regional corporation also has the right to review land transactions proposed by village corporations. Furthermore, the regional corporation must approve any changes in the articles of incorporation of a village corporation for a 10-year period.

## LANG REPORTS CHANGES

" 'An Alaskan native will someday be the president of the state Chamber of Commerce.' That prediction came yesterday from Roger Lang, Alaska Federation of Natives President, in his address here on the future of the people who are to be the state's largest landowners.

" 'Natives will and are now being thought of differently than five and even three years ago,' he said to the Anchorage Republican luncheon group. 'Alaskan natives are coming into their own as a viable economic power.'

"To back his predictions, Lang said recent native development has been snowballing.

" 'Some 200 profit-making native corporate entities have come into being since the signing of the Alaska Native Claims Settlement Act in 1971,' he said. Two hundred and sixty-eight million dollars in contract work on projects around Alaska is now being handled by natives.

"Hotels 'as good as any in Fairbanks and Anchorage,' are being completed in such places as Kotzebue and Barrow, he said. Projects from new apartments in Bethel, to a timber management group to supervise southeastern wood resources are among additional ventures he said are changing the Alaska natives' position in the state's economic and social circles.

" 'Most important,' said Lang, 'is not these things, but the reinstitution in the pride of being an Alaska native!' "

Source: *Anchorage Daily Times*, April 25, 1975.

One of the major limits to self-determination in the settlement act is upon individuals. Natives may not sell or otherwise dispose of their shares in a Native corporation for 20 years after passage of the act. During that time the prohibition is thoroughgoing; the stock may not be alienated. After December 18, 1991, however, a stockholder is free to do as he likes with his stock. He needs no permission of any kind from government.

Kord Roosen-Runge

*The Chenega Corporation is planning resettlement of Chenega on Prince William Sound. Only the school survived the 1964 earthquake's sea waves.*

A second specific limitation in the act relates to the basic control system of the corporations. The original articles of incorporation and bylaws of regional corporations required the approval of the Secretary of the Interior. During the first five years any change to the articles likewise requires his approval. He could deny approval if he believed proposed changes would be unfair to individuals or groups of Natives.

As noted earlier, the act and regulations issued to implement it are also limitations to self-determination. Two illustrations may suffice. The settlement act stood in the way of a merger between NANA Regional Corporation and its village corporations, so amendment of the act by the Congress had to be sought. Second, the regulations issued for land selection would have denied land to a number of villages, so Native leaders pressed for (and won) a number of revisions. Even the revised regulations put limitations upon the lands which villages could choose.

It was regulations issued which led to a reiteration of a belief in self-determination by Sam Kito, the executive vice-president of Doyon, Ltd. in 1973. Kito told a Congressional committee:

> The Native people of Alaska have long been victims of an archaic bureaucratic philosophy that they are unable to regulate their own affairs. Yet the Government who 'sees all, knows all' and 'knows what is best for its Indian people' has been the progenitor of a trustee system of stewardship over American Native peoples, which has succeeded only in robbing them of their heritage, divorcing them from their culture, made them outcasts in their own land, and left them naught but apathy, alcohol, and forgotten graves.

The act had included the Congressional finding that the settlement should be accomplished "with maximum participation by Natives in decisions affecting their rights and property." Through the first few years after the act's adoption Natives made every effort to realize that intention.

Margaret Bauman

*NANA president, John Schaeffer, Jr., meeting with directors of village corporations.*

**Termination**

Some observers have argued that the meaning of the settlement act that should be emphasized is not "self-determination" but "termination." They admit that the act frees Natives from government controls, but warn that the act will bring to an end the special relationship between Natives and the federal government.

One Eskimo who holds this view is Fred Bigjim. With a fellow student at Harvard University, James Ito-Adler, he wrote a series of letters to the *Tundra Times* in 1973, printed later as a book, *Letters to Howard*. Based upon the act's provision for a study of federal programs for Natives, they forecast that these programs would be phased out "now that Natives are such wealthy citizens." They say, further:

> We will be told that if we want these health, education, and welfare services, we should provide them ourselves. That is supposed to be self-determination.
>
> The irony of this whole thing, Howard, is that in the past we were able to provide for ourselves. But our land has been taken, the fish and game destroyed, our children stolen from us, and our culture put on display for the tourists and museums. An ACT will not bring true self-determination, it is really one more step in the plan for termination of the Native way of life in Alaska.

The study which had been required by the act, *2(c) Report: Federal Programs and Alaska Natives*, was completed in December, 1974. Although the Secretary of the Interior was required to make recommendations for "future management and operation" of the programs by that deadline, he did not do so.

Apart from federal services, there is a second aspect to the relationship between Natives and the federal government that may be threatened by the act. This is the federal trust responsibility of the United States to American Indians. It was defined in 1831 by Chief Justice Marshall as the responsibility of a guardian to its ward. In more recent years it has been described as the "fiduciary" responsibility of the United States — the obligation of the government to advance the interests of Indians with great care and skill.

The exercise of this trust responsibility exists because the lands and resources of Indian tribes and communities are typically held "in trust" for them by the Department of the Interior. Except for Native allotments and restricted deed townsite lots, however, Alaska Natives will own their lands in fee simple.

Until the Department of the Interior discharges its responsibilities under the settlement act, its fiduciary responsibility appears to persist. However, in *Law and the American Indian*, law professor Monroe E. Price raised a number of questions once those responsibilities are met. If a village corporation begins to sell its assets at less than fair value, does the Secretary of the Interior have the power or duty to act? Since a stockholder's shares are restricted, can the Secretary bring a court action on behalf of a stockholder against his corporation? These questions and many others like them have yet to be answered. As Price concluded, "No one knows what continues to be the relationship between the Alaska Native and the United States after the implementation of the Alaska Native Claims Settlement Act."

# Chapter 38                    Goals of Corporations

Self-determination in the settlement act meant that Native corporations would set their own goals for the uses of their lands and money. But at least one goal was set for them by the act: making profits for their stockholders. As business corporations, this was to be their fundamental obligation.

# GOALS AND OBJECTIVES
## Calista Corporation, 1974

- Pursue every available employment opportunity for Calista shareholders.
- Establish a Calista Cultural and Educational Foundation.
- Establish within Calista Corporation land department a permanent Renewable Resource Division to continuously research and develop means and ways to protect to the maximum the subsistence lifestyle of Calista people.
- Establish long-range planning for development of subsurface resources of the Calista Region bearing in mind constantly that the first priority of consideration is to maintain the natural state of the land.
- Acquire land in Bethel in order to construct a Calista headquarters and possible commercial center.
- Assist the establishment of a tax-free Fund in conjunction with other native regional corporations to provide shareholders of the participating corporations with pension, medical and educational benefits.
- To assist in the establishment of an Alaska Native Development Corporation with the other native regional corporations to provide a broad base in land and money assets for economic development, throughout the lands owned by the participating regional corporations.
- To pursue the investigation of an integrated fishing study in the Calista Region which could involve Calista shareholders in all phases of this industry inclusive of preservation to insure perpetuity of the migrating fish, the catching of fish, and the processing of fish in such a way so that such processing provides maximum economic yield to the people.
- The investigation of a bottom fisheries industry in the Bering Sea.
- The consideration of hatchery programs in areas of the region where there is an apparent need to build back up salmon stocks.
- To provide full support for revitalization of the reindeer industry in our region.
- To undertake research for alternate port facilities for our region.
- To provide active support of the proposed canal to interconnect the Kuskokwim and Yukon rivers to bring about better transportation for our Region.
- To constantly support in every legal fashion any effort designed to stop foreign national high seas fishing of our Region's salmon stocks.
- To assist any program designed to rehabilitate and revitalize dock and shipping facilities at Bethel.
- Pursue the establishment of a commodity warehouse in our Region to bring needed products closer to the outlying areas and provide this type of service at a cost savings to the area regional retailers.
- Investigate recreational development in prime geographic areas of the Region.
- Support the establishment of a federally chartered credit union for Calista shareholders.
- Join and support the United Bank of Alaska in conjunction with other regional corporations to bring about an Alaskan Native-owned bank.
- Pursue the business feasibility of marketing berry preserves harvested from the Calista Region.
- Pursue the business feasibility of establishing a soft drink bottling plant in the Bethel area.
- Support the establishment of additional bulk petroleum distribution points within the Region.
- Maintain positive support of regional development through a corporate policy to foster joint ventures with village corporations in feasible endeavors.

Source: Calista Corporation, Annual Report 1974.

Statements of this goal take a variety of forms. In the 1973 annual report of the Arctic Slope Regional Corporation, Treasurer Oliver Leavitt told stockholders:

**Making profits**

> Like other business corporations, the Arctic Slope Regional Corporation has as its principal objective the enhancement of the value of its stock — and thus a corresponding increase in the underlying value of your personal estate.

In Sealaska Region's quarterly report to stockholders in late 1974, President and Chairman of the Board John Borbridge, Jr., wrote:

> Under the watchful eyes of your Board of Directors, Sealaska Corporation will continue to shape and refine its corporate objectives and goals to the end purpose that your assets are employed to their maximum earning potential.

In the 1974 report of Koniag, Inc., President Jack Wick advised stockholders:

> Our aim is to make Koniag, Inc. self-sustaining; so it is profitable in its own right and is not dependent on additional money from the Alaska Native Claims Settlement Act . . .

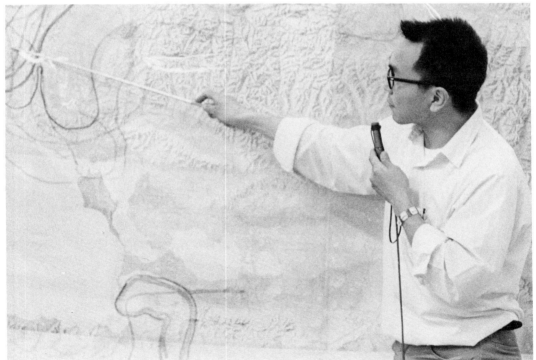

Federal-State Land Use Planning Commission

*NANA Land Director Willie Goodwin points to areas important to subsistence use of land.*

And President Ralph A. Johnson told Cook Inlet Region, Inc. stockholders in the corporation's 1973 report:

> Within twenty years as a result of careful planning of corporate goals, astute investment and revenue sharing, and a caring interest of its people, every Native shareholder should be financially independent.

**Preserving land base**

Profits are important not only so that dividends may be paid to stockholders. Without profits, an accompanying goal of corporations is threatened. This is the goal of preserving each corporation's land base.

Developed land, it will be recalled, is immediately subject to taxation where property taxes exist. But even undeveloped land will be subject to taxation in 1992. Since nearly 44 million acres will be owned by Native corporations, even a modest property tax, if imposed, would be a costly burden. Ability of a corporation to pay such a tax would depend upon its financial successes.

**Other goals**

Even though the goal of making profits is fundamental, the corporations have made clear to their stockholders that other values are important and other goals must also be pursued. An early expression of other values was made in 1972 soon after Doyon, Ltd. was organized and John Sackett was made its president. Speaking to the Tanana Chiefs, Sackett explained that Doyon had a burden that most of the world's profit-making corporations did not have:

> They do not have to worry about whether their stockholders have good educational and transportation facilities, they do not have to worry about obtaining adequate housing for their people, or whether or not there is electricity in the village or adequate health facilities.

In its first annual report, Doyon, Ltd. took those values and expressed them as a goal: "We will be seeking ways to make life better for our stockholders."

Broadly told, other goals of Native corporations include expanding employment opportunities, protecting the environment, maintaining subsistence resources, and preserving the Native way of life.

**Employment**

Just as the annual report of the Arctic Slope Regional Corporation for 1973 told of the goal of profit-making, so it told of the goal of expanding employment opportunities for the people of the region. Leavitt wrote:

> Unlike most other business corporations . . . your Board of Directors and Corporate Officers also recognize as their responsibility the overall development of the Arctic Slope

Region and improving the quality of life of its Inupiat inhabitants. We believe these are compatible goals, and therefore, we have pledged our efforts to their achievement . . .

Consistent with the goals explained above, your Corporation and its subsidiaries are currently involved in and/or pursuing numerous business activities including housing construction, the construction and operation of a hotel, and pipeline road construction. Wherever possible, Inupiat labor is being used in connection with these projects.

Among Calista's goals listed in its 1974 report is "Pursue every available employment for Calista shareholders." Other goals of Calista, and other corporations as well, look to specific economic development projects that may produce jobs for their stockholders.

Ahtna-Rogers-Babler

*Nick Lincoln of Copper Center, employed in soil erosion control work, a joint venture of Ahtna, Inc. and Rogers Babler Construction.*

**Environment**

Concern for the environment is a factor in decision-making and sometimes expressed as a goal in reports of corporations.

In establishing a tug and barge operation in Prince William Sound, Chugach Natives, Inc. was partly motivated by profits and the expansion of job opportunities. In addition, according to its president, Cecil Barnes, the corporation was inspired by environmental concerns. "Other tug and barge operators might want to avoid polluting the Sound because of the law," he explained, "but we want to because it is our water, our home, and we care about it."

Another illustration is to be found in the 1974 Koniag report. After noting the obligation to make profits, the report says:

> ... law or no law, the land and the sea will always mean more to us than dollars and cents. We shall continue to treat them with respect, and we ask all those with whom we do business to do likewise.

Arctic Environmental Information and Data Center

*Caribou grazing.*

**Subsistence**

One of the several corporations which has made maintenance of subsistence resources a goal is NANA Regional Corporation. In recommending its formal adoption to his board of directors, President John Schaeffer called the maintenance of subsistence "the single most important need of all the people."

> ... if subsistence is gone ... NANA undoubtedly will have to pull back from most, if not all, of its activities, with a needed redirection of its cash resources, to meet the void caused by the lack of subsistence resources, such as caribou and fish. The cash resources of

286

NANA, however, are not unlimited and unless there are other activities that will generate additional income, utilizing NANA's cash resources to meet subsistence needs at best will be a short-term solution and a self-defeating one; for when the cash is gone, there will be no substitute for the already lost subsistence, and with its financial resources gone, NANA will see its land start to go. It could be said that the continued existence of NANA and the continued existence of the well-being of its shareholders is based solely on the continued existence of the natural subsistence resources of the Region.

In adopting its goals, the NANA board adopted them subject to future discussion and approval of its stockholders in 1975.

*Byron Mallott of Sealaska Corporation and Yak-tat Kwaan, former Commissioner of Alaska Department of Community and Regional Affairs.*

A goal being increasingly talked about by spokesmen for settlement act corporations is the preservation of the Native way of life. In 1974, Byron Mallott, the State's Commissioner of Community and Regional Affairs, told the convention of the Alaska Federation of Natives, "I think that we as Native people must stop talking glibly of 'the Native way of

**Native way of life**

life' and start doing something to make sure it is sustained." Mallott, a member of the boards of Yak-tat Kwaan, the Yakutat village corporation, and of Sealaska, stresses the importance of defining the Native way of life as first step toward protecting it.

The Native way of life is part of a broader goal of the NANA Regional Corporation. That goal is "instilling pride and confidence in the shareholders and Natives of the NANA Region." As Schaeffer explained:

> ... the most important nonmaterial need is that of giving to each shareholder the pride of being who she or he is, for without that, whatever might follow would be meaningless, would miss the important goal of giving meaning to life. To help achieve this goal, it should be recognized that NANA can contribute to the cultural heritage of the region by seeing that the history and folklore of the people are preserved, making it available to the generations to come.

Such a program, he pointed out, would help an individual to determine what kind of life she or he wants to pursue. But cultural heritage efforts would be just one part of the program. It would include fostering opportunities for employment, self-government, and initiative and other things as well.

# Responsibilities                                     Chapter 39

Most of the responsibility imposed for the achievement of corporate goals rests with directors of the corporations. Their election by stockholders has charged them with the conduct of corporate affairs. They, in turn, choose the president of the corporation and other officers. Under the leadership of the officers, the directors establish goals and set policies which will help achieve the goals.

In their conduct of the corporation, directors are bound by responsibilities established by law. Beyond those responsibilities are the even heavier burdens imposed upon them by those who have given them their votes.

To some extent, these responsibilities are shared by stockholders.

**Legal principles**

There are two basic legal obligations common to directors of all corporations: a director must act in "good faith" and he must act with "reasonable care."

Essentially, acting in good faith means putting loyalty to a corporation above personal gain for oneself. A director who hears of a business opportunity must report it to his corporation to determine whether it is interested, instead of promptly pursuing the opportunity himself. A director should report to his board if he has personal financial interests in any purchase of goods or services being considered by the board; in case of such a conflict he should not vote. Generally speaking, problems of good faith occur when a director tries to obtain personal advantage for himself, his family, or his friends through his board position.

Kord Roosen-Runge

*Eyak Corporation Board members Agnes Nichols, Ted Simeon, Pete Kompkoff (President), Pam Skulstad, Patrick Barnes, Henry Makarka, and Bud Janson are sworn in by Joe Josephson, attorney for Chugach Natives, Inc.*

*Ahtna, Inc. Directors, from left: Mildred Buck, Chitina;
Harding Ewan, Gulkana; Nick Jackson, Gulkana; Christine
Yazzi, Chitina; Robert Marshall (President), Tazlina; Marsha
Major, Tazlina; Ruby John, Cantwell; and Executive Director
Dean Olson.*

Acting with reasonable care means taking the responsibility of the position seriously and working hard to meet the responsibility. A director must be well-informed about the settlement act, regulations, state and federal laws, and his corporation's articles and bylaws. He must also know much about his corporation's activities so that, together with other board members, he can provide oversight and policy direction.

Directors are legally bound to act in good faith and with reasonable care. If they do not, they may be held answerable in court. If one fails to meet his legal obligation, he could be fined, or in serious cases, go to jail.

**Wisdom and fairness**

Another way of viewing responsibilities of directors is to look to what stockholders hope will also be true of their directors: that they will be wise and fair. Perhaps this is what John Sackett was saying in his *Tundra Times* column early in 1972 when he spoke of "the greatest responsibility of leadership." Addressing corporate leaders, he wrote:

> ... because you will be working with your own people's money, their birthright and their settlement, and because in many cases,

*Stockholders hear Ahtna treasurer announce dividend at annual meeting, 1975.*

many of the Native people do not know what decisions to make because of a lack of education, this will be the greatest responsibility of leadership.

And perhaps it is what Howard Rock referred to earlier, immediately after the passage of the settlement act:

... the provisions in it must always be handled carefully, always with feelings that it is being done for the good of the present generation and for the good of the Native people in the future.

If the only goal of settlement act corporations were one of making money, deciding specific issues would be difficult enough. As noted earlier, directors would have to estimate not only how much money a specific investment might earn, but also how safe the investment might be. They would also have to forecast other effects the investment might have — upon the corporation's stockholders and upon the larger community — and take these effects into consideration. In weighing the facts and projections, they would need to act wisely, but questions of fairness would not often arise.

Given the multiplicity of goals which corporations have, however, the question of what is fair is frequently asked. Illustrations may be found in the matter of the distribution of benefits of corporate activity.

The benefits of a corporation's activities are unevenly distributed. Those who work for a corporation obtain more benefit than those who are simply stockholders. Far more dollars will probably go to those on its payrolls than to persons who only receive dividends. Those who sell goods and services to the corporation also obtain more benefits than those who are only stockholders. To assure fairness in management decisions about who will be hired or from whom goods will be purchased, boards of directors of corporations typically establish fixed procedures.

Both wisdom and fairness are certainly required of directors as they seek to balance the interests of resident stockholders and nonresident stockholders. If a regional corporation has a goal of stimulating new jobs in the region, it might decide, for instance, to establish a lumber mill within it. Stockholders who live there might applaud the decision because jobs are scarce for them. Stockholders outside the region who are already employed might criticize it, particularly if greater profits might be earned by investments outside the region.

Kord Roosen-Runge

*Chugach Natives, Inc. Board meeting. From left, around table: Becki Hannon (secretary), Gail Evanoff, Chenega; Carroll Kompkoff, Tatitlek; Roger Wallin, Port Graham; Kathy Anderson, Eyak; Betty Ditman, Eyak; Walter Meganack, Port Graham; Roy Roehl, Seward; and Bud Janson, Eyak.*

It requires a sense of wisdom and fairness for a board to decide how much of the region's money assets ought to be used to protect subsistence resources. The village stockholder would see that goal as a high priority, but the distant stockholder might disagree. Dollars spent to assure continuation of subsistence opportunities would not be available for direct profit-making. On the other hand, as NANA's John Schaeffer points out, the corporation's future may be threatened by a loss of subsistence resources.

Similarly, directors would seek to strike a fair division of the benefits of corporate activity between the present generation of stockholders and future ones. Land or resources of the land sold to produce dividends for stockholders today will not be available for use or lease or sale in the future. But the benefits to most stockholders so far have been few. As one stockholder asked, in a letter critical of her corporation, "Shouldn't those now living have some real benefits from the settlement they helped achieve?"

Wisdom and fairness in decision-making are not objectively measurable. The courts can't help stockholders obtain those qualities in their directors. Honest people might easily disagree on which actions were wise or unwise, fair or unfair; like other personal qualities of directors — integrity, imagination, directness, logical thinking, or a host of others — they can only be subject to the judgments of stockholders.

While most of the responsibility for achievement of corporate goals rests with directors and staffs of corporations, stockholders themselves have a share of it. While their role in corporate affairs is a limited one, they ought to bring to it the same attributes they look for in their directors.

**Individual stockholders**

Arctic Environmental Information Data Center (C. D. Evans)

*Stockholders — Arctic Slope Regional Corporation*

As stockholders they choose directors and influence the course of the corporation's life. And as stockholders, they make their views known to the corporation about what it should be doing or what it should not be doing, and thereby affect it. In these activities a responsible stockholder will try to act in good faith, to show reasonable care, to be wise and fair.

In part, success or failure of Native corporations will be affected by factors beyond their direct control, such as the condition of the nation's economy. In large part, however, the success of corporations will depend upon the quality of persons chosen by stockholders to be their leaders. And this choice depends, in some measure, upon the quality of persons stockholders choose to be themselves.

# EPILOGUE

Alaska Travel Division

Howard Rock can be found just about any day in his crowded little office on Second Avenue in Fairbanks. He is surrounded there by a wall of plaques honoring his work, and a bookcase crammed full of books on many Alaska subjects. His desk is piled high with the day's mail and newspapers from all over the state and the nation.

Rock has been in many discussions on land claims over more than a dozen years and he often speaks about how he loves the land itself. "The land claims act was a defensive action by the Native people . . . when the land they had been living on traditionally was endangered," he said one cold autumn night in 1974. He is more mellow than he used to be, but about the land itself he still is very strong.

"The land claims fight became very emotional and very deep because the land is always very beautiful and wonderful . . . and then when it was in danger of being taken away, tempers sprang up, including over at the *Tundra Times.* Of course I wrote editorials which were rather harsh at times," Rock said, "but we felt it was a very necessary thing."

The *Tundra Times* was heading into its 13th year of publication. Though its editor had suffered a serious illness, the newspaper was still giving Alaska's Native leadership and others a verbal slap when he felt the occasion called for it.

The newspaper had never been able to afford a big celebration on its own, but the fund-raising dinner for it in 1974 capped all the previous ones. Over 1,200 people packed the ballroom of a fashionable Anchorage hotel for the event. It was the largest dinner crowd in the history of Alaska.

Anchorage Daily News (Jane Pender)

*Della Keats tape records a story told by Charlie Goodwin, at 90, the oldest man in Kotzebue (1972).*

One high point of the evening, to be sure, had been Rock's disclosure that the *Tundra Times* was at last operating in the black.

The success of the banquet itself was a sign of change. Looking back on it and on the last few years, Rock says he has noticed a favorable change in the attitude of the business community toward his newspaper and other Native businesses since the land claims act passed. "Businesses are looking at us with a different viewpoint."

At the same time, Rock said, there was little change in his village of Point Hope as a result of the land claims act. And he was finding that to be a stockholder in a Native corporation was "kind of a nebulous thing to a lot of Native people, including," he said, "to myself."

Although the act is complicated and business corporations are new, Rock is optimistic about the ability of Alaska Natives to meet its challenges. When he spoke to the conference of Alaska Native Youth in 1975 he showed this. He told the young people that a "good future for our people" is in their hands. "This is a big assignment, believe me," he said. "What you might have to meet will take every brain tissue, sinew, sense of humor, to make it a reality for the good of your people." And, he asked, "what . . . might help you do it?"

> One thing that I believe that could be important and I'm quite sure it is vital, is your own background. This is one thing that no one can take away from you — the culture of your people . . .

> Your people in the past have sprung to meet life in Alaska with ways or tools to meet one of the most formidable environments this old earth has had to offer.

> The will to survive — what a great story that is, and has been, under the circumstances. It is something you just can't help but be proud of. Your folks in the old days . . . have done some amazing things to meet deadly obstacles, dangers, life and death situations and met them very well indeed. These facts were passed down to us and when they are studied a bit, they can give you a new awakening and spirit, strength to meet difficult situations that might come your way. Believe me, there will be some that will strain your very soul.

> If troublesome obstacles come upon you, think of the achievements of your ancestors. They established cultures that very well met the unkind situations. They won over them and left ample room for fun, arts, and for big shares of lightheartedness.

Some people think that this was not possible under the circumstance our forebears had to live. But they did it through deadly trial and error processes. Who can downgrade such achievements? I for one will never do so.

Looking back and to the future, Rock again showed confidence. "Our ancestors have done amazing things," he said. "They have left us with ways of meeting difficult situations."

Anchorage Daily News

*Kids at play near Ruby.*

# Appendices

# Appendix A

## ALASKA NATIVE CLAIMS SETTLEMENT ACT
### Public Law 92-203
### Guide to Sections

Public Law 92-203
92nd Congress, H. R. 10367
December 18, 1971

# An Act

85 STAT. 688

To provide for the settlement of certain land claims of Alaska Natives, and for other purposes.

*Be it enacted by the Senate and House of Representatives of the United States of America in Congress assembled,* That this Act may be cited as the "Alaska Native Claims Settlement Act".

Alaska Native Claims Settlement Act.

### DECLARATION OF POLICY

SEC. 2. Congress finds and declares that—

(a) there is an immediate need for a fair and just settlement of all claims by Natives and Native groups of Alaska, based on aboriginal land claims;

(b) the settlement should be accomplished rapidly, with certainty, in conformity with the real economic and social needs of Natives, without litigation, with maximum participation by Natives in decisions affecting their rights and property, without establishing any permanent racially defined institutions, rights, privileges, or obligations, without creating a reservation system or lengthy wardship or trusteeship, and without adding to the categories of property and institutions enjoying special tax privileges or to the legislation establishing special relationships between the United States Government and the State of Alaska;

(c) no provision of this Act shall replace or diminish any right, privilege, or obligation of Natives as citizens of the United States or of Alaska, or relieve, replace, or diminish any obligation of the United States or of the State or Alaska to protect and promote the rights or welfare of Natives as citizens of the United States or of Alaska; the Secretary is authorized and directed, together with other appropriate agencies of the United States Government, to make a study of all Federal programs primarily designed to benefit Native people and to report back to the Congress with his recommendations for the future management and operation of these programs within three years of the date of enactment of this Act;

(d) no provision of this Act shall constitute a precedent for reopening, renegotiating, or legislating upon any past settlement involving land claims or other matters with any Native organizations, or any tribe, band, or identifiable group of American Indians;

(e) no provision of this Act shall effect a change or changes in the petroleum reserve policy reflected in sections 7421 through 7438 of title 10 of the United States Code except as specifically provided in this Act;

70A Stat. 457;
76 Stat. 904.

(f) no provision of this Act shall be construed to constitute a jurisdictional act, to confer jurisdiction to sue, nor to grant implied consent to Natives to sue the United States or any of its officers with respect to the claims extinguished by the operation of this Act; and

(g) no provision of this Act shall be construed to terminate or otherwise curtail the activities of the Economic Development Administration or other Federal agencies conducting loan or loan and grant programs in Alaska. For this purpose only, the terms "Indian reservation" and "trust or restricted Indian-owned land areas" in Public Law 89-136, the Public Works and Economic Development Act of 1965, as amended, shall be interpreted to include lands granted to Natives under this Act as long as such lands remain in the ownership of the Native villages or the Regional Corporations.

79 Stat. 552.
42 USC 3121
note.

85 STAT. 689

## DEFINITIONS

Sec. 3. For the purposes of this Act, the term—

(a) "Secretary" means the Secretary of the Interior;

(b) "Native" means a citizen of the United States who is a person of one-fourth degree or more Alaska Indian (including Tsimshian Indians not enrolled in the Metlaktla Indian Community) Eskimo, or Aleut blood, or combination thereof. The term includes any Native as so defined either or both of whose adoptive parents are not Natives. It also includes, in the absence of proof of a minimum blood quantum, any citizen of the United States who is regarded as an Alaska Native by the Native village or Native group of which he claims to be a member and whose father or mother is (or, if deceased, was) regarded as Native by any village or group. Any decision of the Secretary regarding eligibility for enrollment shall be final;

(c) "Native village" means any tribe, band, clan, group, village, community, or association in Alaska listed in sections 11 and 16 of this Act, or which meets the requirements of this Act, and which the Secretary determines was, on the 1970 census enumeration date (as shown by the census or other evidence satisfactory to the Secretary, who shall make findings of fact in each instance), composed of twenty-five or more Natives;

(d) "Native group" means any tribe, band, clan, village, community, or village association of Natives in Alaska composed of less than twenty-five Natives, who comprise a majority of the residents of the locality;

(e) "Public lands" means all Federal lands and interests therein located in Alaska except: (1) the smallest practicable tract, as determined by the Secretary, enclosing land actually used in connection with the administration of any Federal installation, and (2) land selections of the State of Alaska which have been patented or tentatively approved under section 6(g) of the Alaska Statehood Act, as amended (72 Stat. 341, 77 Stat. 223), or identified for selection by the State prior to January 17, 1969;

48 USC
prec. 21 note.

(f) "State" means the State of Alaska;

(g) "Regional Corporation" means an Alaska Native Regional Corporation established under the laws of the State of Alaska in accordance with the provisions of this Act;

(h) "Person" means any individual, firm, corporation, association, or partnership;

(i) "Municipal Corporation" means any general unit of municipal government under the laws of the State of Alaska;

(j) "Village Corporation" means an Alaska Native Village Corporation organized under the laws of the State of Alaska as a business for profit or nonprofit corporation to hold, invest, manage and/or distribute lands, property, funds, and other rights and assets for and on behalf of a Native village in accordance with the terms of this Act.

(k) "Fund" means the Alaska Native Fund in the Treasury of the United States established by section 6; and

(l) "Planning Commission" means the Joint Federal-State Land Use Planning Commission established by section 17.

### DECLARATION OF SETTLEMENT

Prior land conveyances, aboriginal titles and claims, extinguishment.

Sec. 4. (a) All prior conveyances of public land and water areas in Alaska, or any interest therein, pursuant to Federal law, and all tentative approvals pursuant to section 6(g) of the Alaska Statehood Act, shall be regarded as an extinguishment of the aboriginal title thereto, if any.

85 STAT. 690

(b) All aboriginal titles, if any, and claims of aboriginal title in Alaska based on use and occupancy, including submerged land underneath all water areas, both inland and offshore, and including any aboriginal hunting or fishing rights that may exist, are hereby extinguished.

(c) All claims against the United States, the State, and all other persons that are based on claims of aboriginal right, title, use, or occupancy of land or water areas in Alaska, or that are based on any statute or treaty of the United States relating to Native use and occupancy, or that are based on the laws of any other nation, including any such claims that are pending before any Federal or state court or the Indian Claims Commission, are hereby extinguished.

## ENROLLMENT

Sec. 5. (a) The Secretary shall prepare within two years from the date of enactment of this Act a roll of all Natives who were born on or before, and who are living on, the date of enactment of this Act. Any decision of the Secretary regarding eligibility for enrollment shall be final.

(b) The roll prepared by the Secretary shall show for each Native, among other things, the region and the village or other place in which he resided on the date of the 1970 census enumeration, and he shall be enrolled according to such residence. Except as provided in subsection (c), a Native eligible for enrollment who is not, when the roll is prepared, a permanent resident of one of the twelve regions established pursuant to subsection 7(a) shall be enrolled by the Secretary in one of the twelve regions, giving priority in the following order to—

(1) the region where the Native resided on the 1970 census date if he had resided there without substantial interruption for two or more years;

(2) the region where the Native previously resided for an aggregate of ten years or more;

(3) the region where the Native was born; and

(4) the region from which an ancestor of the Native came: The Secretary may enroll a Native in a different region when necessary to avoid enrolling members of the same family in different regions or otherwise avoid hardship.

(c) A Native eligible for enrollment who is eighteen years of age or older and is not a permanent resident of one of the twelve regions may, on the date he files an application for enrollment, elect to be enrolled in a thirteenth region for Natives who are non-residents of Alaska, if such region is established pursuant to subsection 7(c). If such region is not established, he shall be enrolled as provided in subsection (b). His election shall apply to all dependent members of his household who are less than eighteen years of age, but shall not affect the enrollment of anyone else.

## ALASKA NATIVE FUND

Sec. 6. (a) There is hereby established in the United States Treasury an Alaska Native Fund into which the following moneys shall be deposited:

(1) $462,500,000 from the general fund of the Treasury, which are authorized to be appropriated according to the following schedule:

(A) $12,500,000 during the fiscal year in which this Act becomes effective;

(B) $50,000,000 during the second fiscal year;

(C) $70,000,000 during each of the third, fourth, and fifth fiscal years;

(D) $40,000,000 during the sixth fiscal year; and

(E) $30,000,000 during each of the next five fiscal years.

(2) Four percent interest per annum, which is authorized to be appropriated, on any amount authorized to be appropriated by this paragraph that is not appropriated within six months after the fiscal year in which payable.

(3) $500,000,000 pursuant to the revenue sharing provisions of section 9.

Fund expenditures for propaganda or political campaigns, prohibition. Penalty.

(b) None of the funds paid or distributed pursuant to this section to any of the Regional and Village Corporations established pursuant to this Act shall be expended, donated, or otherwise used for the purpose of carrying on propaganda, or intervening in (including the publishing and distributing of statements) any political campaign on behalf of any candidate for public office. Any person who willfully violates the foregoing provision shall be guilty of a misdemeanor and, upon conviction thereof, shall be fined not more than $1,000 or imprisoned not more than twelve months, or both.

Distribution.

(c) After completion of the roll prepared pursuant to section 5, all money in the Fund, except money reserved as provided in section 20 for the payment of attorney and other fees, shall be distributed at the end of each three months of the fiscal year among the Regional Corporations organized pursuant to section 7 on the basis of the relative numbers of Natives enrolled in each region. The share of a Regional Corporation that has not been organized shall be retained in the Fund until the Regional Corporation is organized.

## REGIONAL CORPORATIONS

SEC. 7. (a) For purposes of this Act, the State of Alaska shall be divided by the Secretary within one year after the date of enactment at this Act into twelve geographic regions, with each region composed as far as practicable of Natives having a common heritage and sharing common interests. In the absence of good cause shown to the contrary, such regions shall approximate the areas covered by the operations of the following existing Native associations:

(1) Arctic Slope Native Association (Barrow, Point Hope);

(2) Bering Straits Association (Seward Peninsula, Unalakleet, Saint Lawrence Island);

(3) Northwest Alaska Native Association (Kotzebue);

(4) Association of Village Council Presidents (southwest coast, all villages in the Bethel area, including all villages on the Lower Yukon River and the Lower Kuskokwim River);

(5) Tanana Chiefs' Conference (Koyukuk, Middle and Upper Yukon Rivers, Upper Kuskokwim, Tanana River);

(6) Cook Inlet Association (Kenai, Tyonek, Eklutna, Iliamna);

(7) Bristol Bay Native Association (Dillingham, Upper Alaska Peninsula);

(8) Aleut League (Aleutian Islands, Pribilof Islands and that part of the Alaska Peninsula which is in the Aleut League);

(9) Chugach Native Association (Cordova, Tatitlek, Port Graham, English Bay, Valdez, and Seward);

(10) Tlingit-Haida Central Council (southeastern Alaska, including Metlakatla);

(11) Kodiak Area Native Association (all villages on and around Kodiak Island); and

(12) Copper River Native Association (Copper Center, Glennallen, Chitina, Mentasta).

85 STAT. 692

Any dispute over the boundaries of a region or regions shall be resolved by a board of arbitrators consisting of one person selected by each of the Native associations involved, and an additional one or two persons, whichever is needed to make an odd number of arbitrators, such additional person or persons to be selected by the arbitrators selected by the Native associations involved.

Boundary disputes, arbitration.

(b) The Secretary may, on request made within one year of the date of enactment of this Act, by representative and responsible leaders of the Native associations listed in subsection (a), merge two or more of the twelve regions: *Provided*, That the twelve regions may not be reduced to less than seven, and there may be no fewer than seven Regional Corporations.

Region mergers.

Limitation.

(c) If a majority of all eligible Natives eighteen years of age or older who are not permanent residents of Alaska elect, pursuant to subsection 5(c), to be enrolled in a thirteenth region for Natives who are non-residents of Alaska, the Secretary shall establish such a region for the benefit of the Natives who elected to be enrolled therein, and they may establish a Régional Corporation pursuant to this Act.

Thirteenth region.

(d) Five incorporators within each region, named by the Native association in the region, shall incorporate under the laws of Alaska a Regional Corporation to conduct business for profit, which shall be eligible for the benefits of this Act so long as it is organized and functions in accordance with this Act. The articles of incorporation shall include provisions necessary to carry out the terms of this Act.

Incorporation.

(e) The original articles of incorporation and bylaws shall be approved by the Secretary before they are filed, and they shall be submitted for approval within eighteen months after the date of enactment of this Act. The articles of incorporation may not be amended during the Regional Corporation's first five years without the approval of the Secretary. The Secretary may withhold approval under this section if in his judgment inequities among Native individuals or groups of Native individuals would be created.

(f) The management of the Regional Corporation shall be vested in a board of directors, all of whom, with the exception of the initial board, shall be stockholders over the age of eighteen. The number, terms, and method of election of members of the board of directors shall be fixed in the articles of incorporation or bylaws of the Regional Corporation.

Management.

(g) The Regional Corporation shall be authorized to issue such number of shares of common stock, divided into such classes of shares as may be specified in the articles of incorporation to reflect the provisions of this Act, as may be needed to issue one hundred shares of stock to each Native enrolled in the region pursuant to section 5.

Stock, issuance.

(h)(1) Except as otherwise provided in paragraph (2) of this subsection, stock issued pursuant to subsection (g) shall carry a right to vote in elections for the board of directors and on such other questions as properly may be presented to stockholders, shall permit the holder to receive dividends or other distributions from the Regional Corporation, and shall vest in the holder all rights of a stockholder in a business corporation organized under the laws of the State of Alaska. except that for a period of twenty years after the date of enactment of this Act the stock, inchoate rights thereto, and any dividends paid or distributions made with respect thereto may not be sold, pledged, subjected to a lien or judgment execution, assigned in present or future, or otherwise alienated: *Provided*, That such limitation shall not apply to transfers of stock pursuant to a court decree of separation, divorce or child support.

Stockholders' rights.

Stock
transfer.

(2) Upon the death of any stockholder, ownership of such stock shall be transferred in accordance with his last will and testament or under the applicable laws of intestacy, except that (A) during the twenty-year period after the date of enactment of this Act such stock shall carry voting rights only if the holder thereof through inheritance also is a Native, and (B), in the event the deceased stockholder fails to dispose of his stock by will and has no heirs under the applicable laws of intestacy, such stock shall escheat to the Regional Corporation.

Stock, reissuance.

(3) On January 1 of the twenty-first year after the year in which this Act is enacted, all stock previously issued shall be deemed to be canceled, and shares of stock of the appropriate class shall be issued without restrictions required by this Act to each stockholder share for share.

Certain natural resource revenues, distribution.

(i) Seventy per centum of all revenues received by each Regional Corporation from the timber resources and subsurface estate patented to it pursuant to this Act shall be divided annually by the Regional Corporation among all twelve Regional Corporations organized pursuant to this section according to the number of Natives enrolled in each region pursuant to section 5. The provisions of this subsection shall not apply to the thirteenth Regional Corporation if organized pursuant to subsection (c) hereof.

Corporate funds, distribution.

(j) During the five years following the enactment of this Act, not less than 10% of all corporate funds received by each of the twelve Regional Corporations under section 6 (Alaska Native Fund), and under subsection (i) (revenues from the timber resources and subsurface estate patented to it pursuant to this Act), and all other net income, shall be distributed among the stockholders of the twelve Regional Corporations. Not less than 45% of funds from such sources during the first five-year period, and 50% thereafter, shall be distributed among the Village Corporations in the region and the class of stockholders who are not residents of those villages, as provided in subsection to it. In the case of the thirteenth Regional Corporation, if organized, not less than 50% of all corporate funds received under section 6 shall be distributed to the stockholders.

(k) Funds distributed among the Village Corporations shall be divided among them according to the ratio that the number of shares of stock registered on the books of the Regional Corporation in the names of residents of each village bears to the number of shares of stock registered in the names of residents in all villages.

(l) Funds distributed to a Village Corporation may be withheld until the village has submitted a plan for the use of the money that is satisfactory to the Regional Corporation. The Regional Corporation may require a village plan to provide for joint ventures with other villages, and for joint financing of projects undertaken by the Regional Corporation that will benefit the region generally. In the event of disagreement over the provisions of the plan, the issues in disagreement shall be submitted to arbitration, as shall be provided for in the articles of incorporation of the Regional Corporation.

(m) When funds are distributed among Village Corporations in a region, an amount computed as follows shall be distributed as dividends to the class of stockholders who are not residents of those villages: The amount distributed as dividends shall bear the same ratio to the amount distributed among the Village Corporations that the number of shares of stock registered on the books of the Regional Corporation in the names of nonresidents of villages bears to the number of shares of stock registered in the names of village residents: *Provided*, That an equitable portion of the amount distributed as dividends may be withheld and combined with Village Corporation funds to finance projects that will benefit the region generally.

85 STAT. 694

(n) The Regional Corporation may undertake on behalf of one or more of the Village Corporations in the region any project authorized and financed by them.

(o) The accounts of the Regional Corporation shall be audited annually in accordance with generally accepted auditing standards by independent certified public accountants or independent licensed public accountants, certified or licensed by a regulatory authority of the State or the United States. The audits shall be conducted at the place or places where the accounts of the Regional Corporation are normally kept. All books, accounts, financial records, reports, files, and other papers, things, or property belonging to or in use by the Regional Corporation and necessary to facilitate the audits shall be available to the person or persons conducting the audits; and full facilities for verifying transactions with the balances or securities held by depositories, fiscal agent, and custodians shall be afforded to such person or persons. Each audit report or a fair and reasonably detailed summary thereof shall be transmitted to each stockholder, to the Secretary of the Interior and to the Committees on Interior and Insular Affairs of the Senate and the House of Representatives.

(p) In the event of any conflict between the provisions of this section and the laws of the State of Alaska, the provisions of this section shall prevail.

(q) Two or more Regional Corporations may contract with the same business management group for investment services and advice regarding the investment of corporate funds.

*Annual audit.*

*Report to stockholders and Congressional committees.*
*Federal-state laws, conflict.*

*Business management groups, contracts.*

### VILLAGE CORPORATIONS

SEC. 8. (a) The Native residents of each Native village entitled to receive lands and benefits under this Act shall organize as a business for profit or nonprofit corporation under the laws of the State before the Native village may receive patent to lands or benefits under this Act, except as otherwise provided.

(b) The initial articles of incorporation for each Village Corporation shall be subject to the approval of the Regional Corporation for the region in which the village is located. Amendments to the articles of incorporation and the annual budgets of the Village Corporations shall, for a period of five years, be subject to review and approval by the Regional Corporation. The Regional Corporation shall assist and advise Native villages in the preparation of articles of incorporation and other documents necessary to meet the requirements of this subsection.

(c) The provisions concerning stock alienation, annual audit, and transfer of stock ownership on death or by court decree provided for Regional Corporations in section 7 shall apply to Village Corporations except that audits need not be transmitted to the Committees on Interior and Insular Affairs of the Senate and the House of Representatives.

### REVENUE SHARING

SEC. 9. (a) The provisions of this section shall apply to all minerals that are subject to disposition under the Mineral Leasing Act of 1920, as amended and supplemented.

(b) With respect to conditional leases and sales of minerals heretofore or hereafter made pursuant to section 6(g) of the Alaska Statehood Act, and with respect to mineral leases of the United States that are or may be subsumed by the State under section 6(h) of the Alaska Statehood Act, until such time as the provisions of subsection (c) become operative the State shall pay into the Alaska Native Fund

*Minerals, sale or leases.*
*41 Stat. 437.*
*30 USC 22.*
*Royalties, rentals, bonuses.*
*72 Stat. 341;*
*77 Stat. 223.*
*48 USC prec. 21 note.*

85 STAT. 695

from the royalties, rentals, and bonuses hereafter received by the State (1) a royalty of 2 per centum upon the gross value (as such gross value is determined for royalty purposes under such leases or sales) of such minerals produced or removed from such lands, and (2) 2 per centum of all rentals and bonuses under such leases or sales, excluding bonuses received by the State at the September 1969 sale of minerals from tentatively approved lands and excluding rentals received pursuant to such sale before the date of enactment of this Act. Such payment shall be made within sixty days from the date the revenues are received by the State.

Patents.
72 Stat. 339.
48 USC prec.
21 note.

(c) Each patent hereafter issued to the State under the Alaska Statehood Act, including a patent of lands heretofore selected and tentatively approved, shall reserve for the benefit of the Natives, and for payment into the Alaska Native Fund, (1) a royalty of 2 per centum upon the gross value (as such gross value is determined for royalty purposes under any disposition by the State) of the minerals thereafter produced or removed from such lands, and (2) 2 per centum of all revenues thereafter derived by the State from rentals and bonuses from the disposition of such minerals.

(d) All bonuses, rentals, and royalties received by the United States after the date of enactment of this Act from the disposition by it of such minerals in public lands in Alaska shall be distributed as provided in the Alaska Statehood Act, except that prior to calculating the shares of the State and the United States as set forth in such Act, (1) a royalty of 2 per centum upon the gross value of such minerals produced (as such gross value is determined for royalty purposes under the sale or lease), and (2) 2 per centum of all rentals and bonuses shall be deducted and paid into the Alaska Native Fund. The respective shares of the State and the United States shall be calculated on the remaining balance.

(e) The provisions of this section shall be enforceable by the United States for the benefit of the Natives, and in the event of default by the State in making the payments required, in addition to any other remedies provided by law, there shall be deducted annually by the Secretary of the Treasury from any grant-in-aid or from any other sums payable to the State under any provision of Federal law an amount equal to any such underpayment, which amount shall be deposited in the Fund.

Oil and gas
revenues.

(f) Revenues received by the United States or the State as compensation for estimated drainage of oil or gas shall, for the purposes of this section, be regarded as revenues from the disposition of oil and gas. In the event the United States or the State elects to take royalties in kind, there shall be paid into the Fund on account thereof an amount equal to the royalties that would have been paid into the Fund under the provisions of this section had the royalty been taken in cash.

Fund pay-
ments, cessa-
tion.

(g) The payments required by this section shall continue only until $500,000,000 have been paid into the Alaska Native Fund. Thereafter the provisions of this section shall not apply, and the reservation required in patents under this section shall be of no further force and effect.

Final pay-
ment, compu-
tation.

(h) When computing the final payment into the Fund the respective shares of the United States and the State with respect to payments to the Fund required by this section shall be determined pursuant to this subsection and in the following order:

(1) first, from sources identified under subsections (b) and (c) hereof; and

(2) then, from sources identified under subsection (d) hereof.

(i) The provisions of this section do not apply to mineral revenues received from the Outer Continental Shelf.

STATUTE OF LIMITATIONS

SEC. 10. (a) Notwithstanding any other provision of law, any civil action to contest the authority of the United States to legislate on the subject matter or the legality of this Act shall be barred unless the complaint is filed within one year of the date of enactment of this Act, and no such action shall be entertained unless it is commenced by a duly authorized official of the State. Exclusive jurisdiction over such Jurisdiction. action is hereby vested in the United States District Court for the District of Alaska. The purpose of this limitation on suits is to insure that, after the expiration of a reasonable period of time, the right, title, and interest of the United States, the Natives, and the State of Alaska will vest with certainty and finality and may be relied upon by all other persons in their relations with the State, the Natives, and the United States.

(b) In the event that the State initiates litigation or voluntarily Land selection, becomes a party to litigation to contest the authority of the United suspension of States to legislate on the subject matter or the legality of this Act, all rights. rights of land selection granted to the State by the Alaska Statehood Act shall be suspended as to any public lands which are determined by 72 Stat. 339. the Secretary to be potentially valuable for mineral development, tim- 48 USC prec. ber, or other commercial purposes, and no selections shall be made, no 21 note. tentative approvals shall be granted, and no patents shall be issued for such lands during the pendency of such litigation. In the event of such Extension. suspension, the State's right of land selection pursuant to section 6 of the Alaska Statehood Act shall be extended for a period of time equal 72 Stat. 340; to the period of time the selection right was suspended. 78 Stat. 168.

WITHDRAWAL OF PUBLIC LANDS

SEC. 11. (a)(1) The following public lands are withdrawn, subject to valid existing rights, from all forms of appropriation under the public land laws, including the mining and mineral leasing laws, and from selection under the Alaska Statehood Act, as amended:

(A) The lands in each township that encloses all or part of any Native village identified pursuant to subsection (b) ;

(B) The lands in each township that is contiguous to or corners on the township that encloses all or part of such Native village; and

(C) The lands in each township that is contiguous to or corners on a township containing lands withdrawn by paragraph (B) of this subsection.

The following lands are excepted from such withdrawal: lands in the Exceptions. National Park System and lands withdrawn or reserved for national defense purposes other than Naval Petroleum Reserve Numbered 4.

(2) All lands located within the townships described in subsection (a)(1) hereof that have been selected by, or tentatively approved to, but not yet patented to, the State under the Alaska Statehood Act are withdrawn, subject to valid existing rights, from all forms of appropriation under the public land laws, including the mining and mineral leasing laws, and from the creation of third party interests by the State under the Alaska Statehood Act.

(3)(A) If the Secretary determines that the lands withdrawn by subsections (a)(1) and (2) hereof are insufficient to permit a Village or Regional Corporation to select the acreage it is entitled to select, the Secretary shall withdraw three times the deficiency from the nearest unreserved, vacant and unappropriated public lands. In making this withdrawal the Secretary shall, insofar as possible, withdraw public lands of a character similar to those on which the village is located and

85 STAT. 697

National
Wildlife
Refuge lands.

in order of their proximity to the center of the Native village: *Provided*, That if the Secretary, pursuant to section 17, and 22(e) determines there is a need to expand the boundaries of a National Wildlife Refuge to replace any acreage selected in the Wildlife Refuge System by the Village Corporation the withdrawal under this section shall not include lands in the Refuge.

(B) The Secretary shall make the withdrawal provided for in subsection (3)(A) hereof on the basis of the best available information within sixty days of the date of enactment of this Act, or as soon thereafter as practicable.

(b)(1) The Native villages subject to this Act are as follows:

NAME OF PLACE AND REGION

Afognak, Afognak Island.
Akhiok, Kodiak.
Akiachak, Southwest Coastal Lowland.
Akiak, Southwest Coastal Lowland.
Akutan, Aleutian.
Alakanuk, Southwest Coastal Lowland.
Alatna, Koyukuk-Lower Yukon.
Aleknagik, Bristol Bay.
Allakaket, Koyukuk-Lower Yukon.
Ambler, Bering Strait.
Anaktuvuk, Pass, Arctic Slope.
Andreafsey, Southwest Coastal Lowland.
Aniak, Southwest Coastal Lowland.
Anvik, Koyukuk-Lower Yukon.
Arctic Village, Upper Yukon-Porcupine.
Atka, Aleutian.
Atkasook, Arctic Slope.
Atmautluak, Southwest Coastal Lowland.
Barrow, Arctic Slope.
Beaver, Upper Yukon-Porcupine.
Belkofsky, Aleutian.
Bethel, Southwest Coastal Lowland.
Bill Moore's, Southwest Coastal Lowland.
Biorka, Aleutian.
Birch Creek, Upper Yukon-Porcupine.
Brevig Mission, Bering Strait.
Buckland, Bering Strait.
Candle, Bering Strait.
Cantwell, Tanana.
Canyon Village, Upper Yukon-Porcupine.
Chalkyitsik, Upper Yukon-Porcupine.
Chanilut, Southwest Coastal Lowland.
Cherfornak, Southwest Coastal Lowland.
Chevak, Southwest Coastal Lowland.
Chignik, Kodiak.
Chignik Lagoon, Kodiak.
Chignik Lake, Kodiak.
Chistochina, Copper River.
Chitina, Copper River.
Chukwuktoligamute, Southwest Coastal Lowland.
Circle, Upper Yukon-Porcupine.
Clark's Point, Bristol Bay.
Copper Center, Copper River.
Crooked Creek, Upper Kuskokwim.
Deering, Bering Strait.

Dillingham, Bristol Bay.
Dot Lake, Tanana.
Eagle, Upper Yukon-Porcupine.
Eek, Southwest Coastal Lowland.
Egegik, Bristol Bay.
Eklutna, Cook Inlet.
Ekuk, Bristol Bay.
Ekwok, Bristol Bay.
Elim, Bering Strait.
Emmonak, Southwest Coastal Lowland.
English Bay, Cook Inlet.
False Pass, Aleutian.
Fort Yukon, Upper Yukon-Porcupine.
Gakona, Copper River.
Galena, Koyukuk-Lower Yukon.
Gambell, Bering Sea.
Georgetown, Upper Kuskokwim.
Golovin, Bering Strait.
Goodnews Bay, Southwest Coastal Lowland.
Grayling, Koyukuk-Lower Yukon.
Gulkana, Copper River.
Hamilton, Southwest Coastal Lowland.
Holy Cross, Koyukuk-Lower Yukon.
Hooper Bay, Southwest Coastal Lowland.
Hughes, Koyukuk-Lower Yukon.
Huslia, Koyukuk-Lower Yukon.
Igiugig, Bristol Bay.
Iliamna, Cook Inlet.
Inalik, Bering Strait.
Ivanof Bay, Aleutian.
Kaguyak, Kodiak.
Kaktovik, Arctic Slope.
Kalskag, Southwest Coastal Lowland.
Kaltag, Koyukuk-Lower Yukon.
Karluk, Kodiak.
Kasigluk, Southwest Coastal Lowland.
Kiana, Bering Strait.
King Cove, Aleutian.
Kipnuk, Southeast Coastal Lowland.
Kivalina, Bering Strait.
Kobuk, Bering Strait.
Kokhanok, Bristol Bay.
Koliganek, Bristol Bay.
Kongiganak, Southwest Coastal Lowland.
Kotlik, Southwest Coastal Lowland.
Kotzebue, Bering Strait.
Koyuk, Bering Strait.
Koyukuk, Koyukuk-Lower Yukon.
Kwethluk, Southwest Coastal Lowland.
Kwigillingok, Southwest Coastal Lowland.
Larsen Bay, Kodiak.
Levelock, Bristol Bay.
Lime Village, Upper Kuskokwim.
Lower Kalskag, Southwest Coastal Lowland.
McGrath, Upper Kuskokwim.
Makok, Koyukuk-Lower Yukon.
Manley Hot Springs, Tanana.
Manokotak, Bristol Bay.
Marshall, Southwest Coastal Lowland.

85 STAT. 699

Mary's Igloo, Bering Strait.
Medfra, Upper Kuskokwim.
Mekoryuk, Southwest Coastal Lowland.
Mentasta Lake. Copper River.
Minchumina Lake, Upper Kuskokwim.
Minto, Tanana.
Mountain Village, Southwest Coastal Lowland.
Nabesna Village, Tanana.
Naknek, Bristol Bay.
Napaimute, Upper Kuskokwim.
Napakiak, Southwest Coastal Lowland.
Napaskiak, Southwest Coastal Lowland.
Nelson Lagoon, Aleutian.
Nenana, Tanana.
Newhalen, Cook Inlet.
New Stuyahok, Bristol Bay.
Newtok, Southwest Coastal Lowland.
Nightmute, Southwest Coastal Lowland.
Nikolai, Upper Kuskokwim.
Nikolski, Aleutian.
Ninilchik, Cook Inlet.
Noatak, Bering Strait.
Nome, Bering Strait.
Nondalton, Cook Inlet.
Nooiksut, Arctic Slope.
Noorvik, Bering Strait.
Northeast Cape, Bering Sea.
Northway, Tanana.
Nulato, Koyukuk-Lower Yukon.
Nunapitchuk, Southwest Coastal Lowland.
Ohogamiut, Southwest Coastal Lowland.
Old Harbor, Kodiak.
Oscarville, Southwest Coastal Lowland.
Ouzinkie, Kodiak.
Paradise, Koyukuk-Lower Yukon.
Pauloff Harbor, Aleutian.
Pedro Bay, Cook Inlet.
Perryville, Kodiak.
Pilot Point, Bristol Bay.
Pilot Station, Southwest Coastal Lowland.
Pitkas Point, Southwest Coastal Lowland.
Platinum, Southwest Coastal Lowland.
Point Hope, Arctic Slope.
Point Lay, Arctic Slope.
Portage Creek (Ohgsenakale), Bristol Bay.
Port Graham, Cook Inlet.
Port Heiden (Meshick), Aleutian.
Port Lions, Kodiak.
Quinhagak, Southwest Coastal Lowland.
Rampart, Upper Yukon-Porcupine.
Red Devil, Upper Kuskokwim.
Ruby, Koyukuk-Lower Yukon.
Russian Mission or Chauthalue (Kuskokwim), Upper Kuskokwim.
Russian Mission (Yukon), Southwest Coastal Lowland.
St. George, Aleutian.
St. Mary's, Southwest Coastal Lowland.
St. Michael, Bering Strait.
St. Paul, Aleutian.

Salamatof, Cook Inlet.
Sand Point, Aleutian.
Savonoski, Bristol Bay.
Savoonga, Bering Sea.
Scammon Bay, Southwest Coastal Lowland.
Selawik, Bering Strait.
Seldovia, Cook Inlet.
Shageluk, Koyukuk-Lower Yukon.
Shaktoolik, Bering Strait.
Sheldon's Point, Southwest Coastal Lowland.
Shishmaref, Bering Strait.
Shungnak, Bering Strait.
Slana, Copper River.
Sleetmute, Upper Kuskokwim.
South Naknek, Bristol Bay.
Squaw Harbor, Aleutian.
Stebbins, Bering Strait.
Stevens Village, Upper Yukon-Porcupine.
Stony River, Upper Kuskokwim.
Takotna, Upper Kuskokwim.
Tanacross, Tanana.
Tanana, Koyukuk-Lower Yukon.
Tatilek, Chugach.
Tazlina, Copper River.
Telida, Upper Kuskokwim.
Teller, Bering Strait.
Tetlin, Tanana.
Togiak, Bristol Bay.
Toksook Bay, Southwest Coastal Lowland.
Tulusak, Southwest Coastal Lowland.
Tuntutuliak, Southwest Coastal Lowland.
Tununak, Southwest Coastal Lowland.
Twin Hills, Bristol Bay.
Tyonek, Cook Inlet.
Ugashik, Bristol Bay.
Unalakleet, Bering Strait.
Unalaska, Aleutian.
Unga, Aleutian.
Uyak, Kodiak.
Venetie, Upper Yukon-Porcupine.
Wainwright, Arctic Slope.
Wales, Bering Strait.
White Mountain, Bering Strait.

(2) Within two and one-half years from the date of enactment of  *Review.*
this Act, the Secretary shall review all of the villages listed in subsection (b) (1) hereof, and a village shall not be eligible for land benefits under subsections 14 (a) and (b), and any withdrawal for such
village shall expire, if the Secretary determines that—

(A) less than twenty-five Natives were residents of the village
on the 1970 census enumeration date as shown by the census or
other evidence satisfactory to the Secretary, who shall make findings of fact in each instance; or,

(B) the village is of a modern and urban character, and the
majority of the residents are non-Native.

Any Native group made ineligible by this subsection shall be considered under subsection 14(h).

(3) Native villages not listed in subsection (b) (1) hereof shall be
eligible for land and benefits under this Act and lands shall be withdrawn pursuant to this section if the Secretary within two and one-

313

half years from the date of enactment of this Act, determines that—
 (A) twenty-five or more Natives were residents of an established village on the 1970 census enumeration date as shown by the census or other evidence satisfactory to the Secretary, who shall make findings of fact in each instance; and
 (B) the village is not of a modern and urban character, and a majority of the residents are Natives.

NATIVE LAND SELECTIONS

SEC. 12. (a)(1) During a period of three years from the date of enactment of this Act, the Village Corporation for each Native village identified pursuant to section 11 shall select, in accordance with rules established by the Secretary, all of the township or townships in which any part of the village is located, plus an area that will make the total selection equal to the acreage to which the village is entitled under section 14. The selection shall be made from lands withdrawn by subsection 11(a): *Provided*, That no Village Corporation may select more than 69,120 acres from lands withdrawn by subsection 11(a)(2), and not more than 69,120 acres from the National Wildlife Refuge System, and not more than 69,120 acres in a National Forest: *Provided further*, That when a Village Corporation selects the surface estate to lands within the National Wildlife Refuge System or Naval Petroleum Reserve Numbered 4, the Regional Corporation for that region may select the subsurface estate in an equal acreage from other lands withdrawn by subsection 11(a) within the region, if possible.

*Acreage limitation.*

(2) Selections made under this subsection (a) shall be contiguous and in reasonably compact tracts, except as separated by bodies of water or by lands which are unavailable for selection, and shall be in whole sections and, wherever feasible, in units of not less than 1,280 acres.

*Allocation.*

(b) The difference between twenty-two million acres and the total acreage selected by Village Corporations pursuant to subsection (a) shall be allocated by the Secretary among the eleven Regional Corporations (which excludes the Regional Corporation for southeastern Alaska) on the basis of the number of Natives enrolled in each region. Each Regional Corporation shall reallocate such acreage among the Native villages within the region on an equitable basis after considering historic use, subsistence needs, and population. The action of the Secretary or the Corporation shall not be subject to judicial review. Each Village Corporation shall select the acreage allocated to it from the lands withdrawn by subsection 11(a).

(c) The difference between thirty-eight million acres and the 22 million acres selected by Village Corporations pursuant to subsections (a) and (b) shall be allocated among the eleven Regional Corporations (which excludes the Regional Corporation for southeastern Alaska) as follows:

*Computation.*

(1) The number of acres each Regional Corporation is entitled to receive shall be computed (A) by determining on the basis of available data the percentage of all land in Alaska (excluding the southeastern region) that is within each of the eleven regions, (B) by applying that percentage to thirty-eight million acres reduced by the acreage in the southeastern region that is to be selected pursuant to section 16, and (C) by deducting from the figure so computed the number of acres within that region selected pursuant to subsections (a) and (b).

(2) In the event that the total number of acres selected within a region pursuant to subsections (a) and (b) exceeds the percentage of the reduced thirty-eight million acres allotted to that region pursuant

85 STAT. 702

to subsection (c)(1)(B), that region shall not be entitled to receive
any lands under this subsection (c). For each region so affected the
difference between the acreage calculated pursuant to subsection (c)
(1)(B) and the acreage selected pursuant to subsections (a) and (b)
shall be deducted from the acreage calculated under subsection (c)
(1)(C) for the remaining regions which will select lands under this
subsection (c). The reductions shall be apportioned among the remaining regions so that each region's share of the total reduction bears the
same proportion to the total reduction as the total land area in that
region (as calculated pursuant to subsection (c)(1)(A) bears to the
total land area in all of the regions whose allotments are to be reduced
pursuant to this paragraph.

(3) Before the end of the fourth year after the date of enactment of
this Act, each Regional Corporation shall select the acreage allocated
to it from the lands within the region withdrawn pursuant to subsection 11(a)(1), and from the lands within the region withdrawn pursuant to subsection 11(a)(3) to the extent lands withdrawn pursuant
to subsection 11(a)(1) are not sufficient to satisfy its allocation: *Provided*, That within the lands withdrawn by subsection 11(a)(1) the
Regional Corporation may select only even numbered townships in
even numbered ranges, and only odd numbered townships in odd numbered ranges.

(d) To insure that the Village Corporation for the Native village at
Dutch Harbor, if found eligible for land grants under this Act, has
a full opportunity to select lands within and near the village. no federally owned lands, whether improved or not, shall be disposed of pursuant to the Federal surplus property disposal laws for a period of
two years from the date of enactment of this Act. The Village Corporation may select such lands and improvements and receive patent to
them pursuant to subsection 14(a) of this Act.

(e) Any dispute over the land selection rights and the boundaries
of Village Corporations shall be resolved by a board of arbitrators
consisting of one person selected by each of the Village Corporations
involved, and an additional one or two persons, whichever is needed
to make an odd number of arbitrators, such additional person or persons to be selected by the arbitrators selected by the Village Corporations.

Disputes,
arbitration.

## SURVEYS

SEC. 13. (a) The Secretary shall survey the areas selected or designated for conveyance to Village Corporations pursuant to the provisions of this Act. He shall monument only exterior boundaries of
the selected or designated areas at angle points and at intervals of
approximately two miles on straight lines. No ground survey or monu-
mentation will be required along meanderable water boundaries. He
shall survey within the areas selected or designated land occupied as a
primary place of residence, as a primary place of business, and for
other purposes, and any other land to be patented under this Act.

(b) All withdrawals, selections, and conveyances pursuant to this
Act shall be as shown on current plats of survey or protraction diagrams of the Bureau of Land Management, or protraction diagrams of
the Bureau of the State where protraction diagrams of the Bureau of
Land Management are not available, and shall conform as nearly as
practicable to the United States Land Survey System.

## CONVEYANCE OF LANDS

SEC. 14. (a) Immediately after selection by a Village Corporation for a Native village listed in section 11 which the Secretary

315

85 STAT. 703

finds is qualified for land benefits under this Act, the Secretary shall issue to the Village Corporation a patent to the surface estate in the number of acres shown in the following table:

| If the village had on the 1970 census enumeration date a Native population between— | It shall be entitled to a patent to an area of public lands equal to— |
|---|---|
| 25 and 99 | 69,120 acres. |
| 100 and 199 | 92,160 acres. |
| 200 and 399 | 115,200 acres. |
| 400 and 599 | 138,240 acres. |
| 600 or more | 161,280 acres. |

The lands patented shall be those selected by the Village Corporation pursuant to subsection 12(a). In addition, the Secretary shall issue to the Village Corporation a patent to the surface estate in the lands selected pursuant to subsection 12(b).

(b) Immediately after selection by any Village Corporation for a Native village listed in section 16 which the Secretary finds is qualified for land benefits under this Act, the Secretary shall issue to the Village Corporation a patent to the surface estate to 23,040 acres. The lands patented shall be the lands within the township or townships that enclose the Native village, and any additional lands selected by the Village Corporation from the surrounding townships withdrawn for the Native village by subsection 16(a).

Patent requirements.

(c) Each patent issued pursuant to subsections (a) and (b) shall be subject to the requirements of this subsection. Upon receipt of a patent or patents:

(1) the Village Corporation shall first convey to any Native or non-Native occupant, without consideration, title to the surface estate in the tract occupied as a primary place of residence, or as a primary place of business, or as a subsistence campsite, or as headquarters for reindeer husbandry;

(2) the Village Corporation shall then convey to the occupant, either without consideration or upon payment of an amount not in excess of fair market value, determined as of the date of initial occupancy and without regard to any improvements thereon, title to the surface estate in any tract occupied by a nonprofit organization;

(3) the Village Corporation shall then convey to any Municipal Corporation in the Native village or to the State in trust for any Municipal Corporation established in the Native village in the future, title to the remaining surface estate of the improved land on which the Native village is located and as much additional land as is necessary for community expansion, and appropriate rights-of-way for public use, and other foreseeable community needs: *Provided*, That the amount of lands to be transferred to the Municipal Corporation or in trust shall be no less than 1,280 acres;

(4) the Village Corporation shall convey to the Federal Government, State or to the appropriate Municipal Corporation, title to the surface estate for existing airport sites, airway beacons, and other navigation aids, together with such additional acreage and/or easements as are necessary to provide related services and to insure safe approaches to airport runways; and

(5) for a period of ten years after the date of enactment of this Act, the Regional Corporation shall be afforded the opportunity to review and render advice to the Village Corporations on all land sales, leases or other transactions prior to any final commitment.

(d) the Secretary may apply the rule of approximation with respect to the acreage limitations contained in this section.

(e) Immediately after selection by a Regional Corporation, the Secretary shall convey to the Regional Corporation title to the surface and/or the subsurface estates, as is appropriate, in the lands selected.

(f) When the Secretary issues a patent to a Village Corporation for the surface estate in lands pursuant to subsections (a) and (b), he shall issue to the Regional Corporation for the region in which the lands are located a patent to the subsurface estate in such lands, except lands located in the National Wildlife Refuge System and lands withdrawn or reserved for national defense purposes, including Naval Petroleum Reserve Numbered 4, for which in lieu rights are provided for in subsection 12(a)(1): *Provided*, That the right to explore, develop, or remove minerals from the subsurface estate in the lands within the boundaries of any Native village shall be subject to the consent of the Village Corporation.

*Subsurface estate, patent.*

*Mineral rights.*

(g) All conveyances made pursuant to this Act shall be subject to valid existing rights. Where, prior to patent of any land or minerals under this Act, a lease, contract, permit, right-of-way, or easement (including a lease issued under section 6(g) of the Alaska Statehood Act) has been issued for the surface or minerals covered under such patent, the patent shall contain provisions making it subject to the lease, contract, permit, right-of-way, or easement, and the right of the lessee, contractee, permittee, or grantee to the complete enjoyment of all rights, privileges, and benefits thereby granted to him. Upon issuance of the patent, the patentee shall succeed and become entitled to any and all interests of the State or the United States as lessor, contractor, permitter, or grantor, in any such leases, contracts, permits, rights-of-way, or easements covering the estate patented, and a lease issued under section 6(g) of the Alaska Statehood Act shall be treated for all purposes as though the patent had been issued to the State. The administration of such lease, contract, permit, right-of-way, or easement shall continue to be by the State or the United States, unless the agency responsible for administration waives administration. In the event that the patent does not cover all of the land embraced within any such lease, contract, permit, right-of-way, or easement, the patentee shall only be entitled to the proportionate amount of the revenues reserved under such lease, contract, permit, right-of-way, or easement by the State or the United States which results from multiplying the total of such revenues by a fraction in which the numerator is the acreage of such lease, contract, permit, right-of-way, or easement which is included in the patent and the denominator is the total acreage contained in such lease, contract, permit, right-of-way, or easement.

*72 Stat. 341;
77 Stat. 323.
48 USC prec.
21 note.*

(h) The Secretary is authorized to withdraw and convey 2 million acres of unreserved and unappropriated public lands located outside the areas withdrawn by sections 11 and 16, and follows:

*Land conveyance, authorization.*

(1) The Secretary may withdraw and convey to the appropriate Regional Corporation fee title to existing cemetery sites and historical places;

(2) The Secretary may withdraw and convey to a Native group that does not qualify as a Native village, if it incorporates under the laws of Alaska, title to the surface estate in not more than 23,040 acres surrounding the Native group's locality. The subsurface estate in such land shall be conveyed to the appropriate Regional Corporation;

(3) The Secretary may withdraw and convey to the Natives residing in Sitka, Kenai, Juneau, and Kodiak, if they incorporate under the laws of Alaska, the surface estate of lands of a similar

character in not more than 23,040 acres of land, which shall be located in reasonable proximity to the municipalities. The subsurface estate in such lands shall be conveyed to the appropriate Regional Corporation unless the lands are located in a Wildlife Refuge;

(4) The Secretary shall withdraw only such lands surrounding the villages and municipalities as are necessary to permit the conveyance authorized by paragraphs (2) and (3) to be planned and effected;

(5) The Secretary may convey to a Native, upon application within two years from the date of enactment of this Act, the surface estate in not to exceed 160 acres of land occupied by the Native as a primary place of residence on August 31, 1971. Determination of occupancy shall be made by the Secretary, whose decision shall be final. The subsurface estate in such lands shall be conveyed to the appropriate Regional Corporations;

(6) The Secretary shall charge against the 2 million acres authorized to be conveyed by this section all allotments approved pursuant to section 18 during the four years following the date of enactment of this Act;

(7) The Secretary may withdraw and convey lands out of the National Wildlife Refuge System and out of the National Forests, for the purposes set forth in subsections (h) (1), (2), (3), and (5); and

(8) Any portion of the 2 million acres not conveyed by this subsection shall be allocated and conveyed to the Regional Corporations on the basis of population.

### TIMBER SALE CONTRACTS

SEC. 15. Notwithstanding the provisions of existing National Forest timber sale contracts that are directly affected by conveyances authorized by this Act, the Secretary of Agriculture is authorized to modify any such contract, with the consent of the purchaser, by substituting, to the extent practicable, timber on other national forest lands approximately equal in volume, species, grade, and accessibility for timber standing on any land affected by such conveyances, and, on request of the appropriate Village Corporation the Secretary of Agriculture is directed to make such substitution to the extent it is permitted by the timber sale contract without the consent of the purchaser.

### THE TLINGIT-HAIDA SETTLEMENT

SEC. 16. (a) All public lands in each township that encloses all or any part of a Native village listed below, and in each township that is contiguous to or corners on such township, except lands withdrawn or reserved for national defense purposes, are hereby withdrawn, subject to valid existing rights, from all forms of appropriation under the public land laws, including the mining and mineral leasing laws, and from selection under the Alaska Statehood Act, as amended:

72 Stat. 339.
48 USC
prec. 21. note.

Angoon, Southeast.
Craig, Southeast.
Hoonah, Southeast.
Hydaburg, Southeast.
Kake, Southeast.
Kasaan, Southeast.
Klawock, Southeast.
Klukwan, Southeast.
Saxman, Southeast.
Yakutat, Southeast.

(b) During a period of three years from the date of enactment of this Act, each Village Corporation for the villages listed in subsection (a) shall select, in accordance with rules established by the Secretary, an area equal to 23,040 acres, which must include the township or townships in which all or part of the Native village is located, plus, to the extent necessary, withdrawn lands from the townships that are contiguous to or corner on such township. All selections shall be contiguous and in reasonably compact tracts, except as separated by bodies of water, and shall conform as nearly as practicable to the United States Lands Survey System.

(c) The funds appropriated by the Act of July 9, 1968 (82 Stat. 307), to pay the judgment of the Court of Claims in the case of The Tlingit and Haida Indians of Alaska, et al. against The United States, numbered 47,900, and distributed to the Tlingit and Haida Indians pursuant to the Act of July 13, 1970 (84 Stat. 431), are in lieu of the additional acreage to be conveyed to qualified villages listed in section 11.

25 USC 1211.

### JOINT FEDERAL-STATE LAND USE PLANNING COMMISSION FOR ALASKA

SEC. 17. (a)(1) There is hereby established the Joint Federal-State Land Use Planning Commission for Alaska. The Planning Commission shall be composed of ten members as follows:

Establishment.<br>Membership.

(A) The Governor of the State (or his designate) and four members who shall be appointed by the Governor. During the Planning Commission's existence at least one member appointed by the Governor shall be a Native as defined by this Act.

(B) One member appointed by the President of the United States with the advice and consent of the Senate, and four members who shall be appointed by the Secretary of the Interior.

(2) The Governor of the State and the member appointed by the President pursuant to subsection (a)(1)(B), shall serve as cochairmen of the Planning Commission. The initial meeting of the Commission shall be called by the cochairmen. All decisions of the Commission shall require the concurrence of the cochairmen.

(3) Six members of the Planning Commission shall constitute a quorum. Members shall serve at the pleasure of the appointing authority. A vacancy in the membership of the Commission shall not affect its powers, but shall be filled in the same manner in which the original appointment was made.

(4)(A) Except to the extent otherwise provided in subparagraph (B) of this subsection, members of the Planning Commission shall receive compensation at the rate of $100 per day for each day they are engaged in the performance of their duties as members of the Commission. All members of the Commission shall be entitled to reimbursement for travel, subsistence, and other necessary expenses incurred by them in the performance of their duties as members of the Commission.

Compensation.

(B) Any member of the Planning Commission who is designated or appointed from the Government of the United States or from the Government of the State shall serve without compensation in addition to that received in his regular employment. The member of the Commission appointed by the President pursuant to subsection (a)(1)(B) shall be compensated as provided by the President at a rate not in excess of that provided for level V of the Executive Schedule in title 5, United States Code.

(5) Subject to such rules and regulations as may be adopted by the Planning Commission, the cochairmen, without regard to the provisions of title 5, United States Code, governing appointments in the

80 Stat. 463;<br>83 Stat. 864.<br>5 USC 5316.<br>5 USC 101<br>et seq.

80 Stat.443,
467.
5 USC 5101,
5331.
5 USC 5332
note.

80 Stat. 416.
Hearings.

competitive service, and without regard to the provisions of chapter 51 and subchapter III of chapter 53 of such title relating to classification and General Schedule pay rates, shall have the power—

(A) to appoint and fix the compensation of such staff personnel as they deem necessary, and

(B) to procure temporary and intermittent services to the same extent as is authorized by section 3109 of title 5, United States Code, but at rates not to exceed $100 a day for individuals.

(6) (A) The Planning Commission or, on the authorization of the Commission, any subcommittee or member thereof, may, for the purpose of carrying out the provisions of this section, hold such hearings, take such testimony, receive such evidence, print or otherwise reproduce and distribute so much of its proceedings and reports thereon, and sit and act at such times and places as the Commission, subcommittee, or member deems advisable.

Information,
availability.

(B) Each department, agency, and instrumentality of the executive branch of the Federal Government, including independent agencies, is authorized and directed to furnish to the Commission, upon request made by a cochairman, such information as the Commission deems necessary to carry out its functions under this section.

(7) The Planning Commission shall—

(A) undertake a process of land-use planning, including the identification of and the making of recommendations concerning areas planned and best suited for permanent reservation in Federal ownership as parks, game refuges, and other public uses, areas of Federal and State lands to be made available for disposal, and uses to be made of lands remaining in Federal and State ownership;

72 Stat. 339.
48 USC
prec. 21 note.

(B) make recommendations with respect to proposed land selections by the State under the Alaska Statehood Act and by Village and Regional Corporations under this Act;

(C) be available to advise upon and assist in the development and review of land-use plans for lands selected by the Native Village and Regional Corporations under this Act and by the State under the Alaska Statehood Act;

(D) review existing withdrawals of Federal public lands and recommend to the President of the United States such additions to or modifications of withdrawals as are deemed desirable;

(E) establish procedures, including public hearings, for obtaining public views on the land-use planning programs of the State and Federal Governments for lands under their administration;

(F) establish a committee of land-use advisers to the Commission, made up of representatives of commercial and industrial land users in Alaska, recreational land users, wilderness users, environmental groups, Alaska Natives, and other citizens;

(G) make recommendations to the President of the United States and the Governor of Alaska as to programs and budgets of the Federal and State agencies responsible for the administration of Federal and State lands;

(H) make recommendations from time to time to the President of the United States, Congress, and the Governor and legislature of the State as to changes in laws, policies, and programs that the Planning Commission determines are necessary or desirable;

(I) make recommendations to insure that economic growth and development is orderly, planned and compatible with State and national environmental objectives, the public interest in the public lands, parks, forests, and wildlife refuges in Alaska, and the economic and social well-being of the Native people and other residents of Alaska;

85 STAT. 708

(J) make recommendations to improve coordination and consultation between the State and Federal Governments in making resource allocation and land use decisions; and

(K) make recommendations on ways to avoid conflict between the State and the Native people in the selection of public lands.

(8) (A) On or before January 31 of each year, the Planning Commission shall submit to the President of the United States, the Congress, and the Governor and legislature of the State a written report with respect to its activities during the preceding calendar year.

(B) The Planning Commission shall keep and maintain accurate and complete records of its activities and transactions in carrying out its duties under this Act, and such records shall be available for public inspection.

(C) The principal office of the Planning Commission shall be located in the State.

(9) (A) The United States shall be responsible for paying for any fiscal year only 50 per centum of the costs of carrying out subsections (a) and (b) for such fiscal year.

(B) For the purpose of meeting the responsibility of the United States in carrying out the provisions of this section, there is authorized to be appropriated $1,500,000 for the fiscal year ending June 30, 1972, and for each succeeding fiscal year.

(10) On or before May 30, 1976, the Planning Commission shall submit its final report to the President of the United States, the Congress, and the Governor and Legislature of the State with respect to its planning and other activities under this Act, together with its recommendations for programs or other actions which it determines should be taken or carried out by the United States and the State. The Commission shall cease to exist effective December 31, 1976.

(b) (1) The Planning Commission shall identify public easements across lands selected by Village Corporations and the Regional Corporations and at periodic points along the courses of major waterways which are reasonably necessary to guarantee international treaty obligations, a full right of public use and access for recreation, hunting, transportation, utilities, docks, and such other public uses as the Planning Commission determines to be important.

(2) In identifying public easements the Planning Commission shall consult with appropriate State and Federal agencies, shall review proposed transportation plans, and shall receive and review statements and recommendations from interested organizations and individuals on the need for and proposed location of public easements: *Provided,* That any valid existing right recognized by this Act shall continue to have whatever right of access as is now provided for under existing law and this subsection shall not operate in any way to diminish or limit such right of access.

(3) Prior to granting any patent under this Act to the Village Corporation and Regional Corporations, the Secretary shall consult with the State and the Planning Commission and shall reserve such public easements as he determines are necessary.

(c) In the event that the Secretary withdraws a utility and transportation corridor across public lands in Alaska pursuant to his existing authority, the State, the Village Corporations and the Regional Corporations shall not be permitted to select lands from the area withdrawn.

(d) (1) Public Land Order Numbered 4582, 34 Federal Register 1025, as amended, is hereby revoked. For a period of ninety days after the date of enactment of this Act all unreserved public lands in Alaska are hereby withdrawn from all forms of appropriation under the public land laws, including the mining (except locations for metalliferous

Report to President and Congress of U.S., Governor and legislature of Alaska.
Recordkeeping.

Appropriation.

Final report.

Termination date.

Public easements.

Unreserved public land, withdrawal.

85 STAT. 709

minerals) and the mineral leasing laws. During this period of time the Secretary shall review the public lands in Alaska and determine whether any portion of these lands should be withdrawn under authority provided for in existing law to insure that the public interest in these lands is properly protected. Any further withdrawal shall require an affirmative act by the Secretary under his existing authority, and the Secretary is authorized to classify or reclassify any lands so withdrawn and to open such lands to appropriation under the public land laws in accord with his classifications. Withdrawals pursuant to this paragraph shall not affect the authority of the Village Corporations, the Regional Corporations, and the State to make selections and obtain patents within the areas withdrawn pursuant to section 11.

72 Stat. 339.
48 USC
prec. 21 note.

(2) (A) The Secretary, acting under authority provided for in existing law, is directed to withdraw from all forms of appropriation under the public land laws, including the mining and mineral leasing laws, and from selection under the Alaska Statehood Act, and from selection by Regional Corporations pursuant to section 11, up to, but not to exceed, eighty million acres of unreserved public lands in the State of Alaska, including previously classified lands, which the Secretary deems are suitable for addition to or creation as units of the National Park, Forest, Wildlife Refuge, and Wild and Scenic Rivers Systems: *Provided*, That such withdrawals shall not affect the authority of the State and the Regional and Village Corporations to make selections and obtain patents within the areas withdrawn pursuant to section 11.

Final with-
drawal date.

(B) Lands withdrawn pursuant to paragraph (A) hereof must be withdrawn within nine months of the date of enactment of this Act. All unreserved public lands not withdrawn under paragraph (A) or subsection 17(d)(1) shall be available for selection by the State and for appropriation under the public land laws.

Report to
Congress.

(C) Every six months, for a period of two years from the date of enactment of this Act, the Secretary shall advise the Congress of the location, size and values of lands withdrawn pursuant to paragraph (A) and submit his recommendations with respect to such lands. Any lands withdrawn pursuant to paragraph (A) not recommended for addition to or creation as units of the National Park, Forest, Wildlife Refuge, and Wild and Scenic Rivers Systems at the end of the two years shall be available for selection by the State and the Regional Corporations, and for appropriation under the public land laws.

(D) Areas recommended by the Secretary pursuant to paragraph (C) shall remain withdrawn from any appropriation under the public land laws until such time as the Congress acts on the Secretary's recommendations, but not to exceed five years from the recommendation dates. The withdrawal of areas not so recommended shall terminate at the end of the two year period.

(E) Notwithstanding any other provision of this subsection, initial identification of lands desired to be selected by the State pursuant to the Alaska Statehood Act and by the Regional Corporations pursuant to section 12 of this Act may be made within any area withdrawn pursuant to this subsection (d), but such lands shall not be tentatively approved or patented so long as the withdrawals of such areas remain in effect: *Provided*, That selection of lands by Village Corporations pursuant to section 12 of this Act shall not be affected by such withdrawals and such lands selected may be patented and such rights granted as authorized by this Act. In the event Congress enacts legislation setting aside any areas withdrawn under the provisions of this subsection which the Regional Corporations or the State desired to select, then other unreserved public lands shall be made available for alternative selection by the Regional Corporations and the State. Any time periods established by law for Regional Corporations or State selections are hereby extended to the extent that delays are caused by compliance with the provisions of this subsection (2).

(3) Any lands withdrawn under this section shall be subject to administration by the Secretary under applicable laws and regulations, and his authority to make contracts and to grant leases, permits, rights-of-way, or easements shall not be impaired by the withdrawal.

### REVOCATION OF INDIAN ALLOTMENT AUTHORITY IN ALASKA

SEC. 18. (a) No Native covered by the provisions of this Act, and no descendant of his, may hereafter avail himself of an allotment under the provisions of the Act of February 8, 1887 (24 Stat. 389), as amended and supplemented, or the Act of June 25, 1910 (36 Stat. 363). Further, the Act of May 17, 1906 (34 Stat. 197), as amended, is hereby repealed. Notwithstanding the foregoing provisions of this section, any application for an allotment that is pending before the Department of the Interior on the date of enactment of this Act may, at the option of the Native applicant, be approved and a patent issued in accordance with said 1887, 1910, or 1906 Act, as the case may be, in which event the Native shall not be eligible for a patent under subsection 14(h)(5) of this Act.

25 USC 334.
36 Stat. 863.
25 USC 337.
Repeal.
70 Stat. 954.
43 USC 270-1
to 270-3.

(b) Any allotments approved pursuant to this section during the four years following enactment of this Act shall be charged against the two million acre grant provided for in subsection 14(h).

### REVOCATION OF RESERVATIONS

SEC. 19. (a) Notwithstanding any other provision of law, and except where inconsistent with the provisions of this Act, the various reserves set aside by legislation or by Executive or Secretarial Order for Native use or for administration of Native affairs, including those created under the Act of May 31, 1938 (52 Stat. 593), are hereby revoked subject to any valid existing rights of non-Natives. This section shall not apply to the Annette Island Reserve established by the Act of March 3, 1891 (26 Stat. 1101) and no person enrolled in the Metlakatla Indian community of the Annette Island Reserve shall be eligible for benefits under this Act.

25 USC 497.

25 USC 495.

(b) Notwithstanding any other provision of law or of this Act, any Village Corporation or Corporations may elect within two years to acquire title to the surface and subsurface estates in any reserve set aside for the use or benefit of its stockholders or members prior to the date of enactment of this Act. If two or more villages are located on such reserve the election must be made by all of the members or stockholders of the Village Corporations concerned. In such event, the Secretary shall convey the land to the Village Corporation or Corporations, subject to valid existing rights as provided in subsection 14(g), and the Village Corporation shall not be eligible for any other land selections under this Act or to any distribution of Regional Corporation funds pursuant to section 7, and the enrolled residents of the Village Corporation shall not be eligible to receive Regional Corporation stock.

### ATTORNEY AND CONSULTANT FEES

SEC. 20. (a) The Secretary of the Treasury shall hold in the Alaska Native Fund, from the appropriation made pursuant to section 6 for the second fiscal year, moneys sufficient to make the payments authorized by this section.

85 STAT. 711

Claims.

(b) A claim for attorney and consultant fees and out-of-pocket expenses may be submitted to the Chief Commissioner of the United States Court of Claims for services rendered before the date of enactment of this Act to any Native tribe, band, group, village, or association in connection with:

(1) the preparation of this Act and previously proposed Federal legislation to settle Native claims based on aboriginal title, and

(2) the actual prosecution pursuant to an authorized contract or a cause of action based upon a claim pending before any Federal or State Court or the Indians Claims Commission that is dismissed pursuant to this Act.

Filing date.

(c) A claim under this section must be filed with the clerk of the Court of Claims within one year from the date of enactment of this Act, and shall be in such form and contain such information as the Chief Commissioner shall prescribe. Claims not so filed shall be forever barred.

Rules.

(d) The Chief Commissioner or his delegate is authorized to receive, determine, and settle such claims in accordance with the following rules:

(1) No claim shall be allowed if the claimant has otherwise been reimbursed.

(2) The amount allowed for services shall be based on the nature of the service rendered, the time and labor required, the need for providing the service, whether the service was intended to be a voluntary public service or compensable, the existence of a bona fide attorney-client relationship with an identified client, and the relationship of the service rendered to the enactment of proposed legislation. The amount allowed shall not be controlled by any hourly charge customarily charged by the claimant.

(3) The amount allowed for out-of-pocket expenses shall not include office overhead, and shall be limited to expenses that were necessary, reasonable, unreimbursed and actually incurred.

(4) The amounts allowed for services rendered shall not exceed in the aggregate $2,000,000, of which not more than $100,000 shall be available for the payment of consultants' fees. If the approved claims exceed the aggregate amounts allowable, the Chief Commissioner shall authorize payment of the claims on a pro rata basis.

(5) Upon the filing of a claim, the clerk of the Court of Claims shall forward a copy of such claims to the individuals or entities on whose behalf services were rendered or fees and expenses were allegedly incurred, as shown by the pleadings, to the Attorney General of the United States, to the Attorney General of the State of Alaska, to the Secretary of the Interior, and to any other person who appears to have an interest in the claim, and shall give such persons ninety days within which to file an answer contesting the claim.

(6) The Chief Commissioner may designate a trial commissioner for any claim made under this section and a panel of three commissioners of the court to serve as a reviewing body. One member of the review panel shall be designated as presiding commissioner of the panel.

(7) Proceedings in all claims shall be pursuant to rules and orders prescribed for the purpose by the Chief Commissioner who is hereby authorized and directed to require the application of the pertinent rules of practice of the Court of Claims insofar as feasible. Claimants may appear before a trial commissioner in person or by attorney, and may produce evidence and examine witnesses. In the discretion of the Chief Commissioner or his designate, hearings may be held in the localities where the claimants reside if convenience so demands.

(8) Each trial commissioner and each review panel shall have authority to do and perform any acts which may be necessary or proper for the efficient performance of their duties, and shall have the power of subpena, the power to order audit of books and records, and the power to administer oaths and affirmations. Any sanction authorized by the rules of practice of the Court of Claims, except contempt, may be imposed on any claimant, witness, or attorney by the trial commissioner, review panel, or Chief Commissioner. None of the rules, regulations, rulings, findings, or conclusions authorized by this section shall be subject to judicial review.

(9) The findings and conclusions of the trial commissioner shall be submitted by him, together with the record in the case, to the review panel of commissioners for review by it pursuant to such rules as may be provided for the purpose, which shall include provision for submitting the decision of the trial commissioner to the claimant and any party contesting the claim for consideration, exception, and argument before the panel. The panel, by majority vote, shall adopt or modify the findings or the conclusions of the trial commissioner.

(10) The Court of Claims is hereby authorized and directed, under such conditions as it may prescribe, to provide the facilities and services of the office of the clerk of the court for the filing, processing, hearing, and dispatch of claims made pursuant to this section and to include within its annual appropriations the costs thereof and other costs of administration, including (but without limitation to the items herein listed) the salaries and traveling expenses of its auditors and the commissioners serving as trial commissioners and panel members, mailing and service of process, necessary physical facilities, equipment, and supplies, and personnel (including secretaries, reporters, auditors, and law clerks).

(e) The Chief Commissioner shall certify to the Secretary of the Treasury, and report to the Congress, the amount of each claim allowed and the name and address of the claimant. The Secretary of the Treasury shall pay to such person from the Alaska Native Fund the amounts certified. No award under this section shall bear interest.

(f)(1) No remuneration on account of any services or expenses for which a claim is made or could be made pursuant to this section shall be received by any person for such services and expenses in addition to the amount paid in accordance with this section, and any contract or agreement to the contrary shall be void.

(2) Any person who receives, and any corporation or association official who pays, on account of such services and expenses, any remuneration in addition to the amount allowed in accordance with this section shall be guilty of a misdemeanor and, upon conviction thereof, shall be fined not more than $5,000, or imprisoned not more than twelve months, or both.

(g) A claim for actual costs incurred in filing protests, preserving land claims, advancing land claims settlement legislation, and presenting testimony to the Congress on proposed Native land claims may be submitted to the Chief Commissioner of the Court of Claims by any bona fide association of Natives. The claim must be submitted within six months from the date of enactment of this Act, and shall be in such form and contain such information as the Chief Commissioner shall prescribe. The Chief Commissioner shall allow such amounts as he determines are reasonable, but he shall allow no amount for attorney and consultant fees and expenses which shall be compensable solely under subsection (b) through (e). If approved claims under this subsection aggregate more than $600,000, each claim shall be reduced on a pro rata basis. The Chief Commissioner shall certify to the Secretary of the Treasury, and report to the Congress, the amount

*Subpena power.*

*Report to Congress.*

*Restriction.*

*Penalty.*

*Filing costs, claim.*

*Report to Congress.*

of each claim allowed and the name and address of the claimant. The Secretary of the Treasury shall pay to such claimant from the Alaska Native Fund the amount certified. No award under this subsection shall bear interest.

TAXATION

SEC. 21. (a) Revenues originating from the Alaska Native Fund shall not be subject to any form of Federal, State, or local taxation at the time of receipt by a Regional Corporation, Village Corporation, or individual Native through dividend distributions or in any other manner. This exemption shall not apply to income from the investment of such revenues.

(b) The receipt of shares of stock in the Regional or Village Corporations by or on behalf of any Native shall not be subject to any form of Federal, State or local taxation.

(c) The receipt of land or any interest therein pursuant to this Act or of cash in order to equalize the values of properties exchanged pursuant to subsection 22(f) shall not be subject to any form of Federal, State or local taxation. The basis for computing gain or loss on subsequent sale or other disposition of such land or interest in land for purposes of any Federal, State or local tax imposed on or measured by income shall be the fair value of such land or interest in land at the time of receipt.

(d) Real property interests conveyed, pursuant to this Act, to a Native individual, Native group, or Village or Regional Corporation which are not developed or leased to third parties, shall be exempt from State and local real property taxes for a period of twenty years after the date of enactment of this Act: *Provided*, That municipal taxes, local real property taxes, or local assessments may be imposed upon leased or developed real property within the jurisdiction of any governmental unit under the laws of the State: *Provided further*, That easements, rights-of-way, leaseholds, and similar interests in such real property may be taxed in accordance with State or local law. All rents, royalties, profits, and other revenues or proceeds derived from such property interests shall be taxable to the same extent as such revenues or proceeds are taxable when received by a non-Native individual or corporation.

(e) Real property interests conveyed pursuant to this Act to a Native individual, Native group, or Village or Regional Corporation shall, so long as the fee therein remains not subject to State or local taxes on real estate, continue to be regarded as public lands for the purpose of computing the Federal share of any highway project pursuant to title 23 of the United States Code, as amended and supplemented, for the purpose of the Johnson-O'Malley Act of April 16, 1934, as amended (25 U.S.C. 452), and for the purpose of Public Laws 815 and 874, 81st Congress (64 Stat. 967, 1100), and so long as there are also no substantial revenues from such lands, continue to receive forest fire protection services from the United States at no cost.

23 USC 101 et seq.
49 Stat. 1458.
72 Stat. 548.
79 Stat. 27.
20 USC 631, 236.

MISCELLANEOUS

SEC. 22. (a) None of the revenues granted by section 6, and none of the lands granted by this Act to the Regional and Village Corporation and to Native groups and individuals shall be subject to any contract which is based on a percentage fee of the value of all or some portion of the settlement granted by this Act. Any such contract shall not be enforceable against any Native as defined by this Act or any Regional or Village Corporation and the revenues and lands granted by this Act shall not be subject to lien, execution or judgment to fulfill such a contract.

85 STAT. 714

(b) The Secretary is directed to promptly issue patents to all persons who have made a lawful entry on the public lands in compliance with the public land laws for the purpose of gaining title to homesteads, headquarters sites, trade and manufacturing sites, or small tract sites (43 U.S.C. 682), and who have fulfilled all requirements of the law prerequisite to obtaining a patent. Any person who has made a lawful entry prior to August 31, 1971, for any of the foregoing purposes shall be protected in his right of use and occupancy until all the requirements of law for a patent have been met even though the lands involved have been reserved or withdrawn in accordance with Public Land Order 4582, as amended, or the withdrawal provisions of this Act: *Provided*, That occupancy must have been maintained in accordance with the appropriate public land law: *Provided further*, That any person who entered on public lands in violation of Public Land Order 4582, as amended, shall gain no rights. | 34 Stat. 1052.

(c) On any lands conveyed to Village and Regional Corporations, any person who prior to August 31, 1971, initiated a valid mining claim or location under the general mining laws and recorded notice of said location with the appropriate State or local office shall be protected in his possessory rights, if all requirements of the general mining laws are complied with, for a period of five years and may, if all requirements of the general mining laws are complied with, proceed to patent. | Mining claims, possessory rights.

(d) The provisions of Revised Statute 452 (43 U.S.C. 11) shall not apply to any land grants or other rights granted under this Act.

(e) If land within the National Wildlife Refuge System is selected by a Village Corporation pursuant to the provisions of this Act, the secretary shall add to the Refuge System other public lands in the State to replace the lands selected by the Village Corporation.

(f) The Secretary, the Secretary of Defense, and the Secretary of Agriculture are authorized to exchange any lands or interests therein in Alaska under their jurisdiction for lands or interests therein of the Village Corporations, Regional Corporations, individuals, or the State for the purpose of effecting land consolidations or to facilitate the management or development of the land. Exchanges shall be on the basis of equal value, and either party to the exchange may pay or accept cash in order to equalize the value of the properties exchanged. | Land exchanges.

(g) If a patent is issued to any Village Corporation for land in the National Wildlife Refuge System, the patent shall reserve to the United States the right of first refusal if the land is ever sold by the Village Corporation. Notwithstanding any other provision of this Act, every patent issued by the Secretary pursuant to this Act—which covers lands lying within the boundaries of a National Wildlife Refuge on the date of enactment of this Act shall contain a provision that such lands remain subject to the laws and regulations governing use and development of such Refuge.

(h) (1) All withdrawals made under this Act, except as otherwise provided in this subsection, shall terminate within four years of the date of enactment of this Act: *Provided*, That any lands selected by Village or Regional Corporations or by a Native group under section 12 shall remain withdrawn until conveyed pursuant to section 14. | Withdrawals, termination dates.

(2) The withdrawal of lands made by subsection 11(a)(2) and section 16 shall terminate three years from the date of enactment of this Act.

(3) The provisions of this section shall not apply to any withdrawals made under section 17 of this Act.

(4) The Secretary is authorized to terminate any withdrawal made by or pursuant to this Act whenever he determines that the withdrawal is no longer necessary to accomplish the purposes of this Act.

(i) Prior to a conveyance pursuant to section 14, lands withdrawn by or pursuant to sections 11, 14, and 16 shall be subject to administration by the Secretary, or by the Secretary of Agriculture in the case of National Forest lands, under applicable laws and regulations, and their authority to make contracts and to grant leases, permits, rights-of-way, or easements shall not be impaired by the withdrawal.

(j) In any area of Alaska for which protraction diagrams of the Bureau of Land Management or the State do not exist, or which does not conform to the United States Land Survey System, or which has not been surveyed in a manner adequate to withdraw and grant the lands provided for under this Act, the Secretary shall take such actions as are necessary to accomplish the purposes of this Act, and the deeds granted shall note that upon completion of an adequate survey appropriate adjustments will be made to insure that the beneficiaries of the land grants receive their full entitlement.

Land patents in national forests, conditions.

(k) Any patents to lands under this Act which are located within the boundaries of a national forest shall contain such conditions as the Secretary deems necessary to assure that:

(1) the sale of any timber from such lands shall, for a period of five years, be subject to the same restrictions relating to the export of timber from the United States as are applicable to national forest lands in Alaska under rules and regulations of the Secretary of Agriculture; and

(2) such lands are managed under the principle of sustained yield and under management practices for protection and enhancement of environmental quality no less stringent than such management practices on adjacent national forest lands for a period of twelve years.

Land selection limitation.

(l) Notwithstanding any provision of this Act, no Village or Regional Corporation shall select lands which are within two miles from the boundary, as it exists on the date of enactment of this Act, of any home rule or first class city (excluding boroughs) or which are within six miles from the boundary of Ketchikan.

## REVIEW BY CONGRESS

Reports to Congress.

SEC. 23. The Secretary shall submit to the Congress annual reports on implementation of this Act. Such reports shall be filed by the Secretary annually until 1984. At the beginning of the first session of Congress in 1985 the Secretary shall submit, through the President, a report of the status of the Natives and Native groups in Alaska, and a summary of actions taken under this Act, together with such recommendations as may be appropriate.

## APPROPRIATIONS

SEC. 24. There are authorized to be appropriated such sums as may be necessary to carry out the provisions of this Act.

## PUBLICATIONS

Publication in Federal Register.
60 Stat. 237.
5 USC 551
et seq.

SEC. 25. The Secretary is authorized to issue and publish in the Federal Register, pursuant to the Administrative Procedure Act, such regulations as may be necessary to carry out the purposes of this Act.

### SAVING CLAUSE

SEC. 26. To the extent that there is a conflict between any provision of this Act and any other Federal laws applicable to Alaska, the provisions of this Act shall govern.

**SEPARABILITY**

SEC. 27. If any provision of this Act or the applicability thereof is held invalid the remainder of this Act shall not be affected thereby.

Approved December 18, 1971.

---

LEGISLATIVE HISTORY:

HOUSE REPORTS: No. 92-523 (Comm. on Interior and Insular Affairs) and No. 92-746 (Comm. of Conference).
SENATE REPORTS: No. 92-405 accompanying S. 35 (Comm. on Interior and Insular Affairs) and No. 92-581 (Comm. of Conference).
CONGRESSIONAL RECORD, Vol. 117 (1971):
    Oct. 19, 20, considered and passed House.
    Nov. 1, considered and passed Senate, amended, in lieu of S. 35.
    Dec. 14, House and Senate agreed to conference report.

# Appendix B

## VILLAGE CORPORATIONS
## ELIGIBLE FOR LAND AND MONEY BENEFITS

| village name | name of village corporation | enroll-ment 9-14-74 | regional corporation |
|---|---|---|---|
| Afognak | Natives of Afognak, Inc. | 392 | Koniag |
| Akhiok | Natives of Akhiok, Inc. | 100 | Koniag |
| Akiachak | Akiachak, Ltd. | 332 | Calista |
| Akiak | Kokarmiut Corporation | 211 | Calista |
| Akutan | Akutan Corporation | 106 | Aleut |
| Alakanuk | Alakanuk Native Corporation | 467 | Calista |
| Alatna | Alatna Endeavors, Inc. | 30 | Doyon |
| Aleknagik | Aleknagik Natives, Ltd. | 231 | Bristol Bay |
| Allakaket | Aala Kaa K'a, Inc. | 147 | Doyon |
| Ambler | Ivisaapaagmiit Corporation | 166 | NANA |
| Anaktuvuk Pass | Nunamiut Corporation | 132 | Arctic Slope |
| Andreafski | Nerklikmute Native Corporation | 84 | Calista |
| Angoon | Kootznoowoo, Inc. | 620 | Sealaska |
| Aniak | Aniak, Ltd. | 250 | Calista |
| Anvik | Central Native Corporation | 129 | Doyon |
| Atka | Atxam Corporation | 145 | Aleut |
| Atkasook | Atkasook Corporation | 71 | Arctic Slope |
| Atmauthluak | Atmauthluak, Ltd. | 120 | Calista |
| Barrow | Ukpeagvik Inupiat Corporation | 2041 | Arctic Slope |
| Beaver | Beaver Kwit' chin Corporation | 190 | Doyon |
| Belkofski | Belkofski Corporation | 34 | Aleut |
| Bethel | Bethel Native Corporation | 1725 | Calista |
| Bettles Field/ Evansville | Evansville, Inc. | 77 | Doyon |
| Bill Moores | Kongnikilnomiut Yuita Corp. | 46 | Calista |
| Birch Creek | Tihteet' Aii, Inc. | 52 | Doyon |
| Brevig Mission | Brevig Mission Native Corp. | 135 | Bering Straits |
| Buckland | Nunachiak Corporation | 159 | NANA |
| Cantwell | Cantwell Yedetena Na Corp. | 72 | Ahtna |
| Chalkyitsik | Chalkyitsik Native Corporation | 90 | Doyon |
| Chefornak | Chefarnrmute, Inc. | 162 | Calista |
| Chenega | Chenega Corporation | 68 | Chugach |
| Chevak | Chevak Company | 423 | Calista |
| Chickaloon | Chickaloon-Moose Creek Native Association, Inc. | 42 | Cook Inlet |
| Chignik | Far West, Inc. | 286 | Bristol Bay |
| Chignik Lagoon | Chignik Lagoon Native Corp. | 103 | Bristol Bay |
| Chignik Lake | Chignik Lake Natives, Inc. | 104 | Bristol Bay |
| Chistochina | Cheesh-na, Inc. | 32 | Ahtna |
| Chitina | Chitina Native Corporation | 237 | Ahtna |
| Chuathbaluk | Chuathbaluk Company | 114 | Calista |
| Chuloonawick | Chuloonawick Corporation | 27 | Calista |
| Circle | Danzhit Hanlaii Corporation | 104 | Doyon |

| | | | |
|---|---|---|---|
| Clark's Point | Saguyak, Inc. | 111 | Bristol Bay |
| Copper Center | Kluti-kaah Corporation | 260 | Ahtna |
| Council | Council Native Corporation | 72 | Bering Straits |
| Craig | Shaan-Seet, Inc. | 317 | Sealaska |
| Crooked Creek | Kipchaughpuk, Ltd. | 127 | Calista |
| Deering | Deering Ipnatchiak Corporation | 159 | NANA |
| Dillingham | Choggiung, Ltd. | 925 | Bristol Bay |
| Dot Lake | Dot Lake Native Corporation | 45 | Doyon |
| Eagle | Hungwitchin Corporation | 101 | Doyon |
| Eek | Iqfijouaq Company | 200 | Calista |
| Egegik | Becharof Corporation | 166 | Bristol Bay |
| Eklutna | Eklutna, Inc. | 126 | Cook Inlet |
| Ekuk | Ekuk Natives, Ltd. | 39 | Bristol Bay |
| Ekwok | Ekwok Natives, Ltd. | 113 | Bristol Bay |
| Emmonak | Emmonak Corporation | 478 | Calista |
| English Bay | English Bay Corporation | 71 | Chugach |
| Eyak | Eyak Corporation | 323 | Chugach |
| False Pass | False Pass Corporation | 66 | Aleut |
| Ft. Yukon | Gwitchyaazhee Corporation | 737 | Doyon |
| Gakona | Gakona Corporation | 35 | Ahtna |
| Galena | Notaaghleedin, Ltd. | 344 | Doyon |
| Georgetown | Georgetown, Inc. | 45 | Calista |
| Golovin | Golovin Native Corporation | 171 | Bering Straits |
| Goodnews Bay/ Mumtrak | Kiutsarak, Inc. | 223 | Calista |
| Grayling | Hee-yea-lingde Corporation | 178 | Doyon |
| Gulkana | Sta-keh Corporation | 106 | Ahtna |
| Hamilton | Nunapiglluraq Corporation | 35 | Calista |
| Healy Lake | Mendas Chax-aq Native Corp. | 27 | Doyon |
| Holy Cross | Deloycheet, Inc. | 429 | Doyon |
| Hoonah | Huna Totem | 868 | Sealaska |
| Hooper Bay | Sea Lion Corporation | 623 | Calista |
| Hughes | Hadohdleekaga, Inc. | 96 | Doyon |
| Huslia | Bin Googa, Inc. | 217 | Doyon |
| Hydaburg | Haida Corporation | 570 | Sealaska |
| Inalik/Diomede | Diomede Native Corporation | 104 | Bering Straits |
| Igiugig | Igiugig Native Corporation | 37 | Bristol Bay |
| Iliamna | Iliamna Natives, Ltd. | 75 | Bristol Bay |
| Ivanof Bay | Bay View, Inc. | 47 | Bristol Bay |
| Kaguyak | Kaguyak, Inc. | 48 | Koniag |
| Kake | Kake Tribal Corporation | 552 | Sealaska |
| Kaktovik | Kaktovik Inupiat Corporation | 112 | Arctic Slope |
| Kaltag | Takathlee-todin, Inc. | 253 | Doyon |
| Karluk | Karluk Native Corporation | 186 | Koniag |
| Kasaan | Kavilco, Inc. | 121 | Sealaska |
| Kasigluk | Kasigluk, Inc. | 309 | Calista |
| Kiana | Katyaak Corporation | 339 | NANA |
| King Cove | The King Cove Corporation | 343 | Aleut |
| King Island | King Island Native Corporation | 205 | Bering Straits |
| Kipnuk | Kugkaktlik, Ltd. | 359 | Calista |
| Kivalina | Kivalina Sinuakmeut Corporation | 191 | NANA |
| Klawock | Klawock Heenya | 507 | Sealaska |

| | | | |
|---|---|---|---|
| Knik | Knikatnu, Inc. | 29 | Cook Inlet |
| Kobuk | Koovukmeut, Inc. | 63 | NANA |
| Kokhanok | Kokhanok Native Corporation | 106 | Bristol Bay |
| Koliganek | Koliganek, Ltd. | 131 | Bristol Bay |
| Kongiganak | Qenirtalet Coast Corporation | 248 | Calista |
| Kotlik | Kotlik Yupik Corporation | 220 | Calista |
| Kotzebue | Kikiktagruk Inupiat Corp. | 1983 | NANA |
| Koyuk | Koyuk Native Corporation | 188 | Bering Straits |
| Koyukuk | Mineelghaadza', Ltd. | 164 | Doyon |
| Kwethluk | Kwethluk, Inc. | 450 | Calista |
| Kwigillingok | Kwik, Inc. | 229 | Calista |
| Larsen Bay | Nu-Nachk Pit, Inc. | 201 | Koniag |
| Levelock | Levelock Natives, Ltd. | 100 | Bristol Bay |
| Lime Village | Lime Village Company | 26 | Calista |
| Lower Kalskag | Lower Kalskag, Inc. | 168 | Calista |
| Manley Hot Springs | Bean Ridge Corporation | 42 | Doyon |
| Manokotak | Manokotak Natives, Ltd. | 227 | Bristol Bay |
| Marshall/ Fortuna Ledge | Maserculiq, Inc. | 214 | Calista |
| Mary's Igloo | Mary's Igloo Native Corporation | 109 | Bering Straits |
| McGrath | Chamai, Inc. | 176 | Doyon |
| Mekoryuk | Nima Corporation | 306 | Calista |
| Mentasta Lake | Mentasta, Inc. | 97 | Ahtna |
| Minto | Seth-de-ya-ah Corporation | 286 | Doyon |
| Mountain Village | Azachorok, Inc. | 488 | Calista |
| Naknek | Paug-vik Incorporated, Ltd. | 293 | Bristol Bay |
| Napaimute | Napaimute, Ltd. | 43 | Calista |
| Napakiak | Napakiak Corporation | 260 | Calista |
| Napaskiak | Napaskiak, Inc. | 218 | Calista |
| Nelson Lagoon | Nelson Lagoon Corporation | 54 | Aleut |
| Nenana | Toghetthele Corporation | 452 | Doyon |
| New Stuyahok | Stuyahok, Ltd. | 229 | Bristol Bay |
| Newhalen | Newhalen Native Corporation | 74 | Bristol Bay |
| Newtok | Newtok Corporation, Inc. | 126 | Calista |
| Nightmute | NGTA, Inc. | 99 | Calista |
| Nikolai | DonLee Corporation | 93 | Doyon |
| Nikolski | Chaluka Corporation | 74 | Aleut |
| Ninilchik | Ninilchik Native Assoc., Inc. | 203 | Cook Inlet |
| Noatak | Noatak Napaaktukmeut Corp. | 281 | NANA |
| Nome | Sitnasuak Native Corporation | 2060 | Bering Straits |
| Nondalton | Nondalton Native Corporation | 253 | Bristol Bay |
| Noorvik | Putoo Corporation | 487 | NANA |
| Northway | Northway Natives, Inc. | 207 | Doyon |
| Nuiqsut | Kuukpik Corporation | 206 | Arctic Slope |
| Nulato | Nik'aghun, Ltd. | 388 | Doyon |
| Nunapitchuk | Nunapitchuk, Ltd. | 325 | Calista |
| Ohogamiut | OHOG, Inc. | 22 | Calista |
| Old Harbor | Old Harbor Native Corporation | 335 | Koniag |
| Oscarville | Oscarville Native Corporation | 53 | Calista |
| Ouzinkie | Ouzinkie Native Corporation | 333 | Koniag |
| Paimiut | Paimiut Corporation | 22 | Calista |

| | | | |
|---|---|---|---|
| Pedro Bay | Pedro Bay Corporation | 105 | Bristol Bay |
| Perryville | Oceanside Corporation | 130 | Bristol Bay |
| Pilot Point | Pilot Point Native Corporation | 146 | Bristol Bay |
| Pilot Station | Pilot Station, Inc. | 322 | Calista |
| Pitka's Point | Pitka's Point Native Corporation | 89 | Calista |
| Platinum | ARVIG, Inc. | 68 | Calista |
| Point Hope | Tigara Corporation | 500 | Arctic Slope |
| Point Lay | Cully Corporation | 88 | Arctic Slope |
| Port Graham | Port Graham Corporation | 190 | Chugach |
| Port Heiden | Meshik, Inc. | 70 | Bristol Bay |
| Port Lions | Port Lions Native Corporation | 112 | Koniag |
| Portage Creek | Ohgsenakle Corporation | 78 | Bristol Bay |
| Quinhagak | Qanirtuug, Inc. | 346 | Calista |
| Rampart | Baan o yeel kon Corporation | 175 | Doyon |
| Red Devil | Red Devil, Inc. | 35 | Calista |
| Ruby | Dineega Corporation | 288 | Doyon |
| Russian Mission (Yukon) | Russian Mission Native Corp. | 127 | Calista |
| St. George | St. George Tanaq Corporation | 215 | Aleut |
| St. Mary's | St. Mary's Native Corporation | 297 | Calista |
| St. Michael | St. Michael Native Corporation | 256 | Bering Straits |
| St. Paul | Tanadgusix Corporation | 549 | Aleut |
| Sand Point | Shumagin Corporation | 402 | Aleut |
| Saxman | Cape Fox Corporation | 191 | Sealaska |
| Scammon Bay | Askinuk Corporation | 192 | Calista |
| Selawik | Akuliuk, Inc. | 477 | NANA |
| Seldovia | Seldovia Native Assoc., Inc. | 254 | Cook Inlet |
| Shageluk | Zho-tse, Inc. | 185 | Doyon |
| Shaktoolik | Shaktoolik Native Corporation | 207 | Bering Straits |
| Sheldon's Point | Swan Lake Corporation | 131 | Calista |
| Shishmaref | Shishmaref Native Corporation | 310 | Bering Straits |
| Shungnak | Isingnakmeut, Inc. | 161 | NANA |
| Sleetmute | Sleetmute, Ltd. | 164 | Calista |
| South Naknek | Quinuyang, Ltd. | 180 | Bristol Bay |
| Stebbins | Stebbins Native Corporation | 273 | Bering Straits |
| Stevens Village | Dinyea Corporation | 166 | Doyon |
| Stony River | Stony River, Ltd. | 82 | Calista |
| Takotna | Gold Creek, Ltd. | 38 | Doyon |
| Tanacross | Tanacross, Inc. | 167 | Doyon |
| Tanana | Tozitna, Ltd. | 595 | Doyon |
| Tatitlek | Tatitlek Corporation | 215 | Chugach |
| Tazlina | Tazlina, Inc. | 121 | Ahtna |
| Telida | Seseui, Inc. | 25 | Doyon |
| Teller | Teller Native Corporation | 272 | Bering Straits |
| Togiak | Togiak Natives, Ltd. | 400 | Bristol Bay |
| Toksook Bay | Nunakauiak Yupik Corporation | 280 | Calista |
| Tuluksak | Tulkisarmute, Inc. | 183 | Calista |
| Tuntutuliak | Tuntutuliak Land, Ltd. | 211 | Calista |
| Tununak | Tununrmiut Rinit Corporation | 296 | Calista |
| Twin Hills | Twin Hills Native Corporation | 61 | Bristol Bay |
| Tyonek | Tyonek Native Corporation | 303 | Cook Inlet |
| Ugashik | Ugashik Native Corporation | 31 | Bristol Bay |

| Umkumuite | Umkumuite, Ltd. | 27 | Calista |
| Unalakleet | Unalakleet Native Corporation | 839 | Bering Straits |
| Unalaska | Ounalashka Corporation | 268 | Aleut |
| Unga | Unga Corporation | 58 | Aleut |
| Upper Kalskag | Upper Kalskag, Inc. | 159 | Calista |
| Wainwright | Olgoonik Corporation | 371 | Arctic Slope |
| Wales | Wales Native Corporation | 167 | Bering Straits |
| White Mountain | White Mountain Native Corp. | 202 | Bering Straits |
| Woody Island | Leisnoi, Inc. | 296 | Koniag |
| Yakutat | Yak-tat Kwaan, Inc. | 334 | Sealaska |

## Appendix C
### VILLAGE CORPORATIONS
### WHICH CHOSE FORMER RESERVES

| village name | name of village corporation | enroll- ment 9-14-74 | name of former reserve |
|---|---|---|---|
| Arctic Village | Neets'ai Corporation | 147 | Venetie |
| Elim | Elim Native Corporation | 238 | Elim |
| Gambell | Gambell Native Corporation | 429 | St. Lawrence Island |
| Klukwan | Klukwan Corporation | 251 | Klukwan |
| Savoonga | Savoonga Native Corporation | 412 | St. Lawrence Island |
| Tetlin | Tetlin Native Corporation | 125 | Tetlin |
| Venetie | Venetie Indian Corporation | 156 | Venetie |

## Appendix D
### LOCAL CORPORATIONS,
### FOUR NAMED CITIES

| city | name of corporation | enrollment 9-14-74 |
|---|---|---|
| Juneau | Goldbelt, Inc. | 2640 |
| Kenai | Kenai Native Association, Inc. | 477 |
| Kodiak | Natives of Kodiak | 500 |
| Sitka | Shee Atika, Inc. | 1804 |

## Appendix E
### LOCAL CORPORATIONS
### CERTIFIED AS GROUPS

| location | name of corporation | enroll- ment | regional corporation |
|---|---|---|---|
| Caswell | Caswell Native Corporation | 35 | Cook Inlet |
| Montana Creek | Montana Creek Native Corporation | 45 | Cook Inlet |

## Appendix F

## VILLAGE CORPORATIONS APPEALING INELIGIBILITY,
## FILING FOR LAND

| village name | name of village corporation | enroll- ment 9-14-74 | regional corporation |
|---|---|---|---|
| Alexander Creek | Alexander Creek Native Corporation | 37 | Cook Inlet |
| Anton Larsen Bay | Anton Larsen, Inc. | 31 | Koniag |
| Attu | (not formed) | 11 | Aleut |
| Ayakulik | Ayakulik, Inc. | 31 | Koniag |
| Bells Flats | Bells Flats Natives, Inc. | 27 | Koniag |
| Litnik | Litnik, Inc. | 37 | Koniag |
| Little Afognak | Kitoi, Inc. | 0 | Koniag |
| Point Possession | Point Possession, Inc. | 36 | Cook Inlet |
| Port William | Shuyak, Inc. | 43 | Koniag |
| Salamatoff | Salamatoff Native Assoc., Inc. | 127 | Cook Inlet |
| Sanak | Sanak Corporation | 25 | Aleut |
| Solomon | Solomon Native Corporation | 38 | Bering Straits |
| Uganik | Uganik Natives, Inc. | 31 | Koniag |
| Uyak | Uyak Natives, Inc. | 34 | Koniag |

## Appendix G

## INCORPORATORS OF THE TWELVE REGIONAL CORPORATIONS

The Alaska Native Claims Settlement Act provided that each of the regional associations was to name five persons whose responsibility was to incorporate as a business for profit under the act and Alaska law. The associations named the following persons as incorporators for what became the 12 regional corporations:

### Ahtna, Incorporated

Lillian Boston, Chistochina
Hector Ewan, Copper Center
Norman Ewan, Gakona

Roy Ewan, Anchorage
George Hobson, Copper Center
Christine Yazzie, Glennallen

### The Aleut Corporation

Charles A. Hoff, Anchorage
Lillie McGarvey, Anchorage
Alvin Osterback, Anchorage

Iliodor Philemonof, Anchorage
Michael Swetzof, Anchorage

### Arctic Slope Regional Corporation

Wesley Aiken, Barrow
Edward E. Hopson, Sr., Barrow
Warren Matumeak, Barrow

Lester Suvulu, Barrow
Joseph Upicksoun, Barrow

## Bering Straits Native Corporation

George Bell, Nome
Charles W. Fagerstrom, Nome
Fred Katchatag, Sr., Unalakleet

Martin Olson, Golovin
Jerome Trigg, Nome

## Bristol Bay Native Corporation

Fred Theodore Angasan, Dillingham
William Peter Johnson, Dillingham
Harold Harvey Samuelsen, Dillingham

John Jack Knutsen, Dillingham
Donald Fredrick Nielsen, Naknek

## Calista Corporation

Elizabeth Beans, Nightmute
Phillip Guy, Kwethluk
Robert Nick, Nunapitchuk

Fred A. Notti, Aniak
William Tyson, St. Marys

## Chugach Natives, Inc.

Cecil Barnes, Cordova
John Borodkin, Tatillek
Mary Gordaoff, Cordova

Vincent Kvasnikoff, English Bay
Walter Meganack, Port Graham

## Cook Inlet Region, Inc.

Mike Alex, Eklutna
Douglas Bryan, Anchorage
Adam Kroto, Tyonek

George Miller, Jr., Kenai
Larry Oskolkoff, Anchorage

## Doyon, Ltd.

Roger Huntington, Galena
Sam Kito, Jr., Fairbanks
John Sackett, Fairbanks

Tim Wallis, Fairbanks
Jules Wright, Fairbanks

## Koniag, Inc.

Nick Anderson, Kodiak
Karl Armstrong, Kodiak
Robert Erickson, Kodiak

Sven Haakanson, Old Harbor
Ted Velanis, Kodiak

## NANA Regional Corporation, Inc.

Grant Ballot, Selawik
Roland Booth, Noatak
Stanley Custer, Shungnak

Robert Newlin, Noorvik
Vincent Schuerch, Kiana

## Sealaska Corporation

John Borbridge, Jr., Juneau
Clarence Jackson, Sr., Kake
Marlene Johnson, Hoonah

Leonard Kato, Klawock
Richard Kito, Petersburg

# Appendix H

## ALASKA FEDERATION OF NATIVES
### First Board of Directors—1967

Cecil Barnes, Anchorage
John Borbridge, Jr., Juneau
Oscar Craig, Glennallen
Frank Degnan, Unalakleet
Andrew Demoski, Nulato
Charles Franz, Port Moeller
Tom Gregoroff, Kodiak
William Hensley, Kotzebue
Eben Hopson, Barrow
Axel Johnson, Emmonak
Flore Lekanof, Anchorage

Tony Lewis, Bethel
Emil McCord, Tyonek
Hugh Nicholls, Barrow
Emil Notti, Anchorage
George Olson, Cordova
John Sackett, Huslia
Harvey Samuelsen, Dillingham
Rev. Walter Soboleff, Juneau
Seraphim Stephan, Jr., Tyonek
Jerome Trigg, Nome
Jules Wright, Fairbanks

### Officers

**1967-1970**  Emil Notti, president

Don Wright, vice-president (1967)
John Borbridge, Jr., vice-president (1968-1969)

Elva Naanes, secretary (1967-1969)
Margaret Nick, secretary (1969-1970)

**1970-1972**  Donald Wright, president

Phillip Guy, vice-president (1970-1972)

Margaret Nick, secretary (1970-1972)

**1972-1973**  William Hensley, president

Joe Upicksoun, chairman of the board (1972)
John Sackett, chairman of the board (1972-1973)

Frances Degnan, secretary (1972)
Henry Eaton, secretary (1972-1973)

**1974-1975**  Roger Lang, president

Jack Wick, chairman of the board (1974-1975)

Ralph A. Johnson, secretary (1974)
Carl Moses, secretary (1975)

**1975-**  Sam Kito, president

Jack Wick, chairman of the board (1975-    )

Carl Moses, secretary (1975-    )

# References

Andrews, C. L. *The Story of Alaska.* Caxton Printers, Ltd. Caldwell, Idaho, 1953.

Bancroft, Hubert Howe. *History of Alaska 1730-1885.* A. L. Bancroft and Co., New York, 1886. Reprinted. Arno Press, New York.

Bigjim, Frederick Seagayak and Ito-Adler, James. *Letters to Howard.* Alaska Methodist University Press, Anchorage, Alaska, 1974.

Cohen, Felix S. *Handbook of Federal Indian Law.* University of New Mexico Press, Albuquerque, New Mexico, reprint of 1942 original edition.

Collier, John. *Indians of the Americas.* The New American Library, New York, 1947.

Collins, Henry B., Jr. *The Aleutian Islands: Their People and Natural History.* Smithsonian Institution, Washington, D. C., 1945.

Driver, Harold E. *Indians of North America.* The University of Chicago Press, Chicago, Illinois, first edition, 1961, revised, 1969.

Drucker, Philip. *The Native Brotherhoods: Modern Intertribal Organizations on the Northwest Coast.* Bureau of American Ethnology Bulletin 168, U. S. Government Printing Office, Washington, D. C., 1958.

Fedorova, Svetlana G. *The Russian Population in Alaska and California: Late 18th Century — 1867.* Limestone Press, Kingston, Ontario, 1973. (Translated by Richard A. Pierce and Alton S. Donnelly.)

Fey, Harold E. and McNickle, D'Arcy. *Indians and Other Americans.* Harper and Row, New York, 1959.

Forbes, Jack D., ed. *The Indian in America's Past.* Prentice Hall, Inc., Englewood Cliffs, New Jersey, 1964.

Gallagher, Hugh. *Etok: A Story of Eskimo Power.* G. P. Putnam's Sons, New York, 1974.

Gruening, Ernest. *The State of Alaska.* Random House, New York, 1968.

Gsovski, Vladimir. "Russian Administration of Alaska and the Status of Alaskan Natives." 81st Congress, 2nd Session, Senate Document No. 152, U. S. Government Printing Office, Washington, D. C., 1950.

Hamilton, Charles. *Cry of the Thunderbird: The American Indian's Own Story.* University of Oklahoma Press, Norman, Oklahoma, second edition, 1972.

Hanke, Lewis. *Aristotle and the American Indians.* Henry Regnery and Company, Chicago, 1959.

Hinckley, Ted C. *The Americanization of Alaska, 1867-1897.* Pacific Books, Publishers, Palo Alto, California, 1972.

Hopkins, David M., editor. *The Bering Land Bridge.* Stanford University Press, Palo Alto, California, 1967.

Institute for the Development of Indian Law. *American Indian Treaty Series.* 8 Volumes. 927 - 15th Street, N.W., Washington, D. C. 20005.

Jackson, Helen Hunt. *A Century of Dishonor: The Early Crusade for Indian Reform.* Harper and Row, Publishers, New York, first edition, 1881, reprinted, 1965.

Krause, Aurel, *The Tlingit Indians.* Results of a trip to the Northwest Coast of America and the Bering Straits. Translated by Erna Gunther. University of Washington Press, Seattle, 1956.

Martin, Guy. "The Politics of Passage," *Series on the Native Land Claims.* Department of Education and Center for Northern Educational Research, Juneau, Alaska, 1975.

McNickle, D'Arcy. *The Indian Tribes of the United States: Ethnic and Cultural Survival.* Oxford University Press, London, 1962.

Mooney, James. *The Aboriginal Population of America North of Mexico.* Smithsonian Miscellaneous Collection, Vol. 80, No. 7, Washington, D. C., 1928.

Morris, William Gouverneur. "Report on the Customs District, Public Service, and Resources of Alaska," *Alaska Industries: Seal and Salmon Fisheries.* U. S. Government Printing Office, Washington, D. C., 1898.

Moser, Jefferson F. *The Salmon and Salmon Fisheries of Alaska.* United States Fish Commission, Washington, D. C., 1898.

Oswalt, Wendell. *Alaskan Eskimos.* Chandler Publishing Company, San Francisco, 1967.

Patty, Stanton H. "A Conference with the Tanana Chiefs," *Alaska Journal.* Spring, 1971.

Pearce, Roy Harvey. *The Savages of America.* Johns Hopkins University Press, Baltimore, 1953.

Price, Monroe E. *Law and the American Indian.* The Bobbs-Merrill Company, Inc., Indianapolis, 1973.

Prucha, Francis Paul. *American Indian Policy in the Formative Years.* University of Nebraska Press, Lincoln, Nebraska, 1962.

Ransom, J. Ellis. "Derivation of the word Alaska," *American Anthropologist.* 1940.

Ray, Dorothy Jean. "Land Tenure and Polity of the Bering Strait Eskimos," *Journal of the West.* Volume 6, No. 3, pp. 311-394.

Robert R. Nathan Associates, Inc. *2(c) Report: Federal Programs and Alaska Natives.* Introduction and Summary. Prepared for the United States Department of the Interior. United States Government Printing Office, Washington, D. C., 1975.

Rogers, George, ed. *Change in Alaska.* University of Alaska Press, College, Alaska, 1970.

*Tundra Drums* (newspaper) Bethel, Alaska, 1975.

*Tundra Times* (newspaper) Fairbanks, Alaska, 1962-1975.

Tyler, S. Lyman. *A History of Indian Policy.* Bureau of Indian Affairs, U. S. Government Printing Office, Washington, D. C., 1973.

U. S. Federal Field Committee for Development Planning in Alaska. *Alaska Natives and the Land.* U. S. Government Printing Office, Washington, D.C., 1968.

Vanderwerth, W. C. *Indian Oratory: Famous Speeches by Noted Indian Chieftains.* University of Oklahoma Press, Norman, Oklahoma, 1971.

Van Stone, James W. *Athapaskan Adaptations: Hunters and Fishermen of the Subarctic Forests.* Aldine Publishing Company, (529 South Wabash Avenue.) Chicago, Illinois, 1974.

Wissler, Clark. *Indians of the United States: Four Centuries of Their History and Culture.* Doubleday and Company, Inc., Garden City, New York, 1953.

# Index

## Pronunciation Key

The following list is suggested as a guide for pronouncing words or names which appear in the index.

| | | |
|---|---|---|
| A | as in | cat |
| AA | as in | plate |
| AH | as in | calm |
| AI | as in | pie |
| AW | as in | jaw |
| E | as in | Ben |
| EE | as in | feet |
| EH | as in | met |
| I | as in | if |
| IE | as in | pie or sky |
| OH | as in | boat |
| OO | as in | boot |
| U | as in | buck |
| Y | as in | feet |

Creoles, (CREE' OHL), 22, 26
Crow, Lucy, 263
Custer, George A., 36

## D

Dall, William, 74
Davis, Jeff C., 62, p 63
Dawes, Henry, 54
Dawes Act. See General Allotment Act.
Deficiency lands, 244
Degnan, Frances, p 136, p 141
Degnan, Frank, p 88, 89, p 113, p 126, p 132
Demientieff (DUH MEN' TEE EHF), Daisy, 209
Demmert, Dennis, 275
Dena Nena Henash (DU NAH' NU NAH' HUH NASH'), 98, 109
Diomede, 87
Ditman, Betty, p 292
Doyon (DOY' ON), Ltd., 166, 187, 232, 259, 284
Drake, Carol, 281
Drake, Tom, 281
Duncan, William, 80

## E

Easements (ANCSA) [ANCSA Sec. 17(b)(1)], 269-270
Eaton, Hank, p 141, 233
Edwardsen, Jr., Charles, p 110, 111, p 132, 137, p 141, 162
*Edwardsen vs. Morton*, 162
Egan, William A., 135, p 135, 140
Egegik (EE GEH GIK) land selections. See Becharof Corporation.
Eklutna, Inc., 238, 239
Eligibility for ANCSA benefits (ANCSA Sec. 5), 146
Elim, 208
Encroachments upon Alaska Native lands, 79
English legal system of land ownership, 41-42
Enrollment (ANCSA) (ANCSA Sec. 5), 146
Eskimos, 15-17
Evanoff, Gail, p 292
Evans, John, p 109
Ewan, (EE WAN), Harding, p 290
Ewan, Roy, 209
Eyak (EE' YAK), 13, 183
Eyak Corporation, 183, 248
Ezi (EE' ZIE), Pete, p 164

## F

Fairbanks Native Association, 108, 117
Federal Field Committee for Development Planning in Alaska, 126
Federal guardian, 57
Federal programs for Alaska Natives (ANCSA), 146-147
    See ANCSA Sec. 2(c).

Federal-State Land Use Planning Commission. See Joint Federal-State Land Use Planning Commission.
Fee simple title, 146, 147, 150, 276
Field, George, p 83
First Americans, 3
Fischer, Victor, 90
Fish, Darryl, p 265
FitzGerald, Joseph H., 126
Forbes, Dr. Henry S., p 99, 99-100
Ford, James A., 7
Frank, Richard, 100-101, p 101, 119, p 141
Franz, Charles, 119, p 126
French, Stewart, 145

## G

Gambell, 208
General Allotment Act (Dawes Act), 51, 54-56, 83, 86
Goldbelt, Inc., 200
Goldberg, Arthur J., 132, p 133
Goldberg, Robert M., p 265
Gold rush in Alaska, 72-74
Goodwin, Willie, p 283
Gorsuch, Lee, 227
Gravel, Mike, p 135, 142, 276
Gray, Jerry, p 132
Gray, Nick, 112, p 113
Greely, Major General A. W., 79
Gregory, Mary, p 156
Groh, Clifford, 120, p 141
Gross, Avrum, 162
Ground Hog Bay, 5, p 5
Gruenberg, Max, p 141
Gruening (GREENING), Ernest, 65, 103, 112, 120
Guarrick (GWAHR' IK), Tom, 74
Guy, Philip, p 136, p 141
Gwitchya Gwitchin Ginkhye (GWITCH'YA GWICH'IN GHIN HEE), 110

## H

Haidas (HIE' DUHS), 11-12
    See also Tlingit-Haida court case.
Hammond, Bella, 273
Hannon, Becki, p 292
Hansen, Erik, p 234
Harris, Fred, 137
Havelock, John, 141
Hawley, Bob, 209
Healy (HEE' LEE) Lake, 6, p 6
Hensley, William (Willie), 93, 112, 114, p 114, 117, 119, 121, p 126, p 132, 203, p 274
Hickel, Walter, 118, 119, 123-124, 125-126
Hobson, William, p 83
Hoffman, Sr., Edward, 263
Homestead Act, 244
Hope, Andrew, 88, p 88, 110
Hope, John, 110
Hopson, Eben, 109, p 125, p 132

village Native corporations (business) (ANCSA) (ANCSA Sec. 11, 12, 14 and 19)

    See Village Native corporations (business) (ANCSA),

        Village Native corporations: 4 named cities (Juneau, Kenai, Kodiak, and Sitka) (business) (ANCSA),

        Village Native corporations: groups, and

        Village Native corporations (business) on revoked reserves (ANCSA).

    See Taxation of ANCSA lands.

    See Tlingit-Haida court settlement.

Land use

    comparison of European and American Indian attitudes, 43-47

    in Alaska before Russian traders, 2-17

Lang, Roger, 205, p 205, 270, 277

Leavitt, Oliver, p 157, 283, 284

Lekanof (LEH' KAN OFF), Flore, p 109, 117, p 126, p 207

Levine, Roy, p 132

Liberty, Paul, p 83

Lincoln, Nick, p 285

Lisburne, Dan, p 113

Lively, Lew, p 260


## M

Major, Marsha, p 290

Makarka, Henry, 289

Mallott, (MAH LOT'), Byron, 119, 287, p 287

Malutin, Radion X., 77

Marshall, Chief Justice John, 57, 280

Marshall, Robert, 168, p 168, p 265, p 290

Martin, Guy, 139-140

Mauneluk (MAH NEE' LYUK) Corporation, 206

McCutcheon, Stanley J., 112, p 114

McVee, Curtis V., p 260

Meeds, Lloyd, 137

Meganack, (MEH GAN' ACK), Walter, p 292

Mercer, Frank, p 83

Merculieff (MER COO' LEE EHF), Larry, 163, 252

Metlakatla. See Annette Island Reserve.

Migrations to western hemisphere from Asia, 2

Military occupation of Alaska, 63, 65, 68

Miller, Jr., George, p 132, p 141, 186, 208

Miller, Keith, 132, 135

Montana Creek Native Corporation, 201

Morton, Rogers C. B., 162

Moser, Jefferson, 77

Moses, Carl E., p 115, 117, 172, p 172

Municipalities

    land acquired through ANCSA [ANCSA Sec. 14(c)], 150, 271-272

    relationship to village corporations, 160

## N

Nageak (NAG EE AK), James, p 111

Nakak, Al, p 141

NANA Regional Corporation, Inc., 192, 228, 231, 232, p 231, 259, 278, 286-287, 288

Napoleon, Harold, 227

National Council on Indian Affairs, 105

National Council on Indian Opportunity, 138

National Congress of American Indians, 135

National interest lands (ANCSA), 147, 150, 247, 248, 251, 255, 266-271, 283

    See ANCSA Sec. 17(d)(1, 2).

Native Allotment Act (1906), 80-81, 98, 146, 244

    See ANCSA Sec. 18.

Natives of Afognak, Inc., 190

Native Townsite Act (1926), 81

Navigable waters problem (ANCSA), 244-245

Nenana Native Council, 118

Newlin, Robert, 192

Nicholls, Hugh, 120

Nichols, Agnes, p 289

Nixon, Richard M., 124, 138, 139, 140-141, 144

Nopawhotak, Lester, p 91

North Pacific Rim Native Corporation, 206

Northwest Alaska Native Association, 117, 158

Notti, Emil (NAH TEE, EE' MILL), p 109, 112, p 113, 117, 119, 121, 125, p 126, p 127, 130, p 132, 133, 136, 206, p 206, 276

Notti (NAH TEE), Fred, p 109

Nunakaviak Yupik Corporation (Toksook Bay), 247, 248

Nunamiut (NOO' NAH MYOOT), 16

Nunivak Kaluiat Native Corporation, 228

Nusungingya (NOO SUNG GHEENGE' YA), John, 95

## O

Oil lease sale, (North Slope, 1969), 130, 131

Oil pipeline, 139

Okakok (OH KAH KOHK), Guy, 96, p 96

Old Crow Flats, 3

Olson, Dean, p 290

Onion Portage, 4, p 4

Oomituk (UM MEE' TOOK), Otthneil, p 111

Operation Grassroots, 111

Organic Act of 1884, 68-71, 91, 107, 118

Oskolkoff, Larry, p 132

Overselection, 238

## P

Paneak (PAN EE AK), Simon, p 252

Paul, Fred, p 141

Paul, Sr., William L., 83, 85, p 85, 90, p 108, 109, 121

Pearce, Roy Harvey, 47

People of Alaska, mid-18th century, 8-14

Stockholders at large (ANCSA) [ANCSA Sec. 7(m)], 153, 159, 217, 219-221, 223

Stone, David, p 158

Subsistence, 268-269, 286-287

Subsurface ownership (ANCSA), 150, 238, 251, 253-255, 260

Sugcestun (SYOOK' STOON) people, 10

Surface estate ownership (ANCSA) [ANCSA Sec. 14(a)], 150, 238, 250, 253, 256, 260

Swetzof, Mike, 172

Swineford, Governor A. P., 67

### T

Taalak (TAW LUK), Sam, 111, p 111

Tanadgusix (TAN AH GOO' SIKH) Corporation, 172, 242-243, 244

Tanaina (TAH NIE' NAH) people, 13, 14

Tanana (TAN' UH NAW) people, 13

Tanana Chiefs Conference, 109, 158, 206

Tanana Survival School, 207

Tangle Lakes, 4, p 4

Taxation of ANCSA
  of cash compensation to Natives [ANCSA Sec. 21(a, b)], 221, 225
  of Native lands [ANCSA Sec. 21(c, d, e)], 240, 260, 284

Ten Bears, 31, p 31

Termination, 134, 275, 279-280

Tetlin, 187, 208

Thiele (THEE' L), Otto, p 164

Thirteenth regional corporation (ANCSA) [ANCSA Sec. 5(c)], 159, 164, 165, 196, 216, 223

Thomas of Nenana, p 81

Thompson, Morris, p 132, p 207

Tlingit-Haida Central Council, 110, 158, 206

Tlingit-Haida court settlement (land settlement case) (1959), 91-92, 106-107, 150, 151
  See ANCSA Sec. 16(a, b), 236.

Tlingits (CLINK' ET), 11-12, 62, 68
  Aukwan, 70, 72
  Cape Fox, 80
  Chilkat, 75

Togotthele (TAWG AH TEE LEE) Corporation, 226

Toksook (TOOK SOOK) Bay. See Nunakaviak Yupik Corporation.

Top-filing, 238

Township, 248

Treaties, 47-51

Treaty of Cession, 25

Trigg, Barbara, p 132

Trigg, Jerome, 176, p 176

Tsimshians (SIM' SHEE AN), 80, 146

Tucker, Shirley, p 109

*Tundra Times*, 99-100

Tyonek Corporation, 134, 186

### U

Udall (YOU' DALL), Morris, 142

Udall, Stewart, 102, 103, p 117, 117, 124

Ukpeagvik Inupiat (OOK PYAHG VIK INOO' PYAHT) Village Corporation (Barrow), 231, 236-237

Unalakleet, 87

United Bank of Alaska, 232

United States Atomic Energy Commission, 94

United States Congress
  ANCSA intent, 146
  appropriations to the Alaska Native Fund, 151, 211-212
  land claims hearings, 120-124
  legislation on Alaska Native land claims, 119, 120, 129-130, 132-134, 136-138, 140-144

United States Constitution, 57

United States Department of the Interior, 96, 112, 119, 139, 196
  Alaska Native Claims Appeal Board, 202-203
  approval of settlement act corporations, 157
  national interest land withdrawals (ANCSA), [ANCSA Sec. 17(d)(2)], 147
  Native land withdrawals (ANCSA), 148-151
  *2(c) Report: Federal Programs and Alaska Natives* [ANCSA Sec. 2(c)], 280
  See Bureau of Indian Affairs (U. S.).
  See Bureau of Land Management (U. S.).

United States military in Alaska (1867), 62

United States government
  policies toward American Indians, 33-36, 51-56, 70
  See also Treaties.

United States Office of Economic Opportunity (OEO), 111

Upicksoun (UH PICK SUN), Joseph, p 125, 137, p 141, p 158, 173, p 173

### V

Venetie reserve, 87, 187, 208

Village Native corporations (business) (ANCSA), 196-199
  cash compensation (ANCSA) [ANCSA Sec. 7(k, 1, m)], 153, 224-226
  eligibility [ANCSA Sec. 11(b)(2)], 159
  land entitlements (ANCSA Sec. 12), 148-151
  land selections [ANCSA Sec. 11(b)(3), Sec. 12(a), and Sec. 14(a)], 235-250
  responsibilities, 159-160
  uses of cash compensation, 225-228
  See Land Settlement: Conveyance of land.

Village Native corporations (business): 4 named cities (Juneau, Kenai, Kodiak, and Sitka) (ANCSA)
  cash compensation (ANCSA) [ANCSA Sec. 7(k)], 200-201, 225